ENCYCLOPEDIA OF
MOVIE STARS

RUDOLPH VALENTINO & VILMA BANKY.
IN "THE SON OF THE SHEIK".
'FAMOUS CINEMA STAR' SERIES.

ALLIED ARTISTS
PICTURE.

BEAG

ENCYCLOPEDIA OF
MOVIE
STARS

DANIEL AND SUSAN COHEN

Bison Books

Published by
Bison Books Ltd.
176 Old Brompton Road,
London, SW 5
England.

ISBN 0 86124 221 1

Printed in Hong Kong

Reprinted 1987

CREDITS

CONTENTS
Introduction
6
A-Z of Movie Stars
8

Page 1
Left: James Dean.
Right: Lauren Bacall.

Page 2-3
Top row, left to right: Brigitte Bardot, Burt Reynolds.
Bottom row, left to right: Ginger Rogers and Fred Astaire; Rudolph Valentino and Vilma Banky; Meryl Streep and Kevin Kline; Marlene Dietrich.

Page 4 5
Top: James Caan.
Bottom row, left to right: Elizabeth Taylor; Clint Eastwood; Robert Redford.

Clark Gable and Vivien Leigh.

Shirley Maclaine.

INTRODUCTION

At first it sounded like lots of fun. Pick about 400 of the world's top movie stars to be included in an *Encyclopedia of Movie Stars.* When we began it was easy, almost too easy – Garbo, Bogart, Marilyn Monroe, John Wayne – the legendary figures are obvious – Cary Grant, Alec Guinness, Katharine Hepburn, Dustin Hoffman. Then you have to start digging a bit: Robert Donat, Doris Day, Dick Powell, Diane Keaton.

But movie 'stars,' those who made the time spent in front of the screen more real to us than real life itself, were often not those who received top billing. What about C Aubrey Smith? Perhaps you don't remember the name immediately, but anyone devoted to the films of the 1930s and 1940s will remember the face – this bushy-eyebrowed old character actor was the personification of the crusty old English gentleman to a generation of movie goers. Or Sydney Greenstreet; at 300 pounds he was an unlikely star, particularly since he didn't start making films until he was 61, and only made a handful – but oh that sinister chuckle, who can forget it?

Though this is a book heavily weighted toward American and British stars, there are certain international figures who could not be ignored. Marcello Mastroianni has stoutly resisted tempting offers from Hollywood. Toshiro Mifune has occasionally appeared in an American film or on television, but it is his Japanese films such as *Rashomon* and *Seven Samurai* for which he is justly famous.

We had to be careful not to slight the great figures of other eras. Of course the acting of Lillian Gish and even John Barrymore looks melodramatic and stilted to us today but, given the styles and film techniques of the time, both could be superb.

Some may not yet have reached their peak as these words are written. Ben Kingsley and Eddie Murphy have only made a few films each, but each in his own way has the potential to make film history.

Then there was the temptation of picking only those individuals who we happened to like. Neither of us are fans of the singing cowboy but Gene Autry and Roy Rogers had huge followings. Elvis Presley made films strictly for Elvis Presley fans – nobody else went to see them. Yet for years he was one of the top box-office draws – he could not be left out.

In the end, of course, we had too many names, far too many. Then came the heartbreaking task of pruning the list. We consulted with editors, friends, even enemies and finally came up with a list with which no one was satisfied. How could we be? We have always had a passionate attachment to films, and to leave out anyone who ever contributed to the movies we love was painful. You will argue with the final choices – any movie fan will.

Yet in the end the project was fun. It gave us a chance to reminisce and recall the lives and careers of so many who have given us so much pleasure and to catch up on some of today's stars. We hope you have nearly as much fun reading this book as we had in putting it together.

Charlton Heston.

Warren Beatty.

Montgomery Clift and Marilyn Monroe.

ABBOTT, Bud 1895-1947 and COSTELLO, Lou 1906-1959

Abbott was the snide straight man, Costello the pudgy funnyman. The pair teamed up in the early 1930s and knocked around in vaudeville, burlesque, Broadway and radio for a decade before making it very big in their second film *Buck Privates* (1941). All of their more than 30 films relied on the same basic characterizations, the same broad, slapstick humor. Yet throughout the 1940s and early 1950s they were consistently among Hollywood's top box-office draws.

Their personal lives were marred by tragedy and the friction between the pair finally exploded in 1956 when they split. Costello finally made one film on his own, *The Thirty-Foot Bride of Candy Rock* (1959), but it was not a success at the box office.

FILMOGRAPHY
One Night in the Tropics 1940
Buck Privates 1941
Hold That Ghost 1941
Who Done It? 1942
The Wistful Widow of Wagon Gap 1947
The Noose Hangs High 1948
Abbott and Costello Meet Frankenstein 1948
Abbott and Costello Meet the Invisible Man 1951
Jack and the Beanstalk 1952
Dance with me Henry 1955

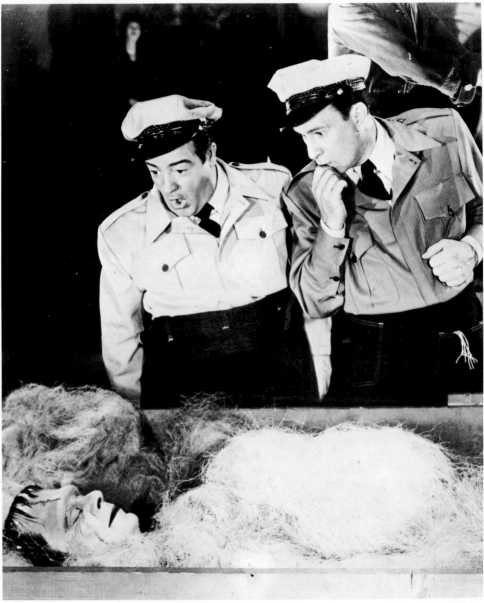

Bud Abbott (right) and Lou Costello come across Frankenstein's monster (Glenn Strange).

Eddie Albert and Catherine Deneuve in *Hustle* (1975).

FILMOGRAPHY
Brother Rat 1938
Four Wives 1939
Smash Up 1947
Roman Holiday 1953
I'll Cry Tomorrow 1955
Attack 1956
The Heartbreak Kid 1972
The Longest Yard 1974

ALBERT, Eddie 1908-

Eddie Albert is a durable character actor who has worked in several media: stage, radio, and television. Albert was usually Mr Nice Guy, a hearty friendly hail-fellow-well-met type, the second lead, the hero's best friend. Getting the girl was distinctly not his forté. But every once in a while he'd land a good role, shake off his clean-cut image, and play a really villainous character.

Born Edward Albert Heimberger in Rock Island, Illinois, he attended the University of Minnesota. A circus trapeze artist, he made his film debut in 1938, later earning Oscar nominations for *Roman Holiday* (1953) and *The Heartbreak Kid* (1972). He appeared in the successful television series *Green Acres* with Eva Gabor. In 1945 Eddie Albert married the Mexican-born actress and dancer Margo.

ALDA, Alan 1936-

Alan Alda – his is the deceptively bland style of a natural screen talent. The son of actor Robert Alda, Alan Alda projects a quiet charm and low-key dignity. His private persona has also helped him win fans, for Alda is an intelligent, decent, compassionate man with solid values whom the public can respect.

Born in New York City, Alda made his film debut at 27 in *Gone Are the Days* (1963), a remake of *Purlie Victorious*. Alda made more movies but it was television which catapulted him to stardom. He played Hawkeye Pierce in the revered television series, *M*A*S*H**. When he returned to films he chose wisely, making *Same Time Next Year* (1978) with Ellen Burstyn and *The Seduction of Joe Tynan* (1979) with Meryl Streep. His best and biggest success so far is *The Four Seasons* (1981), a witty movie about middle-aged marriage.

FILMOGRAPHY
Gone Are the Days 1963
Same Time Next Year 1978
California Suite 1978
The Seduction of Joe Tynan 1979
The Four Seasons 1981
Sweet Liberty 1986

Alan Alda and Ellen Burstyn in *Same Time Next Year* (1978).

Robert Alda (with Joan Leslie) played George Gershwin in *Rhapsody in Blue* (1945).

ALDA, Robert 1914-1986

Robert Alda was awfully handsome in *Rhapsody in Blue* (1945), the life and times of George Gershwin, Hollywood style. It was his first role in a picture and big things were expected of him on the screen. But he never equalled the promise of his impressive debut and he really made his mark on Broadway in *Guys and Dolls* and *What Makes Sammy Run*.

Born Alphonso Giuseppe Giovanni Roberto D'Abruzzo in New York City, Alda was a barber's son and architectural draftsman who took a shot at singing in vaudeville. Radio and burlesque followed. Next came films. In the early 1960s Robert Alda settled in Rome, appearing in European film productions. He was the father of film and television actor Alan Alda.

FILMOGRAPHY
Rhapsody in Blue 1945
The Beast with Five Fingers 1947
April Showers 1948
Imitation of Life 1959
The Girl Who Knew Too Much 1968

ALLEN, Woody 1935-

Woody Allen, the 98-pound weakling with the superman brain, is a comic genius, America's most original movie actor, writer and director rolled into one. A master at zinging one-liners, the epitome on screen of the modern bungler tormented by self-doubt, neuroses, and unswervable lusts, Allen is the eternal aging Brooklyn adolescent set adrift in Manhattan's chic set. Beneath the hilarity there is always pain.

Born Allen Stewart Königsberg in Brooklyn, Allen attended New York University and City College of New York. An early flowerer, Allen wrote television comedy while still in his teens. Writing for Sid Caesar's *Your Show of Shows* put him at the top. In 1961 Woody Allen began appearing in Greenwich Village cafes as a stand up comic. Soon he was a popular TV talk-show guest and night-club performer.

Allen co-wrote and appeared in *What's New, Pussycat?* (1965), his first film. He dubbed an English sound track on to a Japanese movie and came up with *What's Up, Tiger Lily?* (1967), and with his wife, Louise Lasser, scored a hit with *Bananas* (1971). His *Play it Again, Sam* (1972), based on his own hit play, with Diane Keaton, was the plaintive cry of a man who never got the girl and a tribute to Humphrey Bogart who usually did.

Allen continued making movies which were strong on gags until *The Front* (1976), but it was *Annie Hall* (1977), also with Keaton, which represented a major change for him. Though humorous, this film definitely had its serious side and it won the Oscar for best picture. Allen also won the Academy Awards for best director and co-screen writer. *Manhattan* (1979) was even wittier and more poignant than *Annie Hall*. Allen spoofed himself and his generation, hitting home a lot of truths along the way. *Zelig* (1983), with Mia Farrow, used old black-and-white film footage, with novel and brilliant results. *Broadway Danny Rose* (1984) is vintage Allen as is *Hannah and Her Sisters* (1986). You can never tell what Woody Allen, the man with the funny face and baroque fears, will serve up next, but whatever it is, it's probably worth seeing.

FILMOGRAPHY
What's New, Pussycat? 1965
What's Up, Tiger Lily? 1967
Take the Money and Run 1969
Bananas 1971
Everything You Always Wanted to Know About Sex (But Were Afraid to Ask) 1972
Play it Again, Sam 1972
Sleeper 1973
Love and Death 1976
Annie Hall 1977
Manhattan 1979
Stardust Memories 1980
A Midsummer Night's Sex Comedy 1982
Zelig 1983
Broadway Danny Rose 1984
Hannah and Her Sisters 1986
Radio Days 1987

Woody Allen with Diane Keaton in *Annie Hall* (1977), which won the best picture Oscar.

The legendary cowboy star, 'Broncho Billy' Anderson.

turned to movies in 1902, appearing in and directing one-reelers. He played several roles in *The Great Train Robbery* (1903).

In 1907 he began producing films starring Ben Turpin. In 1911 he was the producer of Charlie Chaplin comedies. He starred in and directed his first Broncho (later Bronco) Billy serial in 1907. All told there were over 400 episodes in this series.

In 1916 Anderson retired, returning to Hollywood to direct Stan Laurel shorts in the 1920s. Forgotten for decades, he received a special Oscar in 1957 for his contribution to movies. A cameo appearance in *The Bounty Killer* (1965) completed his career.

FILMOGRAPHY
The Great Train Robbery 1903
Raffles, the American Cracksman 1905
The Bandit Makes Good 1907
Broncho Billy's Redemption 1910
Broncho Billy's Marriage 1915
The Bounty Killer 1965

ALLYSON, June 1917-

When allowed to play spiteful or nasty characters June Allyson (born Ella Geisman) did them very well, but most of the time she was either the pretty, peppy girl-next-door sort, or else she was a perfect and devoted wife. Allyson could tackle light comedy, melodramas or musicals with equal skill.

She got her start as a Broadway showgirl and dancer in the chorus, breaking into films in the late 1930s in two-reel shorts. The widow of movie star Dick Powell, whom she married in 1945, Allyson appeared in nightclubs, and had her own television series in the late 1950s.

FILMOGRAPHY
Best Foot Forward 1943
Two Girls and a Sailor 1944
Good News 1947
The Three Musketeers 1948
Little Women 1949
The Stratton Story 1949
The Glenn Miller Story 1954
Executive Suite 1954
The Shrike 1955
Interlude 1957
They Only Kill Their Masters 1972
Blackout 1978

AMECHE, Don 1908-

Don Ameche, the gifted light comedian and romantic lead of stage, screen, and radio, was born Dominic Felix Amici. He appeared in numerous movie musicals with Alice Faye. In 1985 he won the Academy Award for Best Supporting Actor for *Cocoon*.

FILMOGRAPHY
Ramona 1936
In Old Chicago 1938
Alexander's Ragtime Band 1938
Midnight 1939
The Story of Alexander Graham Bell 1939
Heaven Can Wait 1943
Happy Land 1943
A Fever in the Blood 1961
The Boatniks 1970
Cocoon 1985

ANDERSON, G M (Broncho Billy) 1882-1971

G M (Broncho Billy) Anderson was born Max Aronson in Little Rock, Arkansas. He was one of the screen's first stars and certainly the screen's first cowboy star. A failed stage actor, he

ANDERSON, Dame Judith 1898-

Fiery passions always seemed to rage under her icy controlled exterior. When Alfred Hitchcock cast her as Mrs Danvers, the evil housekeeper in *Rebecca* (1940), screen history was made. She was born in Adelaide, Australia and became one of the great luminaries of the theater, frequently playing Shakespearian roles. Her 1947 stage performance of *Medea* is legendary. In 1960 she was named Dame Commander of the British Empire.

She was memorable in a number of films, especially in the 1940s, generally playing villainous character parts.

FILMOGRAPHY
Blood Money 1933
Rebecca 1940
King's Row 1942
Laura 1944
And Then There Were None 1945
The Diary of a Chambermaid 1945
The Spectre of the Rose 1946
The Strange Love of Martha Ivers 1947
Pursued 1947
Tycoon 1947
The Red House 1947
The Furies 1950
Salome 1953
Cat On A Hot Tin Roof 1958
Macbeth 1963
A Man Called Horse 1970
Star Trek III: The Search for Spock 1984

ANDRESS, Ursula 1936-

A dazzling blonde sex symbol, Ursula Andress was born in Bern, Switzerland, got her career start in Rome and made it big in the first James Bond movie, *Dr No* (1962). She was married to John Derek until Jean Paul Belmondo entered her life. Many of her later films have been made in Italy.

FILMOGRAPHY
Dr No 1962
She 1964
What's New Pussycat? 1965
The Tenth Victim 1965
Casino Royale 1967
The Lives and Times of Scara-mouche 1976

ANDREWS, Dana 1909-

Dana Andrews, a solid leading man and fine supporting actor in many important films, had a career that peaked during the 1940s. However he has continued to make films and has appeared in many television productions.

FILMOGRAPHY
The Ox Bow Incident 1943
The Purple Heart 1944
Laura 1944
A Walk in the Sun 1945
State Fair 1945
The Best Years of Our Lives 1946
Boomerang 1947
My Foolish Heart 1950
Elephant Walk 1953
Night of the Demon 1957
Crack in the World 1965
Airport 1975 1974
The Pilot 1979

ANDREWS, Harry 1911-

Harry Andrews, the distinguished character actor, began his stage career in 1933, often appearing in Shakespearian roles. He then turned to films where he generally played tough no-nonsense military characters.

FILMOGRAPHY
A Hill in Korea 1956
Ice Cold in Alex 1958
The Hill 1965
The Deadly Affair 1966
Theatre of Blood 1973
Equus 1977

ANDREWS, Julie 1935-

Julie Andrews (born Julia Elizabeth Wells), is a lady with style and a real trouper. What's more she has done the near impossible: she changed her image in mid-career. She came from an English show-business family and began performing as a child in pantomimes.

She became a star when she was cast as Eliza Doolittle in *My Fair Lady* on Broadway. Audrey Hepburn got the role in the 1964 screen version, which saddened Andrews, but it was Andrews who won the Oscar for *Mary Poppins* that year. *The Sound of Music* (1965) was one of Hollywood's all-time big grossers and Andrews hit number one at the box office. After that her film career faltered. Shedding the sugar coating, she altered her persona and recouped her career in the late 1970s by appearing in a contemporary series of comedies directed by husband Blake Edwards.

Julie Andrews in *Mary Poppins* (1964).

FILMOGRAPHY
Mary Poppins 1964
The Americanization of Emily 1964
The Sound of Music 1965
Thoroughly Modern Millie 1967
S.O.B. 1981
Victor Victoria 1982
Duet for One 1987

ANN-MARGRET 1941-

Ann-Margret, this gorgeous Swedish-American performer, born Ann-Margret Olsson, is a real pro. She's done stage, cabaret, television and movies. Ann-Margret has had to battle against her sex-symbol image to receive the recognition she deserves.

FILMOGRAPHY
State Fair 1961
Bye Bye Birdie 1962
The Cincinnati Kid 1965
Carnal Knowledge 1971
Tommy 1975
Magic 1978
The Return of the Soldier 1985
Twice in a Lifetime 1986

ARBUCKLE, Fatty 1887-1933

Roscoe 'Fatty' Arbuckle was a gentle buffoon, a sensitive actor whose baby face and 325-pound body made him one of Hollywood's favorite early funny men. But one night he went to a party and found himself accused of a brutal rape and murder. After that there wasn't very much to smile at anymore.

Arbuckle was born in Smith Center, Kansas. He was a starry-eyed kid when it came to show business and sang, danced, and even collected tickets in a nickelodeon. After a stint in vaudeville he began appearing in one- and two-reelers in 1907. In 1913 Mack Sennett made him a Keystone Kop. For a while it was all roses for Fatty. He and Mabel Normand co-starred in a series of classic comedies heavy on verve, low on subtlety. In 1917 Arbuckle formed his own production company, giving newcomer Buster Keaton his start. Ingenious and innovative, Arbuckle wrote his own material and directed his own films. A move to Famous Players won him a salary of $7000 a week, a staggering sum at the time.

Then in September, 1921, Virginia Rappe, a bit player, collapsed at a party and died a few days later. Arbuckle was charged with manslaughter, but ultimately acquitted. It didn't matter. The press and the public had decided that Arbuckle was guilty. The frightened studios imposed a rigid self-censorship to improve their image. Arbuckle films were banned and withdrawn.

Those who knew Arbuckle stood by him. His wife Minta Durfee, though she divorced him some years later, insisted

Roscoe 'Fatty' Arbuckle and Mabel Normand in *Mabel and Fatty's Married Life* (1916).

continued the trend in movies, making a silent version of *Disraeli* (1921), and a sound version (1929) which won him an Academy Award. He returned to England, and retired in 1937.

FILMOGRAPHY
Disraeli 1921
The Green Goddess 1923
Disraeli 1929
Alexander Hamilton 1931
Voltaire 1933
The House of Rothschild 1934
Cardinal Richelieu 1935
The Iron Duke 1935

ARMSTRONG, Robert 1890-1973

Born Donald Robert Smith, this character actor played cops, tough guys and sheriffs in scores of films. He played movie producer Carl Denham in *King Kong* (1933) who was responsible for bringing the ape to New York.

FILMOGRAPHY
King Kong 1933
Son of Kong 1933
My Favorite Spy 1942
The Paleface 1948
Mighty Joe Young 1949

ARTHUR, Jean 1905-

Jean Arthur (born Gladys Green), with her husky idiosyncratic voice, great charm, comic talent and the feminist strength underlying her blonde petiteness, was one of the most bewitching stars of the films of the 1930s. She quit school at 15 to become a model and actress. After doing low-budget silent pictures she tried the New York stage, then went back to films again, this time after the introduction of sound. The theater had given her confidence and style and by the mid-1930s she was making some of the best comedies Hollywood ever released. A very private person she quit films in the mid-1940s, but toured on stage in 1950. Her final movie was *Shane* (1953).

FILMOGRAPHY
The Saturday Night Kid 1929
The Whole Town's Talking 1935
Mr Deeds Goes to Town 1936
The Plainsman 1936
History is Made at Night 1937
You Can't Take It With You 1938
Mr Smith Goes to Washington 1939
A Foreign Affair 1948
Shane 1953

on his innocence. Keaton offered him a directing job and Marion Davies let him direct her under the alias William B Goodrich, standing for Will B Good. He also directed Eddie Cantor's first films.

The strain destroyed Arbuckle. He lost much of his comic gift, became moody and difficult. An attempt to make an acting tour of Europe in 1932 was a failure. He died the following year.

FILMOGRAPHY
Fatty and Mabel's Simple Life 1915
Mabel and Fatty's Married Life 1916
Fatty's Flirtation 1916
Fickle Fatty's Fall 1917
His Wedding Night 1917
The Life of the Party 1920

ARLEN, Richard 1899-1976

One of film's truly familiar faces, Richard Arlen was born Richard Cornelius van Mattemore. A brawny leading man in Hollywood movies of the 1920s, he made countless 'B' pictures, then did bit parts till his death.

FILMOGRAPHY
Wings 1927
The Four Feathers 1928
Dangerous Curves 1929
The Virginian 1929
Call of the Yukon 1938
When My Baby Smiles at Me 1948
Sex and the College Girl 1970

ARLISS, George 1868-1946

Born George Augustus Andrews, Arliss was a distinguished actor of the British and American theater. He made his London stage debut at age 18 and in 1902 came to America on tour, staying to perform on Broadway for years.

He turned to films in his 50s, astonishing himself and everyone else by becoming a star. On stage he had shone playing kings and statesmen. He

ASTAIRE, Fred 1899–

The studio report on Astaire's first screen test said, 'Can't act. Can't sing: Can dance a little.' Astaire, modest, with a boyish charm, is possibly one of the best dancers who ever lived – elegant, perfectionistic, graceful and professional from the tip of his top hat to the soles of his feet. He squired some of Hollywood's most glamorous female dancers across the screen. His movies still charm today.

Born Frederick Austerlitz in Omaha, Nebraska, he and his sister Adele were brought to New York by their mother to study dancing while still children. They toured the vaudeville circuit and debuted on Broadway in 1917, becoming popular stars. They were big hits in London, too, before Adele retired to marry Lord Charles Cavendish.

Astaire appeared on screen first in *Dancing Lady* (1933) opposite Joan Crawford but his big film break came when he danced with Ginger Rogers in *Flying Down to Rio* (1933). She gave him sex; he gave her class, so the saying goes. They were the most sparkling sight on the silver screen, and they made ten films together which landed them in the box-office top ten. *Top Hat* (1935) and *Swing Time* (1936) are arguably the two best musicals Hollywood ever produced.

After the Astaire and Rogers team split up, Astaire made movies with stars like Eleanor Powell, Rita Hayworth, Judy Garland and Cyd Charisse, retiring periodically but always being wooed back. *Holiday Inn* (1942) with Bing Crosby was a sign Astaire was getting older. He could still dance up a storm but he was no longer the major male lead in every film. When Gene Kelly broke his ankle, Astaire got the lead in MGM's *Easter Parade* (1948). At MGM his dances tended towards the balletic, rather than pure tap, but movie musicals had changed, becoming big, splashy, full-color events, rubies instead of the diamonds of the 1930s.

In 1949 Fred Astaire was given a special Academy Award for his work in musicals. He went right on making them well into the 1950s. In 1959 he began playing straight dramatic roles in films, appearing in movies as late as the 1980s in *Ghost Story* (1981). Fred Astaire has introduced more hit songs than practically anyone else and danced them better. He has indeed left his steps in time.

Right: Fred Astaire and Ginger Rogers in *Flying Down to Rio* (1933).

Bottom: Fred, Nanette Fabray and Jack Buchanan sing 'Triplets' in *The Band Wagon* (1953).

FRED ASTAIRE
GINGER ROGERS
FOLLOW THE FLEET

Above: Fred Astaire in *Follow the Fleet* (1936).

Above: Fred and human piano in *Roberta*.

FILMOGRAPHY
Dancing Lady 1933
Flying Down to Rio 1933
The Gay Divorcee 1934
Roberta 1935
Top Hat 1935
Follow the Fleet 1936
Swing Time 1936
Shall We Dance? 1937
Broadway Melody 1940
Holiday Inn 1942
You Were Never Lovelier 1942
Easter Parade 1948
The Band Wagon 1953
Funny Face 1957
Silk Stockings 1957
On the Beach 1959
The Towering Inferno 1975
Ghost Story 1981

ASTOR, Mary 1906-

Mary Astor (born Lucille Vasconcellos Langhanke) was famous for her antics off screen as well as her characterizations of nasty women on. Opposite Bogart in *The Maltese Falcon* (1941) she was enticingly wicked.

She was a silent-film star before the age of 20. Four marriages, a custody battle, alcoholism, a suicide attempt, revelations from her personal diary in court and much publicized affairs with John Barrymore and George S Kaufman made Mary Astor a prime subject of Hollywood gossip columnists. She won an Academy Award for Best Supporting Actress for her performance in the Bette Davis vehicle *The Great Lie* (1941). She is the author of an autobiography and several novels.

FILMOGRAPHY
Beau Brummell 1924
Don Juan 1926
Red Dust 1932
Dodsworth 1936
The Prisoner of Zenda 1937
Midnight 1939
Turnabout 1940
The Great Lie 1941
The Maltese Falcon 1941
Meet Me in St Louis 1944
Act of Violence 1949
Little Women 1949

Above: Mary Astor was a star for 40 years.
Below: Richard Attenborough in *Guns at Batasi* (1964).

ATTENBOROUGH, Sir Richard 1923-

An actor of splendid range and a director of vision, Attenborough was born in Cambridge, England. He made his professional stage debut in 1941 and played a coward in the Noel Coward film *In Which We Serve* (1942). Typecast as a bounder for some time, he broke out of the mold and went on to play character roles and leads in both British and American films.

In the late 1950s Attenborough began producing and directing movies. His directing debut was the fine *Oh What a Lovely War!* in 1969. He won a British Film Academy Award for *Guns at Batasi* (1964). Knighted in 1976, Sir Richard Attenborough won an Academy Award for Best Director for *Gandhi* in 1982.

FILMOGRAPHY
In Which We Serve 1942
Brighton Rock 1947
Private's Progress 1955
Seance on a Wet Afternoon 1964
Guns at Batasi 1964
Doctor Doolittle 1967
10 Rillington Place 1971
The Human Factor 1979

ATWILL, Lionel 1885-1946

Atwill is best remembered for his role as the wooden-armed police chief in *Son of Frankenstein* (1939) and his usually villainous role in a huge number of other horror films. However, the British-born Atwill was a veteran of the London stage and Broadway before coming to Hollywood.

FILMOGRAPHY
The Mystery of the Wax Museum 1933
Murders in the Zoo 1933
Captain Blood 1935
Lives of a Bengal Lancer 1935
Son of Frankenstein 1939
The Three Musketeers 1939
The Hound of the Baskervilles 1939
To Be or Not to Be 1942
Frankenstein Meets the Wolf Man 1943

AUTRY, Gene 1907-

Gene Autrey, born in Texas, was a radio and film singing cowboy, songwriter and producer. He was top box office in westerns featuring his side-kick Smiley Burnette and his horse Champion. A millionaire, he retired from films in the mid-1950s.

FILMOGRAPHY
Springtime in the Rockies 1937
Under Western Stars 1938
South of the Border 1939
Back in the Saddle 1941
Down Mexico Way 1941
Goldtown Ghost Riders 1953

AYKROYD, Dan 1954-

Comedian and writer Aykroyd was born in Canada. A member of the famous improvisational group Second City in Toronto, Aykroyd worked closely with the late comic John Belushi on the hit television show *Saturday Night Live* and in films. Aykroyd was one of the stars and writers of the blockbuster hit comedy *Ghostbusters* (1984).

FILMOGRAPHY
Blues Brothers 1978
Trading Places 1983
Ghostbusters 1984
Spies Like Us 1986

Above: Dan Aykroyd in *Ghostbusters* (1984) – a lunatic cinema hit.

Below: Gene Autry (with clenched fists) wins out in *Sioux City Sue* (1947).

AYRES, Lew 1908-

Lew Ayres was an overnight success in *The Kiss* (1929) with Garbo and *All Quiet on the Western Front* (1930). He starred in the *Dr Kildare* series but his film career suffered when he became a conscientious objector in World War II.

FILMOGRAPHY
The Kiss 1929
All Quiet on the Western Front 1930
Last Train from Madrid 1937
Holiday 1938
Young Dr Kildare 1938
The Dark Mirror 1946
Johnny Belinda 1948
Donovan's Brain 1953
Damien – Omen II 1978

BACALL, Lauren 1924-

Lauren Bacall (born Betty Jean Perske) was bold and intriguingly sexy, with a hint of vulnerability even though she was wise beyond her years. Compared to her, most of the other beauties in 1940s films seemed like pure treacle. Before she was 20 she was a top-flight model and a star destined for the Hollywood firmament. Today she is a legend in her own time, Bogey's 'Baby,' woman of the year every year.

Born in New York City, she studied dance and briefly attended the American Academy of Dramatic Arts. It was her picture on the cover of *Harper's Bazaar* which won her a movie contract just as it was her striking 'come hither' appearance which won her the nickname 'The Look.'

Bacall debuted in *To Have and Have Not* (1944), which starred Humphrey Bogart. The film gave the world lines like 'If you want anything, all you have to do is whistle.' Bacall married Bogart in 1945 and the marriage was one of the happiest in Hollywood. The couple continued making movies together, becoming one of the premier duos of the screen. Bacall also made movies on her own, most notably *How to Marry a Millionaire* (1953), in which she did some nifty scene-stealing from Marilyn Monroe and Betty Grable, and *The Cobweb* (1955). John Wayne admired her enormously despite their political differences; he was on the far right, she was on the left. He went out of his way to cast her in *Blood Alley* (1955).

Bogart's death from cancer in 1957 left Bacall adrift. But she was steely tough, a born survivor, and with her natural flair for light comedy, her wonderful brass horn of a voice and her sturdy common sense, she rebuilt her life. She found success on Broadway in *Goodbye Charlie* and in 1961 married actor Jason Robards. The couple divorced in 1969. Bacall's best film of the era was *Harper* (1966).

She was the toast of Broadway in *Cactus Flower*, and *Applause*, a musical adaptation of the movie *All About Eve*, won Bacall a Tony Award. She was fabulous in *Murder on the Orient Express* (1974), and her most recent Broadway show, *Woman of the Year* was a smash.

The durable and beautiful Lauren Bacall.

FILMOGRAPHY
To Have and Have Not 1944
The Big Sleep 1946
Dark Passage 1947
Key Largo 1948
Young Man with a Horn 1950
How to Marry a Millionaire 1953
The Cobweb 1955
Blood Alley 1955
Harper 1966
Murder on the Orient Express 1974

BACKUS, Jim 1913-

A noted character actor and comedian, Jim Backus was born in Cleveland, Ohio. He has performed on vaudeville, radio, films, television and the stage. He was the voice of the UPA cartoon character Mr Magoo.

FILMOGRAPHY
Pat and Mike 1952
Rebel Without a Cause 1955
It's a Mad Mad Mad World 1963
Pete's Dragon 1977

BAKER, Carroll 1931-

After her success as the thumb-sucking child-wife in *Baby Doll* (1956), Hollywood groomed Carroll Baker as the new Marilyn Monroe. Though Baker was both beautiful and talented she never caught on. Discouraged, she moved to Europe and has appeared in Italian and Spanish films and on the London stage.

FILMOGRAPHY
Giant 1956
Baby Doll 1956
The Carpetbaggers 1964
Harlow 1965
Star 80 1983

BAKER, Sir Stanley 1927-1976

Stanley Baker started in films as a teenager and rose from character parts to leading roles. During the 1960s Baker co-produced many of his own films. He became enormously popular and was knighted just a month before his death from cancer at the age of 49.

FILMOGRAPHY
The Cruel Sea 1953
Hell Below Zero 1954
Richard III 1956
Campbell's Kingdom 1957
Hell Driver 1957
The Criminal 1960
The Guns of Navarone 1961
Zulu 1963
Accident 1967

BALL, Lucille 1910-

A beautiful and gifted comedienne and dramatic actress who often played

Lucille Ball as the effervescent, irrepressible *Mame* (1973).

featherheads but isn't one, Lucille Ball had to wait for television and her 1950s smash hit *I Love Lucy* show to emerge as a major star.

Born in Jamestown, New York, at 15 she took off for New York City, then went to Hollywood as a bit player, appearing in dozens of films. Bigger roles followed. She shone in *Stage Door* (1937), and opposite frequent co-stars Red Skelton and Bob Hope.

Ball married Cuban bandleader Desi Arnaz in the 1940s. In the following decade the couple put together Desilu Productions. They were divorced in 1960 and Lucille Ball took over full control of the company which grossed millions in television.

FILMOGRAPHY
Stage Door 1937
The Affairs of Annabel 1938
Room Service 1938
The Big Street 1942
Du Barry was a Lady 1943
Sorrowful Jones 1949
Fancy Pants 1950
The Long Long Trailer 1954
Mame 1973

BANKHEAD, Tallulah 1903-1968

This daughter of a leading American senator was born in Alabama. Except for Hitchcock's *Lifeboat* (1943), she was chiefly a stage actress famous for her foghorn voice and vivid personality. She had considerable talent, but she rather wasted it.

FILMOGRAPHY
His House in Order 1928
A Woman's Law 1928
Tarnished Lady 1931
Lifeboat 1943
Royal Scandal 1945
Fanatic 1965

BARA, Theda 1890-1955

Born Theodosia Goodman, this silent-screen femme fatale was the first vamp and possibly the first star to be created via publicity. Born in Cincinnati, Ohio, she took the world by storm in her first major role in *A Fool There Was* (1916), based on the Kipling poem, *The Vampire*. A line from the movie, 'Kiss me, my fool', became the slogan of the day.

Theda Bara (supposedly an anagram of 'Arab Death') wore indigo makeup, kept skulls and ravens and met reporters while caressing a snake. She was an object of mystery and fascination to American audiences – everything they'd always believed about sex but were afraid to find out was true.

After World War I she fell out of fashion but became a Hollywood hostess happily married to director Charles Brabin.

FILMOGRAPHY
A Fool There Was 1916
Destruction 1916
Cleopatra 1917
The Forbidden Path 1918
The Hunchback of Notre Dame 1923
Madame Mystery 1926

BARDOT, Brigitte 1933-

Brigitte Bardot was a blonde sex kitten, playful and sensual. She was the image of the 1960s in the 1950s, a new post-war form of golden youth, scantily clad, free of sexual guilt, ready to enjoy life – the first European star of her era to make it big in the United States. Her films made a fortune.

Bardot was born in Paris, the daughter of a wealthy industrialist. She studied ballet and at age 15 posed for the cover of *Elle*, a leading French magazine. She looked like a sexy fawn. Assistant director Roger Vadim noticed her and decided to promote her career. In 1952 he married her; the marriage lasted until 1957.

She had a series of supporting roles in French films, pouting her famous pout and flashing her famous smile. She had a small part in *Act of Love* (1954), with Kirk Douglas, and appeared in *Doctor at Sea* (1955) enticing Dirk Bogarde. *The Light Across the Street* (1955) provided her with her first starring role. *And God Created Woman* (1956), Vadim's first effort as a director, allowed Bardot's child-woman appeal full scope and the movie became an enormous international success.

From then on the world couldn't get enough of Bardot's public and private life. She set the style for bikinis and put Saint Tropez on the map. Gossip columnists around the earth wrote about her affairs, her moods, her tastes. In 1960 Simone de Beauvoir wrote a treatise about Bardot and 'the Lolita Syndrome.' Teenage Bardot types, aping her clothes and hair, were everywhere, especially on the beaches. Many members of their parents' generation attacked Bardot as if she alone were responsible for the sexual revolution. Her performance in *The Truth* (1961) brought her critical recognition at last.

Today Bardot's name still glitters. Though retired from films, she's appeared on television and has been an active supporter of many worthy causes.

The French sex kitten – Brigitte Bardot.

FILMOGRAPHY
Act of Love 1954
Doctor at Sea 1955
The Light across the Street 1955
Helen of Troy 1955
And God Created Woman 1956
Heaven Fell That Night 1957
Une Parisienne 1957
En Cas de Malheur 1957
Please Mr Balzac 1957
The Devil is a Woman 1958
Mam'zelle Pigalle 1958
Babette Goes to War 1959
Please Not Now 1961
The Truth 1961
Vie Privée 1961
Love on a Pillow 1962
Contempt 1964
Dear Brigitte 1965
Viva Maria 1965
Two Weeks in September 1967
Shalako 1968
The Novices 1970
The Legend of Frenchy King 1972
Don Juan 1973

BARRYMORE, Ethel 1879-1959

A member of the great acting family, Miss Barrymore appeared in films primarily from 1914 to 1919 and again in the 1940s when she established herself as America's image of the gracious and spirited elderly woman. She was born in Philadelphia, Pennsylvania, the daughter of actors Maurice Barrymore (Herbert Blythe) and Georgiana Drew. She was the sister of actors John and Lionel Barrymore.

Miss Barrymore made her stage debut at 15, ultimately becoming 'the first lady of the American theater.' She made many important movies, receiving an Academy Award for Best Supporting Actress for *None But the Lonely Heart* (1944).

FILMOGRAPHY
The Nightingale 1914
Rasputin and the Empress 1932
None but the Lonely Heart 1944
The Spiral Staircase 1946
The Farmer's Daughter 1947
Portrait of Jennie 1949
Kind Lady 1951
Deadline 1952
Young at Heart 1954

BARRYMORE, John 1882-1942

John Barrymore was everything a great stage and screen legend should be: glamorous, debonair, gallant, gifted and even tragic. Though he was a major force in American theater, by the time he reached Hollywood life had begun to catch up with him. Still Barrymore has left us some very fine films to remember him by.

The youngest of the 'fabulous Barrymores' was born in Philadelphia, Pennsylvania, the son of stage actors Maurice Barrymore (Herbert Blythe) and Georgiana Drew and the brother of Lionel and Ethel Barrymore. He began working as a cartoonist but theater tradition won out and Barrymore became a leading light comedian and Shakespearian actor, the Broadway idol of his time.

He began making movies in 1913: romantic dramas, comedies and swashbucklers. Though audiences adored him as the great lover, a role he excelled at off screen as well as on, there were few limits to his range.

Though Barrymore was paid vast sums for his movies, he kept returning to the stage. Hollywood took him on any terms because in one of the first box-office polls ever conducted Barrymore was at the top, ahead of Harold Lloyd, Gloria Swanson and Rin-Tin-Tin. He did not sustain this position. In fact, many critics accused him of hamming it up on screen.

Barrymore's beautiful voice guaranteed he would survive the coming of talking pictures, but alcohol was taking its toll and he suffered acute memory lapses. Still he and Garbo were good in *Grand Hotel* (1932). *A Bill of Divorcement* (1932), the sparkling *Dinner at Eight* (1933), *Twentieth Century* (1934) and *Midnight* (1939) proved that Barrymore still had the old magic.

Towards the end of his film career 'The Great Profile' began to parody himself, playing aging actors dreaming of the past. On stage he sometimes fell into a drunken stupor during performances. John Barrymore died penniless. Ironically, he was later portrayed by Erroll Flynn, also notorious for his roguish life style, in the movie version of *Too Much Too Soon* (1938), based on his daughter Diana's autobiography.

The three Barrymores – John (left), Ethel and Lionel, in *Rasputin and the Empress* (1932).

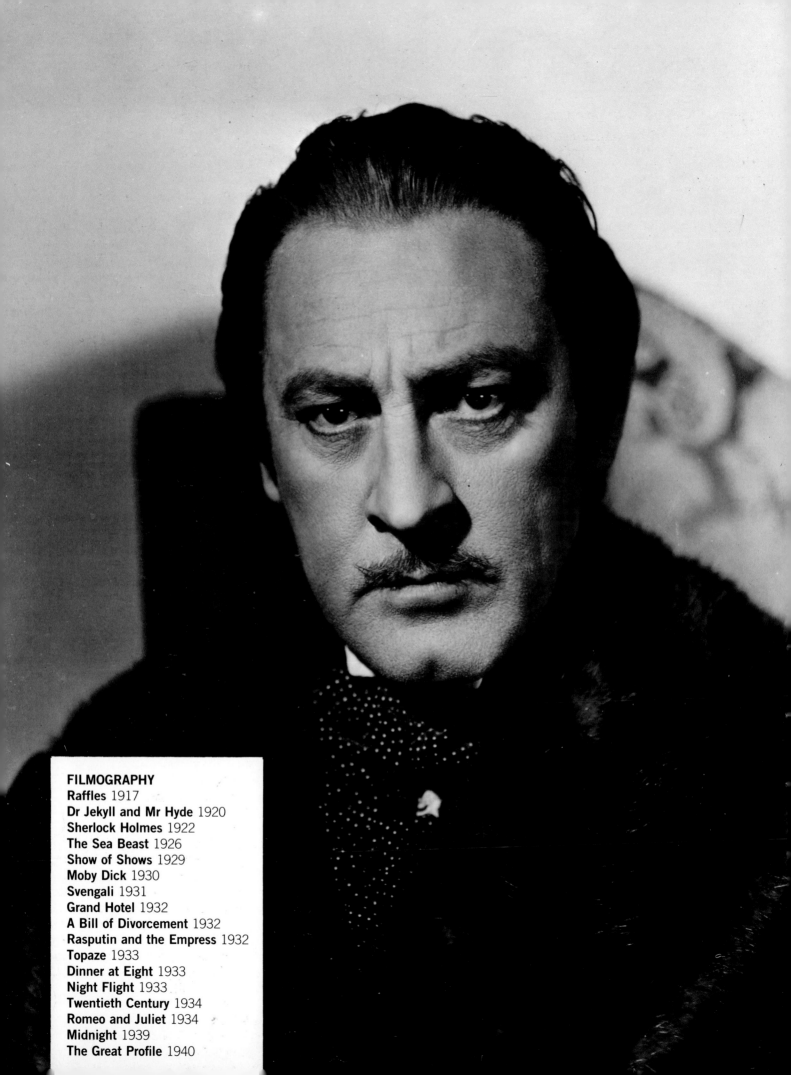

FILMOGRAPHY
Raffles 1917
Dr Jekyll and Mr Hyde 1920
Sherlock Holmes 1922
The Sea Beast 1926
Show of Shows 1929
Moby Dick 1930
Svengali 1931
Grand Hotel 1932
A Bill of Divorcement 1932
Rasputin and the Empress 1932
Topaze 1933
Dinner at Eight 1933
Night Flight 1933
Twentieth Century 1934
Romeo and Juliet 1934
Midnight 1939
The Great Profile 1940

BARRYMORE, Lionel 1878-1954

A member of the great Barrymore acting family, Lionel Barrymore was an actor, director and screenwriter. Born in Philadelphia, Pennsylvania, he was the son of Maurice Barrymore (Herbert Blythe) and Georgiana Drew and brother of Ethel and John Barrymore. He was the first Barrymore to appear in films.

In 1925 Barrymore abandoned theater to devote himself solely to movies. He signed with MGM, remaining with that studio, moving from leading roles to character parts over the years.

Barrymore won an Academy Award for *A Free Soul* (1931). He was especially popular as Dr Gillespie in the Dr Kildare film series. Partially paralyzed by arthritis in the late 1930s Barrymore continued acting in a wheelchair.

FILMOGRAPHY
Friends 1909
A Free Soul 1931
Rasputin and the Empress 1932
Camille 1937
You Can't Take it with You 1938
Young Dr Kildare 1938
It's a Wonderful Life 1946
Duel in the Sun 1946
Key Largo 1948

Left: John Barrymore in *Maytime* (1937).
Below: Richard Barthelmess in 1932.

BARTHELMESS, Richard 1895-1963

Richard Barthelmess was discovered by Alla Nazimova. Lillian Gish thought his face 'the most beautiful of any man who ever went before a camera. D W Griffith thought he'd make a perfect hero, and he did.

Barthelmess was born in New York City, and was in amateur theater productions at Trinity College. He was immensely popular throughout the silent-screen era. He was best as a country boy in *Tol'able David* (1921), and he was nominated for the Academy Award for Best Actor the first year the Oscar was offered, 1927-28. The nomination was based on his work in two films, *The Patent Leather Kid* (1927) and *The Noose* (1928). Barthelmess later turned to character roles before retiring from movies in the 1940s.

FILMOGRAPHY
Broken Blossoms 1919
Tol'able David 1921
The Patent Leather Kid 1927
The Noose 1928
The Dawn Patrol 1930
A Modern Hero 1934
Only Angels Have Wings 1939

BARTHOLOMEW, Freddie 1924-

Born Frederick Llewellyn, this curly-haired, well-bred British child-actor

became a Hollywood star playing the boy hero in movie versions of great adventure novels, and one sugary young dandy named Little Lord Fauntleroy. Born in London, Bartholomew was raised by his aunt, Millicent Bartholomew. He was performing on stage at the age of three.

Freddie appeared in American films for the first time in 1935. The public loved his dimples and his English accent and he became extremely popular. In 1937 he was the focus of two legal battles. One was an attempt by his parents to get him away from his aunt. The other involved his aunt's attempt to get him away from MGM. He wound up with aunt and MGM until his career hit the skids in the 1940s.

FILMOGRAPHY
Fascination 1930
Lily Christine 1932
David Copperfield 1935
Little Lord Fauntleroy 1936
Kidnapped 1938
Tom Brown's Schooldays 1940

BATES, Alan 1934-

Alan Bates is a virile but sensitive leading man who's done films in Britain and America. He was born in Britain and appeared on the London stage before beginning his film career.

FILMOGRAPHY
A Kind of Loving 1962
Whistle down the Wind 1962
Far from the Madding Crowd 1967
The Fixer 1968
Women in Love 1969
An Unmarried Woman 1978
The Rose 1978
Nijinsky 1979
The Return of the Soldier 1985

BAXTER, Anne 1923-1985

Anne Baxter, the granddaughter of architect Frank Lloyd Wright, was born in Michigan City, Indiana. A competent stage and film actress, she won a best supporting Oscar for *The Razor's Edge* (1946), and is best remembered today as the scheming young actress in *All About Eve* (1950).

FILMOGRAPHY
The Magnificent Ambersons 1942
The Razor's Edge 1946
All Above Eve 1950

BEATTY, Warren 1937-

One of Hollywood's more complex talents, Warren Beatty is an innovative director and producer who dreams big, and he's a more than competent actor. Beatty was born in Richmond, Virginia. He was a gifted athlete and actor. His sister, who would one day be famous as Shirley Maclaine, was an aspiring dancer. Beatty attended Northwestern University for a year, then moved to New York, studying acting with Stella Adler. He appeared in William Inge's *A Loss of Roses* on Broadway, then broke into films big when he co-starred opposite Natalie Wood in *Splendour in the Grass* (1961). His good looks and off-screen romance with Wood, who was married to Robert Wagner at the time, didn't hurt Beatty any.

A series of less than memorable films followed until Beatty produced and starred in the smash success *Bonnie and Clyde* (1967), a movie that introduced a new level of violence to the screen. He was nominated for the Oscar for Best Actor for the film.

McCabe and Mrs Miller (1971), with real life lover Julie Christie, got some notice. So did *Shampoo* (1975), about a sexy hair dresser, which Beatty starred in, co-wrote and produced. Feminists labeled the popular film sexist. Beatty denied that it was. Even more popular was the delightful comedy, *Heaven Can Wait* (1978), a remake of *Here Comes Mr Jordan*, co-written by Beatty and Elaine May. Beatty was very good as the football player sent to Heaven by mistake and returned to earth. The movie was nominated for the Academy Award for Best Picture. Beatty himself received two Academy Awards: Best Director (in collaboration) and Best Actor. He won an Academy Award at last for *Reds* (1982), as Best Director.

Reds was an elaborate production and Beatty oversaw each detail. It told the story of American radical John Reed. Beatty has long been active in leftist causes and politics. Co-starring with Beatty was Diane Keaton, his chief romantic interest of the time.

Intellectual and entrepreneurial, Warren Beatty spends years on a project. He's one of the giants of the present movie era.

FILMOGRAPHY
Splendour in the Grass 1961
The Roman Spring of Mrs Stone 1961
All Fall Down 1961
Lilith 1965
Mickey One 1965
Promise Her Anything 1966
Kaleidoscope 1966
Bonnie and Clyde 1967
The Only Game in Town 1969
McCabe and Mrs Miller 1971
The Parallax View 1974
Shampoo 1975
The Fortune 1975
Heaven Can Wait 1978
Reds 1982
Ishtar 1987

Warren Beatty starred with Faye Dunaway in *Bonnie and Clyde* (1967).

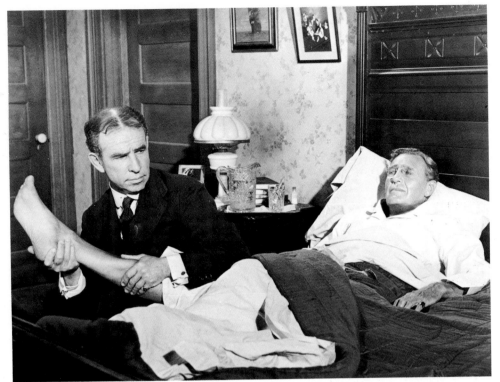

ator in on-screen comedies. In 1916 he married Gloria Swanson, his co-star in a series of Mack Sennett comedies, divorcing her two years later. Then it was chiefly tough guys and villains until sound. He and Marie Dressler became one of Hollywood's memorable movie couples. Beery appeared in several film classics, receiving an Academy Award for *The Champ* (1931).

FILMOGRAPHY
Robin Hood 1921
The Lost World 1924
Min and Bill 1930
The Champ 1931
Grand Hotel 1932
Dinner at Eight 1933
Tugboat Annie 1933
Viva Villa 1934
Treasure Island 1934
The Mighty Barnum 1934
A Message to Garcia 1936

Ralph Bellamy (*right*) as Franklin D Roosevelt in *Sunrise at Campobello* (1960) – with Hume Cronyn.

BEERY, Noah 1884-1946

Noah Beery was a movie villain and scoundrel in the silent era and a character actor in talkies. Beery was born in Kansas City, Missouri. The brother of actor Wallace Beery and father of actor Noah Beery, Jr, he began acting on stage in 1900 and 17 years later he appeared in films.

He became popular as the most villainous of villains and meanest of meanies. Audiences loved him in *The Mark of Zorro* (1920), *The Sea Wolf* (1920) and as the cruel Sergeant Lejaune in *Beau Geste* (1926). He also appeared in many Zane Grey Westerns.

FILMOGRAPHY
The Mark of Zorro 1920
The Sea Wolf 1920
Beau Geste 1926
Don Juan 1926
The Four Feathers 1929
She Done Him Wrong 1933
King of the Damned 1935
Our Fighting Navy 1937
The Girl of the Golden West 1938
Isle of Missing Men 1942

BEERY, Noah Jr 1913-

This American character actor is the son of movie villain Noah Beery and nephew of Wallace Beery. As a child in New York City he appeared in the silent movie *The Mark of Zorro* (1920) with his father and Douglas Fairbanks and continued to perform with his father on stage.

Later Noah Beery, Jr played supporting roles in films, including Westerns starring Tom Mix, Johnny Mack Brown and Buck Jones. He married Jones's daughter Maxine in 1940. He had lead roles in several low-budget movies.

FILMOGRAPHY
The Mark of Zorro 1920
Heroes of the West 1926
Only Angels Have Wings 1939
Of Mice and Men 1940
Riders of Death Valley 1941
Red River 1948
White Feather 1955
Inherit the Wind 1960
The Seven Faces of Dr Lao 1964
Little Fauss and Big Halsy 1970
Walking Tall 1973
The Best Little Whorehouse in Texas 1982

BEERY, Wallace 1885-1949

Wallace Beery had a rubbery face and a gravelly voice yet he became a popular leading man in talkies. Born in Kansas City, he was the brother of Noah Beery and uncle of Noah Beery, Jr. The circus and Broadway musicals preceded his film career.

In 1913 he was a female imperson-

BELLAMY, Ralph 1904-

Bellamy, a versatile stage and screen actor, was born in Chicago, Illinois. Often cast as the guy who loses the girl, he had the title role in the Ellery Queen mystery series, and was Franklin Delano Roosevelt in *Sunrise at Campobello* (1960).

FILMOGRAPHY
The Awful Truth 1937
Ellery Queen, Master Detective 1940
Sunrise at Campobello 1960
Rosemary's Baby 1967
Oh, God! 1977

Wallace Beery in *A Date with Judy* (1948).

BELMONDO, Jean-Paul 1933-

Sexy, charming and appealingly home-ly, this leading French film star was born in Neuilly-sur-Seine, near Paris. He was the son of a sculptor. After studying drama at the Paris Conservatory and appearing on stage, he had supporting roles in films until he sky-rocketed to fame in *Breathless* (1959).

He soon symbolized the New Wave antihero and young rebel to international audiences and by age 30 was president of the French actors' union and had published an autobiography. Talent and skill have kept him at the top ever since. Belmondo has worked with nearly every famous French director, including Jean-Luc Godard, François Truffaut, Alain Resnais and Louis Malle.

FILMOGRAPHY
Breathless 1959
Two Women 1961
Cartouche 1962
A Monkey in Winter 1962
That Man from Rio 1964
Is Paris Burning? 1966
The Mississippi Mermaid 1969
Scoundrel in White 1972
Stavisky 1974
Le Professionnel 1981

BELUSHI, John 1949-1982

Talented comedian Belushi was born in Chicago, Illinois. A member of the Second City improvisational group, Belushi appeared on television's *Saturday Night Live*. His first film, *Animal House* (1978), was one of the most successful comedies of modern times. His subsequent films were only marginally successful. Belushi's death from a drug overdose prompted a national outcry about drugs in the entertainment industry.

FILMOGRAPHY
Animal House 1978
The Blues Brothers 1979
Continental Divide 1981
Neighbors 1981

BENNETT, Joan 1910-

An attractive leading lady in the 1930s and 1940s, sister of Barbara and Constance Bennett, Joan Bennett played

John Belushi was magnificent as the ultimate slob in *Animal House* (1978).

everything from ambitious and mercenary women to motherly types. In the 1960s she starred in the popular Gothic TV soap opera *Dark Shadows*.

FILMOGRAPHY
Little Women 1932
Man Hunt 1941
The Woman in the Window 1944
Scarlet Street 1945
The Secret Beyond the Door 1947
Father of the Bride 1950
House of Dark Shadows 1970

BENNY, Jack 1894-1974

A master comedian, Benny (born Benjamin Kubelsky) was a star of vaudeville, radio, movies and television. Though films were probably his least successful medium (he often joked about this) his performance in *To Be or Not to Be* (1942) was touchingly funny.

FILMOGRAPHY
Charlie's Aunt 1941
To Be or Not to Be 1942
George Washington Slept Here 1942
The Horn Blows at Midnight 1945

BERGEN, Candice 1946-

She's the daughter of ventriloquist Edger Bergen and one of the most beautiful blondes around. Born in Beverly Hills, California, Bergen received an Oscar nomination for *Starting Over* (1979). She was a model before making films and is an accomplished photographer.

FILMOGRAPHY
The Group 1966
Carnal Knowledge 1971
Starting Over 1979
Rich and Famous 1981
Gandhi 1982

BERGMAN, Ingrid 1915-1982

Ingrid Bergman had a natural beauty and warm smile that allowed her to outshine all of Hollywood's female stars. Born in 1915 in Stockholm, Sweden, Bergman was raised by her photographer father and other relatives after the early death of her mother. Bergman's father wanted her to be a performing artist and he encouraged her to follow her own path in life. He

FILMOGRAPHY
Intermezzo 1939
Dr Jekyll and Mr Hyde 1941
Casablanca 1942
For Whom the Bell Tolls 1943
Gaslight 1944
Spellbound 1945
Joan of Arc 1948
Stromboli 1950
Anastasia 1956
The Inn of the Sixth Happiness 1958
The Visit 1964
Cactus Flower 1969
Murder on the Orient Express 1974
Autumn Sonata 1978

The regal Ingrid Bergman – one of the greatest actresses of our time.

Above: Bergman as a concert pianist in *Autumn Sonata* (1978) – her last film.

also helped give her a deep inner confidence. From other relatives she received her passion for order, discipline and hard work.

In 1933 she enrolled in the Royal Theatre of Dramatic Art but switched to films instead and quickly became a well-known screen actress. Bergman was brought to Hollywood by David O Selznick to co-star with Leslie Howard in the American version of the movie *Intermezzo* (1939).

With World War II imminent, Bergman's wholesome freshness and sincerity made her the perfect choice for a new kind of star. She seemed to embody the best of European womanhood and culture at a time when the Nazis were plunging Europe into darkness. Thus, Bergman was cast in a series of important films, most notably *Casablanca* (1942). She won an Academy Award for *Gaslight* (1944).

Her image boomeranged when she left her husband, Dr Peter Lindstrom, and daughter Pia in 1949 to live with Roberto Rossellini, the Italian director. Bergman had Rossellini's child, which created a great hue and cry. Though Bergman married Rossellini in 1950, American moviegoers would not forgive her. She was even called 'Hollywood's apostle of degradation' on the floor of the United States Senate.

In addition to their first born child, a son, Bergman and Rossellini had twin daughters. As actress and director they were not a success and films like *Stromboli* (1950) did not fare well critically or commercially. The couple's marriage was annulled in 1958.

With the passage of time, the public view of Bergman changed and she was welcomed back to America. She won an Academy Award for Best Actress for *Anastasia* (1956), which was Hollywood's way of making amends. An Oscar for Best Supporting Actress and a British Film Academy Award went to her for *Murder on the Orient Express* (1974).

She continued to work in films, on the stage and in television until her death from cancer in 1982.

BISSET, Jacqueline 1944-

A glamorous model and actress, Bisset was born in England, and had bit parts in British films before Hollywood groomed her for a stardom that never quite happened.

FILMOGRAPHY
The Sweet Ride 1967
Bullitt 1968
Murder on the Orient Express 1974
Who is Killing the Great Chefs of Europe? 1978
Under the Volcano 1985

Joan Blondell in *Dames* (1934).

BLONDELL, Joan 1909-1979

Playing a gold-digger with a heart of gold, Blondell was one of Hollywood's top light comediennes and musical stars, especially in the 1930s, when she appeared in as many as ten pictures a year. She spent most of the 1950s on stage, then returned to films in character parts.

FILMOGRAPHY
Gold Diggers of 1933 1933
Footlight Parade 1933
Dames 1934
Stage Struck 1936
A Tree Grows in Brooklyn 1944
The Cincinnati Kid 1965
Grease 1978
The Champ 1979

BOGARDE, Dirk 1920-

Dirk Bogarde is elegant, handsome, and gifted. He has consistently turned in first-rate performances in films, even with weak material. When the material has been worthy of him, he's proved superb. Born Derek Van Den Bogaerde in London, Bogarde's Dutch-born father was art editor for London's *The Times*. Dirk Bogarde began working as a scenic designer and commercial artist but he really wanted to act, and made his stage debut in a small suburban theater in 1939. Only after he returned from the service in World War II, however, did his theatrical career begin in earnest.

A stage play, *Power Without Glory*, won Bogarde a movie contract with Rank Studios and he made a string of pictures. One of them, *The Blue Lamp* (1950), was the most successful British film of the year. Critics praised his performance in *Hunted* (1952), a thriller. Then came Bogarde's big hit, *Doctor in the House* (1953), the first of a series of irreverent 'Doctor' comedies.

Hollywood beckoned but Bogarde resisted. Later he would appear in both American and international films, but in the mid- through late 1950s he was distinctly a British star, the number-one box-office draw. In 1957 *Picturegoer* readers voted him the year's best actor.

In the 1960s Bogarde began receiving the kind of roles he needed to display his subtlety and sensitivity. In *Victim* (1961), he played a gay character, a gutsy move on the part of a major star at a time when the subject of homosexuality was still firmly locked in the closet. His performance as the decadent valet in *The Servant* (1963) won him a British Film Academy Award for Best Actor. He won a second for *Darling* (1965), with Julie Christie.

His performance as a dying composer obsessed with a young boy in *Death in Venice* (1971) is a tour de force. In the early 1970s Bogarde moved to Italy and then to France, in part because he felt he wasn't being offered the kind of roles he craved in Britain. He was by then an international star, highly respected. One of his finest performances was in Alain Resnais's complex *Providence* (1977).

Below: Bogarde in *A Bridge Too Far* (1977).
Bottom: Bogarde and Sarah Miles in the study of decadence, *The Servant* (1963).

FILMOGRAPHY
Quartet 1948
The Blue Lamp 1950
Hunted 1952
Doctor in the House 1953
The Sleeping Tiger 1954
Doctor at Sea 1955
Cast a Dark Shadow 1955
Doctor at Large 1956
The Spanish Gardener 1956
Campbell's Kingdom 1958
A Tale of Two Cities 1958
The Doctor's Dilemma 1959
Song Without End 1960
Victim 1961
The Servant 1963
Doctor in Distress 1964
Darling 1965
The Damned 1969
Death in Venice 1971
The Night Porter 1974
Providence 1977

BOGART, Humphrey 1899-1957

Bogart is 'Bogey,' the most famous male Hollywood star. A cult hero to just about everybody, he is simply one of the best film actors America ever produced. Is there anybody who hasn't seen *Casablanca* (1942)?

He was born Humphrey DeForest Bogart in New York City, the son of a prominent doctor and a famous illustrator. Though Bogart would some day play the common man to perfection he was given a classic education. It didn't stick. Instead he joined the Navy where he received a scar on his lip that presumably gave him his distinctive style of speech.

Bogart broke into acting through the help of a friend, but he had to work hard to make it. A real pro, he spent many years in New York playing the romantic juvenile on stage. In 1930 he tried films. Nothing much came of it and Bogart returned to New York. His big break came when he played gangster Duke Mantee in *The Petrified Forest* on Broadway, then repeated his performance in the 1936 movie version of the play.

Abandoning theater for the next few years, Bogart played mainly gangster roles in lots of films. Then he began working with screenwriter and director John Huston and film history was made. Bogart turned from bad guy to good guy but a cynical good guy, not a saint. Beginning with *High Sierra* (1941), he moved on to *The Maltese Falcon* (1941), a masterpiece. *Casablanca* (1942), with Ingrid Bergman, was absolutely the premier Hollywood movie of World War II. Then there were *To Have and Have Not* (1943), *The Big Sleep* (1946) and *The Treasure of the Sierra Madre* (1947).

On the set of *To Have and Have Not* he met a gorgeous young model named Lauren Bacall and later married her. She was his fourth wife. Bogart and third wife Mayo Methot had been notorious in Hollywood for their fights and were known as 'the battling Bogarts,' but Bogart's marriage to Bacall was immensely successful.

Bogart won an Academy Award for Best Actor for his performance in *The African Queen* (1952), co-starring Katharine Hepburn.

FILMOGRAPHY
The Petrified Forest 1936
Marked Woman 1937
Angels with Dirty Faces 1938
Dark Victory 1939
They Drive by Night 1940
High Sierra 1941
The Maltese Falcon 1941
Across the Pacific 1942
Casablanca 1942
Action in the North Atlantic 1943
Sahara 1943
To Have and Have Not 1943
The Big Sleep 1946
The Treasure of the Sierra Madre 1947
Key Largo 1948
The African Queen 1952
Beat the Devil 1954
The Caine Mutiny 1954
Sabrina 1954
The Barefoot Contessa 1954
We're No Angels 1955
The Desperate Hours 1955

Bogart, Hepburn, *The African Queen* (1951).

Humphrey Bogart and the young Lauren Bacall in *To Have and Have Not* (1943).

BORGNINE, Ernest 1917-

Born Ermes Borgnino, Borgnine's broad frame and broad face got him typecast as a villain in films until *Marty* (1955), a movie about a lonely butcher, where he was able to show what he could do. Born in Connecticut, he spent part of his childhood in Milan, Italy. He joined the US Navy in 1935 and after that he took up acting.

Theater and television followed, and then films including *From Here to Eternity* (1953) and *Bad Day at Black Rock* (1954). *Marty* won Borgnine an Academy Award for Best Actor and a British Film Academy Award, bringing him better roles, both in movies and on television.

FILMOGRAPHY
From Here to Eternity 1953
Vera Cruz 1954
Bad Day at Black Rock 1954
Marty 1955
The Catered Affair 1956
The Vikings 1958
Pay or Die 1960
McHale's Navy 1964
The Dirty Dozen 1967
Willard 1971
The Poseidon Adventure 1972
Escape from New York 1981

BOW, Clara 1905-1965

Clara Bow was the most famous flapper of the jazz age. She was the 'It' girl ('it' for sex appeal) and with her red hair, expressive eyes, coquettish ways and on-screen energy she helped make movie theaters the place to be in the 1920s. Flaming youth never flamed brighter than Bow. Bow's bobbed hair, Bow's bow lips, Bow's bangles and beads became the emblem of the emancipated woman. She lived the wild exuberant life of the Roaring Twenties off screen as well as on and that, in basically prudish America, was to prove her downfall.

Bow's is a rags to riches story. She was born in Brooklyn, New York, where her father was a sometime-waiter at Coney Island, her mother a mentally unstable semi-invalid. At 16 Bow escaped poverty by winning a fan-magazine beauty contest. When New York film studios didn't pan out for her, she went to Hollywood. Nicknamed first 'the Brooklyn bonfire' she churned out movies like crazy, 14 releases in 1925 alone. She was popular but *Mantrap* (1926), her first smash hit, made her a legendary star.

Bow started making big money, though never what she was worth. *It* (1927) captured the imagination of her generation and shop girls and waitresses aped her style. *Rough House Rosie* (1927), *The Wild Party* (1929) and *Dangerous Curves* (1929) drove audiences wild. Bow's list of admirers included an up-and-coming talent — Gary Cooper. She owned a limousine the color of her hair and two red chow dogs dyed to match. In 1928 a national poll declared Clara Bow America's most popular female movie star.

She made the transition to sound easily but by 1930 she was the focus of scandals involving adultery and gambling. Revelations in court about drink, drugs and gigolos turned the public and the press against her; her sizzling career turned to ashes. Clara Bow married cowboy star Rex Bell in 1931. He later became lieutenant governor of Nevada but by then she was in and out of rest homes, suffering from chronic insomnia and recurring breakdowns. In 1962 she claimed Marilyn Monroe as her true successor.

BOYER, Charles 1897-1978

American audiences found Boyer exotic, romantic and possessed of Gallic charm. Born in France, Boyer made his film and stage debut there in 1920, and was chiefly a Paris matinee idol until coming to America in 1934.

In the 1930s and 1940s, Boyer played opposite Hollywood's greatest beauties: stars like Ingrid Bergman and Hedy Lamarr. In 1942 he won a special Academy Award for establishing the French Research Foundation. Despite his film triumphs, his personal life was tinged with tragedy. Boyer's only child committed suicide in 1965. In 1978 Boyer also committed suicide, depressed over the death of his wife of over 30 years, Patricia Paterson.

FILMOGRAPHY
La Barcaolle d'Amour 1928
Red-Headed Woman 1932
Mayerling 1937
Tovarich 1937
Conquest 1937
History is Made at Night 1937
Algiers 1938
Back Street 1941
Gaslight 1944
Cluny Brown 1946
The Happy Time 1952
Fanny 1962
Barefoot in the Park 1968
Stavisky 1974

Clara Bow – the 'It' girl of the 1920s, the vivacious young flapper.

FILMOGRAPHY

Down to the Sea in Ships 1923	**Wings** 1927
Black Oxen 1924	**The Fleet's In** 1928
Kiss Me Again 1925	**The Wild Party** 1929
Dancing Mothers 1926	**Dangerous Curves** 1929
Mantrap 1926	**The Saturday Night Kid** 1929
It 1927	**True to the Navy** 1930
Children of Divorce 1927	**Her Wedding Night** 1930
Rough House Rosie 1927	

BRANDO, Marlon 1924-

Marlon Brando is a deeply talented stage and film actor, original, spontaneous and charismatic. However, moodiness and lack of judgment have hurt him, and Brando's over-all career achievements are not what they should be. Still, he has given us some fiery and memorable film moments.

He was born in Omaha, Nebraska. Ever the rebel, he was expelled from military school and came to New York to study acting, eventually becoming a member of the Actors Studio which stressed the Stanislavsky method. Brando rose to success easily in New York theater, scoring a massive hit with his portrayal of Stanley Kowalski in *A Streetcar Named Desire* in 1947. He played the brutal Kowalski with equal brilliance in the movie version in 1951.

Those were great days for Brando. One of a group of young actors from New York who transformed Hollywood, Brando emerged as the image of nonconformity and individuality at a time when nonconformity was rare. *On the Waterfront* (1954) brought him an Academy Award for Best Actor after three successive nominations. He also received the Cannes Film Festival Prize and his third British Film Academy Award. He had already received British Film Academy Awards for *Viva Zapata* (1952) and as Mark Antony in *Julius Caesar* (1953).

In the 1960s Brando's movies were not up to his achievements in the previous decade. A stormy personal life, including three marriages, added to his image as a temperamental artist. Directors found him difficult to work with and his own attempts at producing and directing films via a company he founded led to financial disaster. Brando made a brilliant comeback as Corleone in *The Godfather*

Marlon Brando was almost 30 when he filmed *The Wild One* (1953).

(1972), winning an Academy Award for Best Actor which he refused to accept, sending in his place a spokesman for the cause of the American Indians. Brando has long been involved with left-wing causes. He created a stir in the bold and sexually explicit *Last Tango in Paris* (1972), and he was Commander Kurtz in *Apocalypse Now* (1979). Lesser roles in the 1970s made money and for the most part Brando prefers to spend his time in Tahiti away from stage or film. We can only hope he will yet give us another magnificent performance. Marlon Brando certainly has the gift.

FILMOGRAPHY
The Men 1950
A Streetcar Named Desire 1951
Viva Zapata 1952
Julius Caesar 1953
The Wild One 1953
On the Waterfront 1954
Desirée 1954
Guys and Dolls 1955
The Teahouse of the August Moon 1956
Sayonara 1957
The Young Lions 1958
One Eyed Jacks 1960
Reflections in a Golden Eye 1967
The Nightcomers 1971
The Godfather 1972
Last Tango in Paris 1972
Superman 1978
Apocalypse Now 1979

Above: Brando and Eva Marie Saint in *On the Waterfront* (1954) – he won an Oscar.

Below: Walter Brennan (left) was the first actor to win three Academy Awards.

BRENNAN, Walter 1894-1974

A popular and versatile character actor, Brennan appeared in over 100 films. He was born in Swampscott, Massachusetts. Appearing first in vaudeville, Brennan came to Hollywood in 1923 and found work as an extra and stuntman. From there he moved on to supporting roles.

Brennan's range was exceptional. He played everything from cowboys to city types, and even villains. While still in his thirties, Brennan was able to play old men convincingly. Brennan was the first actor to win three Academy Awards. He received Oscars for Best Supporting Actor for *Come and Get It* (1936), *Kentucky* (1938) and *The Westerner* (1940).

FILMOGRAPHY
Come and Get It 1936
The Adventures of Tom Sawyer 1938
Kentucky 1938
Stanley and Livingston 1939
The Westerner 1940
Sergeant York 1941
Swamp Water 1941
To Have and Have Not 1944
My Darling Clementine 1946
Rio Bravo 1959
How the West Was Won 1962

34

George Brent in *The Spiral Staircase* (1945).

BRENT, George 1904-1979

George Brent, born George Brent Nolan, was a suave, attractive, romantic leading man who was especially effective when cast with strong leading ladies like Bette Davis and Myrna Loy. A pencil-thin moustache was his trademark. Brent was born in Ireland. A stage actor, he was forced to flee Ireland because of his political activities on behalf of Irish independence. He came to America and continued his acting career in the theater.

Brent's film career, beginning in the early 1930s, spanned 20 years and he appeared opposite some of Hollywood's most famous female stars. He was married six times.

FILMOGRAPHY
Forty Second Street 1933
The Painted Veil 1934
Front Page Woman 1935
Jezebel 1938
Dark Victory 1939
The Rains Came 1939
The Great Lie 1941
The Affairs of Susan 1945
The Spiral Staircase 1945
Born Again 1978

BRONSON, Charles 1921-

Bronson (born Charles Buchinsky), a coal miner's son was born in Ehrenfeld, Pennsylvania. He played villains and tough guys in Hollywood 'B' movies until at age 50 he zoomed to stardom in Europe and then America.

FILMOGRAPHY
Pat and Mike 1952
The Magnificent Seven 1960
The Dirty Dozen 1967
Death Wish 1974
Hard Times 1975
From Ten to Midnight 1982
Murphy's Law 1986

BROOKS, Louise 1906-1985

An intelligent woman and a fine actress, Louise Brooks was born in Cherryvale, Kansas. She was primarily a dancer until her film debut in 1925. Her striking good looks and distinctive brunette bob created the image that she was just another flapper but her performances in *A Girl in Every Port* (1928) and *Beggars of Life* (1928) proved she had real talent.

Brooks came into her own in Germany under the direction of G W Pabst, but upon her return to America she was unwilling or unable to tolerate life in Hollywood. Eventually she abandoned show business completely, becoming a recluse. In the 1950s she was rediscovered by movie buffs and went on to write critically acclaimed articles on films and an interesting autobiography.

FILMOGRAPHY
Love 'Em and Leave 'Em 1927
Rolled Stockings 1927
A Girl in Every Port 1928
Beggars of Life 1928
Pandora's Box 1929
Diary of a Lost Girl 1930

BROOKS, Mel 1926-

A talented comedian, Brooks (born Melvin Kaminsky) is most famous as a producer, director and scriptwriter. He won an Oscar for his screenplay of the 1968 film, *The Producers*. He didn't appear at all in his finest creation, *Young Frankenstein*, which he wrote, produced and co-directed in 1975. Born in Brooklyn, New York, Brooks got his start writing television comedy in the 1950s chiefly for Sid Caesar. A stand-up comic himself, Brooks appeared in Broadway musicals, then in the 1960s created the popular television series, *Get Smart*.

Brooks specializes in broad vulgar humor and slapstick. When he misses he's bad, but when he's on nobody does it better. Brooks is married to gifted actress Anne Bancroft.

FILMOGRAPHY
The Twelve Chairs 1970
Blazing Saddles 1974
Silent Movie 1976
High Anxiety 1977
History of the World – Part I 1981
To Be or Not To Be 1983
Spaceballs 1987

Mel Brooks in *High Anxiety* (1977) – a spoof of the films of Alfred Hitchcock.

Above: Richard Burton with Elizabeth Taylor in *Cleopatra* (1962).

Left: Yul Brynner as the king with Deborah Kerr in *The King and I* (1956).

BRYNNER, Yul 1915-1985

A shaved head was the trademark of Yul Brynner born on Sakhalin, an island east of Siberia, north of Japan. He won an Oscar for Best Actor for *The King and I* (1956) in the role that he had so successfully created on stage.

FILMOGRAPHY
The King and I 1956
Anastasia 1956
The Magnificent Seven 1960
Invitation to a Gunfighter 1964
Westworld 1973

BUCHANAN, Jack 1891-1957

Jack Buchanan was a debonair song and dance man and star of the British musical stage and films. He also appeared on Broadway and in several Hollywood films, most notably the big-budget musical *The Band Wagon* (1953).

FILMOGRAPHY
Monte Carlo 1930
Yes, Mr Brown 1932
Brewster's Millions 1933
The Gang's All Here 1939
The Band Wagon 1953

BURTON, Richard 1925-1984

Richard Burton (born Richard Jenkins) had a reputation as a fine actor that was based chiefly on his stage, not his film, career. Born in South Wales, the son of a coal miner, he won a scholarship to Oxford.

Shakespearian roles and the 1960 Broadway musical *Camelot* followed. Stardom came with the movie *Cleopatra* (1960), a vehicle for Liz Taylor. Burton and Taylor's steamy off-screen romance led to the discarding of spouses and remarriage to each other. They were hot news and they made big money.

The couple divorced in 1976. Burton continued making films but despite his beautiful voice and obvious gifts he frequently appeared in inferior movies.

FILMOGRAPHY
My Cousin Rachel 1952
Alexander the Great 1956
Look Back in Anger 1959
Cleopatra 1962
The VIPs 1963
Becket 1964
The Spy Who Came in from the Cold 1965
Who's Afraid of Virginia Woolf? 1966
The Taming of the Shrew 1967
Anne of the Thousand Days 1970
Equus 1977
1984 1984

BUSHMAN, Francis X 1883-1966

Francis X Bushman was a sculptor's model whose strong body and handsome face paved the way to stardom in silent films. Born in Norfolk, Virginia, he began acting while still a child. In 1911 Bushman started making films, and audiences, particularly female ones, went mad over him.

Bushman worked fiendishly, playing romantic roles in scores of films, but when fans discovered he had secretly married actress Beverly Bayne they deserted him in droves. His career wasn't over, however, and his most famous role came as the Roman Messala in *Ben Hur* (1926).

The heartthrob of the 1920s – Francis X Bushman, as Messala in *Ben Hur* (1926).

FILMOGRAPHY
One Wonderful Night 1914
Romeo and Juliet 1915
Ben Hur 1926
Hollywood Boulevard 1936
David and Bathsheba 1951
Sabrina 1954
The Story of Mankind 1957

CAAN, James 1939-

His riveting performance as the violent Sonny Corleone in *The Godfather* (1972) made Caan one of Hollywood's hottest properties, though he never achieved the sort of stardom he seemed destined for. In recent years he has tried to soften the gangster image and has effectively directed one film.

FILMOGRAPHY
The Rain People 1969
The Godfather 1972
Cinderella Liberty 1973
The Gambler 1975
Funny Lady 1975
Comes a Horseman 1978
Thief 1981

Cagney, as George M Cohan, with the Cohan family, *Yankee Doodle Dandy* (1942).

James Cagney and Frank McHugh (*left*) making Prohibition bathtub gin in *The Roaring Twenties* (1939).

38

CAGNEY, James 1899-1986

Cagney was America's favorite tough guy, a pugnacious little Irish terrier, a whirlwind of energy on screen. Dapper and defiant, Cagney, with his high-pitched rat-a-tat voice and wary eyes, is a Hollywood legend. He was born in New York City, a poor kid but one who had brains, and he attended Columbia University until lack of money forced him to leave.

After working as a waiter and a racker in a pool room, he broke into vaudeville as a female impersonator. He was a chorus boy, did cabaret with his wife June Vernon, and eventually made it to Broadway. Films followed and in *The Public Enemy* (1931)

FILMOGRAPHY
The Public Enemy 1931
Blonde Crazy 1931
Footlight Parade 1933
Lady Killer 1933
Jimmy the Gent 1934
The St Louis Kid 1934
Devil Dogs of the Air 1935
A Midsummer Night's Dream 1935
Boy Meets Girl 1938
Angels with Dirty Faces 1938
The Roaring Twenties 1939
Strawberry Blonde 1941
Yankee Doodle Dandy 1942
13 Rue Madeleine 1946
The Time of Your Life 1948
White Heat 1949
The West Point Story 1950
Love Me or Leave Me 1955
Mister Roberts 1955
Man of a Thousand Faces 1957
One, Two, Three 1961
Ragtime 1981

Cagney lit up the screen shoving a grapefruit in Mae Clarke's face. He did a series of cheap, quickly made but popular tough-guy pictures, fighting Warner Brothers to receive the salary he deserved.

Cagney proved the depth of his talent and sensitivity when he played Bottom in *A Midsummer Night's Dream* (1935), receiving critical acclaim. In *Angels with Dirty Faces* (1938), Cagney was cast with another fine actor playing gangsters, Humphrey Bogart. Cagney was ready for a career change and so he tried romance, difficult because he wasn't the Hollywood stereotyped leading man, tall, dark and handsome. Witty, with a masterful sense of timing, he turned to comedy. Though these

metamorphoses made money for Cagney in a big way he really clicked when, drawing on his vaudeville and musical comedy background, he played George M Cohan in *Yankee Doodle Dandy* (1942). It brought Cagney an Academy Award for Best Actor. His sister, actress Jean Cagney, appeared with him in this film and others.

In the 1950s, though Cagney tried directing, he continued to act, playing Lon Chaney in *Man of a Thousand Faces* (1957). Retiring from the screen while still a star in 1961, he received the American Film Institute's Life Achievement Award in a televised ceremony in 1974. But he came back to do *Ragtime* (1981). Highly respected, James Cagney became the grand old man of American films.

CAINE, Michael 1933-

Michael Caine (born Maurice Micklewhite) is a believable hero and light romantic lead – a witty and attractive presence in films, due in part to his unabashedly Cockney charm. Caine's father was a London fish-market porter and his mother a cleaning-woman. Caine dropped out of school at 15, appearing in amateur theater productions while working as a laborer.

He broke into British television and from there to films, hitting it big in *Zulu* (1963) and *Alfie* (1966). For a few years it looked as if Caine was headed for superstar status. That never happened, but he has proved an able and durable talent who can master a variety of roles.

FILMOGRAPHY
Zulu 1963
The Ipcress File 1965
Alfie 1966
Gambit 1966
Sleuth 1972
The Man Who Would Be King 1976
Dressed to Kill 1980
Deathtrap 1982
Educating Rita 1983
Mona Lisa 1986
Hannah and Her Sisters 1986

CANTOR, Eddie 1892-1964

Eddie Cantor (born Edward Israel Iskowitz) was famous for his rolling eyes, volatile movements and unique high-pitched singing voice. Cantor was a star of burlesque, vaudeville, theater,

movies and radio. He began his career as a singing waiter in New York's Coney Island Amusement Park.

Cantor starred in the Ziegfeld Follies and two of his Broadway successes, *Kid Boots* and *Whoopee*, were made into films. For years he had a popular radio show. Cantor was given a special Academy Award in 1956 for his 'distinguished service to the film industry.' He was married for 48 years to Ida Tobias and his song 'Ida, Sweet as Apple Cider' was written in her honor.

Eddie Cantor in *Roman Scandals* (1933).

FILMOGRAPHY
Kid Boots 1926
Whoopee 1930
The Kid from Spain 1932
Kid Millions 1934
Strike Me Pink 1935
Forty Little Mothers 1940
Thank Your Lucky Stars 1943
Show Business 1944
If You Knew Susie 1948

CAREY, Harry 1878-1947

Harry Carey was born Henry De Witt Carey II. Westerns and action pictures were the forte of this durable and reliable character actor. Though born in New York City he often appeared on the screen as 'Cheyenne Harry.' He did his most memorable work in films directed by John Ford.

FILMOGRAPHY
Ridin' the Trail 1911
The Outcasts of Poker Flat 1919
Trader Horn 1930
Kid Galahad 1937
Mr Smith Goes to Washington 1939
Duel in the Sun 1946

CAREY, Harry Jr 1921-

The son of actor Harry Carey, Carey Jr has appeared chiefly in westerns, including some of the classics of the genre. Like his father, Carey Jr worked closely with director John Ford.

FILMOGRAPHY
Red River 1948
So Dear to My Heart 1949
Rio Grande 1950
The Long Gray Line 1955
Rio Bravo 1959
The Great Imposter 1961
Nickelodeon 1976

CARMICHAEL, Ian 1920-

This delightful actor, light comedian and leading man was born in Hull, England. Carmichael was educated at Scarborough College and appeared on stage in 1939 as a robot in *RUR*. He began making films in the late 1940s.

Carmichael is at his best playing bumbling upper-class fools and his nervous delicacy helped make *Private's Progress* (1955) one of the finest comedies of the era. Carmichael was great fun as Lord Peter Wimsey, the hero of the Dorothy L Sayers mystery novels, in a series of television shows shown in Britain and America.

Ian Carmichael in *Hide and Seek* (1963).

FILMOGRAPHY
Meet Mr Lucifer 1954
Simon and Laura 1955
Private's Progress 1955
Brothers in Law 1957
Lucky Jim 1957
School for Scoundrels 1959
I'm All Right, Jack 1959
The Amorous Prawn 1962
Hide and Seek 1963
Heavens Above 1963
From Beyond the Grave 1975
The Lady Vanishes 1979

Louis Jourdan, Leslie Caron, *Gigi* (1958).

CARON, Leslie 1931-

This French-born dancer and actress became a star in American musicals thanks to Gene Kelly, who discovered her. Caron scored an enormous personal triumph in the musical *Lili* (1953), winning a British Film Academy Award. Later she turned effectively to serious dramatic films winning another BFA Award for *The L-Shaped Room* (1962)

FILMOGRAPHY
An American in Paris 1951
Lili 1953
Daddy Longlegs 1955
Gigi 1958
The L-Shaped Room 1962
The Man Who Loved Women 1977
Contract 1982

CARRADINE, John 1906-

Tall and gaunt with an impressive Shakespearean voice John Carradine, the veteran character actor, has appeared in an enormous number of films. He is best known for his roles in horror films and for his part in *Grapes of Wrath* (1940). He has also appeared frequently on stage and TV.

FILMOGRAPHY
Tol'able David 1930
The Invisible Man 1933
Of Human Bondage 1934
Bride of Frankenstein 1935
The Prisoner of Shark Island 1936
The Hound of the Baskervilles 1939
The Grapes of Wrath 1940
Bluebeard 1944
House of Frankenstein 1945
Johnny Guitar 1954
Around the World in 80 Days 1956
Everything You Always Wanted to Know about Sex but Were Afraid to Ask 1972
The Howling 1982

CASSAVETES, John 1929-

A gifted actor, Cassavetes has become better known as a director of interesting and controversial films. As an actor he started in gritty low-budget melodramas, and delivered impressive performances in *Edge of the City* (1957) and *Rosemary's Baby* (1968).

FILMOGRAPHY
The Night Holds Terror 1955
Edge of the City 1957
Saddle the Wind 1958
The Killers 1964
The Dirty Dozen 1967
Rosemary's Baby 1968
Brass Target 1978
Whose Life is it Anyway? 1981
Tempest 1982

CHANEY, Lon 1883-1930

Lon Chaney (born Alonzo Chaney) was called 'the Man of a Thousand Faces. Director Tod Browning praised him by saying, 'He was the hardest working person in the studio.' Certainly few actors have suffered as much physically for their craft as did Chaney. He had his arms strapped tightly to his body to play the part of an armless knife thrower. In order to look like a vampire he wore a set of false teeth so enormous that he was in constant pain.

Chaney was born in Colorado Springs of deaf mute parents, and he started in the theater early because his brother owned one. For years he toured as a comic and song and dance man before trying to make it in the new film industry. Success was not immediate. Chaney played scores of small parts – usually villains. He had his first major success with *The Miracle Man* (1919) where he played a bogus cripple. After that it was a long series of grotesques mixed in with a few straight parts. His makeup artistry was so good that he often played two parts in one film.

Chaney's greatest success during his lifetime was his performance as Quasimodo in *The Hunchback of Notre Dame* (1924) but the film he is most remembered for today is *The Phantom of the Opera* (1925). There were several changes of directors during the film and, as a result, parts of it really don't make sense – yet it is one of the two or three horror classics of the silent era and Chaney's phantom makeup is instantly recognizable.

It's hard to evaluate Chaney as an actor under the makeup, for many of his non-horror films have been lost, but Victor Sjostrom, a great Swedish director of the silent era, called him, 'without question one of the most marvellous actors in the history of stage or screen.'

Chaney died of throat cancer after completing his first talkie and as he was about to take on the title role in *Dracula*.

FILMOGRAPHY
Where the Forest Ends 1914
The Miracle Man 1919
The Penalty 1921
The Hunchback of Notre Dame 1924
He Who Gets Slapped 1924
The Phantom of the Opera 1925
The Tower of Lies 1925
The Monster 1925
London After Midnight 1927
The Unholy Three 1930

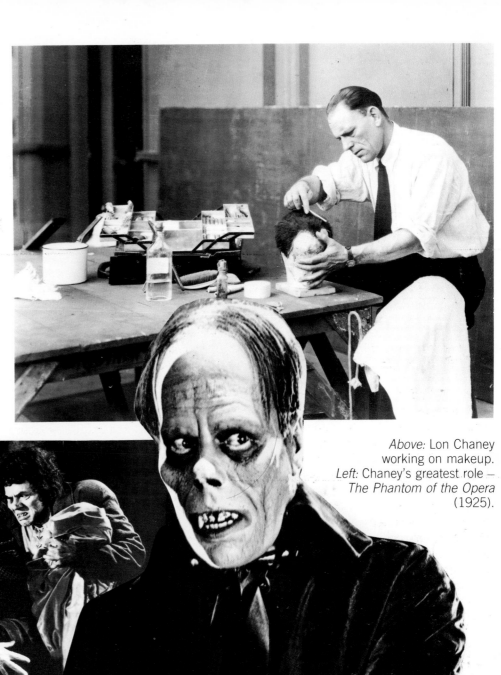

Above: Lon Chaney working on makeup.
Left: Chaney's greatest role — *The Phantom of the Opera* (1925).

Above: Chaney as Quasimodo in *The Hunchback of Notre Dame* (1924).

CHANEY, Lon Jr 1906-1973

Born Creighton Chaney, the son of the great silent-era star had nowhere near his father's ability. He created the role of the werewolf in *The Wolf Man* (1941) but gave his best performance as the simple minded Lenny in *Of Mice and Men* (1939).

FILMOGRAPHY
Bird of Paradise 1932
Of Mice and Men 1939
The Wolf Man 1941
Ghost of Frankenstein 1942
Frankenstein Meets the Wolf Man 1943
Abbott and Costello Meet Frankenstein 1948
High Noon 1952
Buckskin 1968

Colbert in *It Happened One Night* (1934).

heroes. Colbert refused to play the parts usually offered to older actresses and retired from films, though she still makes occasional stage appearances.

FILMOGRAPHY

The Sign of the Cross 1932
I Cover the Waterfront 1933
It Happened One Night 1934
Cleopatra 1934
Imitation of Life 1934
Bluebeard's Eighth Wife 1938
Midnight 1939
Boom Town 1940
The Palm Beach Story 1942
The Egg and I 1947
Sleep My Love 1948
Daughters of Destiny 1953
Parrish 1961

COLMAN, Ronald 1891-1958

Aristocratic, sophisticated and digni-fied, Ronald Colman was a romantic hero women sighed over for nearly three decades. Born in England and orphaned at 16, he got a job with the British Steamship Company. Later he was wounded in World War I and upon returning home decided to become an actor. In 1918 he starred in a play called *Damaged Goods* and this led to films. He did mainly bits until he got the lead in *The Black Spider* (1920), but there was a slump in the British movie in-dustry at the time and he opted for Hollywood.

Again, it was nothing but bit parts until he did a play and was spotted by Lilian Gish. She picked him as her co-star in *The White Sister* (1923). He sported a dashingly attractive mous-tache in the film, and after that it was up and onward. One of the most popu-lar of all silent-screen actors, Colman achieved even greater success when cast with Vilma Banky. With the com-ing of sound, Banky's career tumbled, but Colman carried on.

Ronald Colman was blessed with a beautiful and distinctive voice. Unlike many silent screen stars he understood instinctively that talkies required a less melodramatic style, and he set the tone for acting technique in sound with movies like *Arrowsmith* (1931).

Opposite such stars as Myrna Loy, Loretta Young and Rosalind Russell, Colman remained a heartthrob. He was the definitive Sidney Carton in *A Tale of Two Cities* (1935), and masterful in *Lost Horizon* (1937) or playing the dual role in the *Prisoner of Zenda* (1937). He was unusual in his ability to retain his independence in the Hollywood of the 1930s. While many actors were virtually owned by their studios, Colman moved around, eventually freelancing, choosing only plum roles.

In the 1940s his career began to ebb but he was still impressive. *Random Harvest* (1942), with Greer Garson, was a gem and he won an Academy Award for Best Actor for *A Double Life* (1948). He appeared on radio and television regularly with his second wife, British actress Benita Hume.

FILMOGRAPHY

A Son of David 1919
The Black Spider 1920
The White Sister 1923
The Dark Angel 1925
Stella Dallas 1925
Beau Geste 1926
The Winning of Barbara Worth 1926
Bulldog Drummond 1929
Raffles 1929
Arrowsmith 1931
Clive of India 1935
The Man Who Broke the Bank at Monte Carlo 1935
A Tale of Two Cities 1935
Under Two Flags 1936
Lost Horizon 1937
Prisoner of Zenda 1937
The Talk of the Town 1942
Random Harvest 1942
The Late George Apley 1947
A Double Life 1948
Champagne for Caesar 1950

Ronald Colman – suave, dignified, beloved.

Sean Connery as Agent 007 – the quintessential James Bond in all those fantastic, funny, exciting spy thrillers.

In the early 1960s Connery (born Thomas Connery), then a relative unknown, was given one of the most sought-after roles in filmdom, that of Ian Fleming's superspy James Bond. Connery reputedly got the role over bigger name stars because he couldn't command a huge salary.

At first the decision looked like a mistake, for the initial Bond film *Dr No* (1962) opened to poor reviews, critics saying that the stolid Connery was miscast as the suave Agent 007. The public disagreed and *Dr No* became a huge commercial success. It was followed by an even better Bond film, *From Russia With Love* (1963), and another and another, each being more commercially successful than the last. Sean Connery as James Bond had become an international phenomenon, but Connery was increasingly unhappy with his identification as Bond. He tried other roles and in 1971 announced that he was giving up the Bond part forever. However, he was persuaded to come back in *Never Say Never Again* (1983) as a middle-aged James Bond, and once again was a box-office smash.

Connery was born in Edinburgh, Scotland, and held a wide variety of menial jobs from lifeguard to modelling swimming trunks before going into the theater. He landed a part as a chorus boy in the London production of *South Pacific*, and after that he got small parts in films and somewhat better parts on television. His career, however, was undistinguished until he took the Bond role.

Though he is a serious and competent actor, Sean Connery has shown no inclination to do classical roles or experimental films. In his best non-Bond parts he has delivered solid performances in action films and thrillers like *The Anderson Tapes* (1971), *The Man Who Would Be King* (1976), and *Outland* (1981).

FILMOGRAPHY
No Road Back 1955
Darby O'Gill and the Little People 1959
Dr No 1962
From Russia With Love 1963
Marnie 1964
Goldfinger 1964
Thunderball 1965
You Only Live Twice 1967
Diamonds are Forever 1971
The Man Who Would be King 1976
Robin and Marion 1976
Outland 1981
Never Say Never Again 1983
The Name of the Rose 1986

COOGAN, Jackie 1914-1984

The Kid (1920) with Charlie Chaplin made Coogan a childhood superstar. Coogan earned a fortune but never received the money. The resulting scandal gave rise to the 'Coogan Law' protecting child actors. Briefly married to Betty Grable, Coogan later played heavies in films and comic parts on television.

FILMOGRAPHY
The Kid 1920
Peck's Bad Boy 1921
Oliver Twist 1921
College Swing 1938
High School Confidential 1958

COOPER, Gary 1901-1961

The epitome of 'the strong silent type,' Gary Cooper (born Frank James Cooper) played men you could count on and was tall and good-looking, too, so he appealed to both sexes and was a star for decades. Cooper's father was a state supreme court justice who had emigrated to Helena, Montana from Britain. Often thought of as the quintessential American type, Cooper spent part of his childhood in England. He dreamed of becoming a political cartoonist or illustrator after graduating from Grinnell College in Iowa, but it didn't work out. He went to Hollywood instead.

Cooper had worked on his father's ranch and he was able to pick up jobs as an extra and stuntman in westerns. He won a role in *The Winning of Barbara Worth* (1926), which brought him a lot of notice. So did Cooper's off-screen flings with Clara Bow and Lupe Velez.

Below: Cooper, Brennan in *The Westerner* (1940). *Inset:* The young Gary Cooper.

Cooper was one of the few stars to make the transition to talkies easily. His low-key style suited the new era of sound well, though he was forced to stop sowing his wild oats and settle down to hard work and discipline when a young actor named Cary Grant began to rival him in popularity. Cooper continued to appear in westerns and adventure films, but his light romantic comedies were also popular. Few actors could boast a list of leading ladies like his. Among his co-stars were Marlene Dietrich, Jean Arthur, Claudette Colbert, Ingrid Bergman and later, Grace Kelly and Audrey Hepburn.

Cooper received his first Academy Award for Best Actor in 1942 for *Sergeant York* (1941). He picked up a second one for *High Noon* (1952). He received a special Academy Award in 1961. It was accepted for him by his friend James Stewart because Cooper was dying of cancer. When he died he left behind the wife he had married in the 1930s, socialite Veronica Balfe, their daughter, many friends and some of the most famous movies ever made.

Cotten, the suave southern gentleman.

FILMOGRAPHY
The Winning of Barbara Worth 1926
It 1927
Children of Divorce 1927
Wings 1927
Lilac Time 1928
The Shopworn Angel 1928
The Virginian 1929
Morocco 1930
A Farewell to Arms 1932
City Streets 1932
One Sunday Afternoon 1933
Design for Living 1933
Lives of a Bengal Lancer 1935
Desire 1936
Mr Deeds Goes to Town 1936
The Plainsman 1937
Bluebeard's Eighth Wife 1938
Beau Geste 1939
The Westerner 1940
Meet John Doe 1941
Sergeant York 1941
Pride of the Yankees 1942
For Whom the Bell Tolls 1943
High Noon 1952
Vera Cruz 1954
Friendly Persuasion 1956
Love in the Afternoon 1957
Ten North Frederick 1958
The Naked Edge 1961

COTTEN, Joseph 1905-

His resonant voice and quiet sophistication made this one-time drama critic turned Broadway and Hollywood actor a popular performer. Born in Petersburg, Virginia, Cotten wrote drama reviews for the Miami *Herald* until becoming assistant stage manager to David Belasco in 1930. Later Cotten joined Orson Welles's Mercury Theater, leaving to appear opposite Katharine Hepburn in *The Philadelphia Story* on Broadway.

Welles cast Cotten in some of his major films, including *Citizen Kane* (1941). He also made movies for major directors Alfred Hitchcock and Sir Carol Reed. Cotten shone in romantic films like *Portrait of Jennie* (1948), which earned him a Best Actor Award at the Venice Film Festival.

FILMOGRAPHY
Citizen Kane 1941
The Magnificent Ambersons 1942
Journey into Fear 1942
Shadow of a Doubt 1943
Gaslight 1944
I'll Be Seeing You 1945
Duel in the Sun 1946
The Farmer's Daughter 1947
Portrait of Jennie 1948
Under Capricorn 1949
The Third Man 1949
Niagara 1952
Hush...Hush, Sweet Charlotte 1965
Petulia 1968
Screamers 1981

CRAWFORD, Joan 1906-1977

Crawford proved immensely durable in Hollywood. Hers is a rags to riches story and it took toughness, shrewdness and a formidable single-mindedness to make it happen. She was born Lucille le Sueur in San Antonio, Texas, and later called herself Billie Cassin. She worked as a laundress, waitress and shopgirl, but life got better after she won a Charleston contest and danced her way into clubs, Broadway chorus lines and a Hollywood screen test.

An MGM-sponsored fan-magazine contest came up with the name 'Joan Crawford' for her. After *Our Dancing Daughters* (1928) made her a star, she took over the image of 'number one flapper' from Clara Bow. In the 1930s she played working girls. Her wonder-

Joan Crawford (*right*), with another old professional, Bette Davis, in *Whatever Happened to Baby Jane?* (1962).

ful eyes, high cheek bones and broad shoulders became her trademark as her youthful beauty diminished.

In the 1940s MGM bought the idea she was box-office poison. She fought back, becoming a star at Warner Brothers playing in women's pictures, mostly soap opera stuff ignored by critics. She made them sit up and take notice with *Mildred Pierce* (1945), winning an Academy Award for Best Actress. She later worked again at MGM and at other studios, struggling to remain at the top. Columnist Hedda Hopper said of her, 'She spends 24 hours a day keeping her name in the pupil of the public eye.'

Crawford played aging femme fatales in the 1950s. In the 1960s, with rival Bette Davis, she came up with a winner, *Whatever Happened to Baby Jane?* (1962), a psychological drama. She kept working as long as she was offered roles.

Crawford was married four times: to Douglas Fairbanks, Jr, Franchot Tone, Philip Terry and Alfred Steele, board chairman of Pepsi Cola. After Steele's death she became an active board member of the company. Crawford also had a serious affair with Clark Gable in the 1930s. *Mommie Dearest*, a 1978 biography by her adopted daughter Christina, made her sound like a fiend, but Joan Crawford was one of Hollywood's most glittering stars for over four decades.

FILMOGRAPHY
Our Dancing Daughters 1928
Laughing Sinners 1931
Possessed 1931
Grand Hotel 1932
Rain 1932
Dancing Lady 1933
The Women 1939
Strange Cargo 1940
Susan and God 1940
A Woman's Face 1941
Mildred Pierce 1945

Humoresque 1946
Possessed 1947
Daisy Kenyon 1947
Flamingo Road 1949
Goodbye My Fancy 1951
Sudden Fear 1952
Johnny Guitar 1954
Autumn Leaves 1956
The Story of Esther Costello 1957
The Best of Everything 1959
Whatever Happened to Baby Jane?
    1962

CROSBY, Bing 1904-1977

Bing Crosby, born Harry Lillis Crosby, was Mr Nice Guy personified, a crooner, an amiable and relaxed singer and light comedian whose warbling style made him a superstar. Born in Tacoma, Washington, he took the name Bing from a comic-strip character. While at Gozanga University in Spokane, Washington, he began singing and playing drums with a small combo. By 1926 he had made it to the Paul Whiteman band as part of a trio called 'Paul Whiteman's Rhythm Boys.'

Going solo, Crosby began making records and doing Mack Sennett shorts but his real break came with radio. In 1931 he starred in his own show and his theme song, 'When the Blue of the Night,' swept America. Crosby's records set records; sales were in the millions. His on-screen efforts won him a spot in the box-office top ten by 1934. In 1945 he was number one.

Crosby's 1930s films were bits of fluff filled with songs. In the 1940s he and comedian Bob Hope did a series of 'Road' pictures with Dorothy Lamour which were immensely popular and irresistibly entertaining. Crosby also made movies on his own, combining humor and sentimentality. *Holiday Inn* (1942), with the song 'White Christmas' is a classic. In *Going My Way* (1944) he played a singing priest, winning an Academy Award for Best Actor. He was a priest again in *The Bells of St Mary's* (1945), with Ingrid Bergman, and after that the aura of the friendly neighborhood priest seemed to cling to him. Actually Crosby was considerably more worldly and complex than he appeared.

Crosby proved his abilities as a serious actor in *The Country Girl* (1954), with Grace Kelly. By now his singing career had declined, but he was immensely rich, having invested his fortune wisely. In 1930 Crosby had married singer Dixie Lee. The couple had four sons. It was a stormy marriage and she died an alcoholic in 1953. Crosby married a young actress named Kathryn Grant in 1957 who bore him three children. One is actress Mary Frances Crosby. In his day, Bing was one of the most widely loved stars in the world.

Crosby (*left*) in *Going My Way* (1944).

FILMOGRAPHY
King of Jazz 1930
The Big Broadcast 1932
The Big Broadcast of 1936 1936
Anything Goes 1936
Rhythm on the Range 1936
Pennies from Heaven 1936
Sing You Sinners 1938
Road to Singapore 1940
Road to Zanzibar 1941
Birth of the Blues 1941
Holiday Inn 1942
Road to Morocco 1942
Going My Way 1944
Road to Utopia 1945
The Bells of St Mary's 1945
Blue Skies 1946
Road to Rio 1947
**A Connecticut Yankee in King
   Arthur's Court** 1949
The Country Girl 1954
High Society 1956

Bing Crosby (*right*) with Bob Hope in *The Road to Rio* (1947).

CURTIS, Tony 1925-

Tony Curtis (born Bernard Schwartz), was a teen idol in the 1950s, a good-looking, curly haired, ex-juvenile delinquent who made young girls swoon. But he proved he had staying power and later turned in several sensitive performances in important films.

He was born in the Bronx, New York, the son of an immigrant tailor from Hungary. Curtis spent his early years in poverty and joined a street gang at age 11. A neighborhood settlement house rescued him from his potential life of crime and taught him a love of theater.

Curtis served in the navy during World War II and when he returned to New York he studied at the City College of New York and took acting classes at the Dramatic Workshop. Next he toured the Catskill Mountains 'Borscht Circuit,' a time-honored training ground for young comedians and actors. Off-Broadway followed and then he got a lucky break. Universal Studios signed him in 1949, decided he was right for stardom, and put real muscle into getting him there. He was one of the last movie actors to make it big via the Hollywood studio buildup.

Despite his Bronx accent, Curtis played swashbuckling types, wowing the girls as *The Prince Who Was a Thief* (1951), an Arabian Nights dream fantasy if ever there was one. That same year Curtis married Hollywood glamor girl Janet Leigh. They are the parents of actress Jamie Lee Curtis. Leigh and Curtis were divorced in 1962.

Tony Curtis was an admirer of Cary Grant and hoped to emulate his career. But to become a star of that rank Curtis had to shed his bobby soxer following without taking a fall at the box office. Though he never became a second Cary Grant, when he teamed up with Burt Lancaster to do *The Sweet Smell of Success* (1957), he won critical recognition for the first time. Curtis was excellent as an unctious fawning press agent. *The Defiant Ones* (1958) won him an Oscar nomination. He was also excellent as a musician in drag pursuing Marilyn Monroe in *Some Like It Hot* (1959).

Since then Curtis has done serious roles and light films as well as television. In 1977 he published his first novel, *Kid Andrew Cody and Julie Sparrow*.

Right: The young Tony Curtis.

FILMOGRAPHY
City Across the River 1949
The Prince Who Was a Thief 1951
Houdini 1953
Trapeze 1956
The Sweet Smell of Success 1957
The Vikings 1958
Kings Go Forth 1958
The Defiant Ones 1958
Some Like it Hot 1959
Operation Petticoat 1959
Spartacus 1960
The Great Imposter 1960
The Outsider 1962
The List of Adrian Messenger 1963
Captain Newman, MD 1963
The Boston Strangler 1968
Sextette 1978
The Mirror Crack'd 1980

Above right: Tony Curtis in *Some Like It Hot* (1959) with Billy Wilder, the director.

DAVIES, Marion 1897-1961

A gifted light comedienne in silent pictures Davies (born Marion Douras) was the long-time mistress of William Randolph Hearst, who used his newspaper empire to try to make her a star. It didn't work. The costume dramas which Hearst favored buried her bubbly talent and probably destroyed her career.

FILMOGRAPHY
Cecilia of the Pink Roses 1918
Show People 1928
Page Miss Glory 1935

DAVIS, Bette 1908-

For many fans Bette Davis (born Ruth Elizabeth Davis) is 'the first lady of films.' A superb actress and a charismatic personality, Davis has played all kinds of women: drunks, belles, old maids, rich girls, waitresses and hags, a gallery of screen portraits second to none.

Born in Lowell, Massachusetts, she had acting ambitions that were encouraged by her mother, but Davis found the going rough. Short, with a high-pitched voice, she wasn't the sort to win beauty contests. Universal Studios' boss Carl Laemmle described her as having 'as much sex appeal as Slim Summerville.' Only by fighting like a tiger did Davis win the recognition she deserved.

In 1928 she appeared with the Provincetown Players and in 1929 debuted on Broadway in *Broken Dishes*, a comedy, but by 1930 she was in Hollywood. She spent many stormy years at Warner Brothers, even suing the studio because she had been offered better roles by a British film company. She lost the case but she won the war. *Of Human Bondage* (1934) and *Dangerous* (1935), which won her an Academy Award for Best Actress, had made her a box-office attraction with clout.

Women in particular flocked to Davis films and she appeared in a series of vehicles tailored specifically for her. Audiences liked her best when she was bright and bitchy but she was also effective in weepy soaps. *Jezebel* (1938) won her a second Academy Award.

In the late 1940s Davis's career took a dive but she again fought back, appearing with fourth husband Gary Merrill in *All About Eve* (1950), playing a character based on Tallulah Bankhead. The movie took an Oscar for Best Picture and put Davis back on top. When her career faltered again in the late 1950s Davis boldly advertised for work, accepting roles in horror films and on television. She later referred to herself during this era as 'Boris Karloff in skirts.' However *Whatever Happened to Baby Jane?* (1962), with Joan Crawford, was a huge success. A real pro, Davis continued acting and in 1977 was the first woman to achieve the American Film Institute Life Achievement Award.

DAVIS, Sammy Jr 1925-

Dynamism and energy are the stock in trade of this one-eyed black singer and entertainer, a convert to Judaism. He was performing in vaudeville before he was three. Primarily a nightclub entertainer, he has sometimes appeared in films with his friend Frank Sinatra.

FILMOGRAPHY
Anna Lucasta 1958
Porgy and Bess 1959
Ocean's Eleven 1960
Robin and the Seven Hoods 1964
The Cannonball Run 1981

DAY, Doris 1924-

Peppy and pure, that was Doris Day's persona. She was a well-known recording star in the 1940s who skyrocketed to movie stardom overnight in the musical *Romance on the High Seas* (1948).

Doris Day (born Doris Kappelhoff) was America's leading lady of movie musicals until the 1960s when she switched to glamorous romantic comedies. It looked as if she had the world on a string until at the death of her third husband Marty Melcher in 1968 it was revealed that he had either mismanaged her career or embezzled all her money. She recouped her fortunes with *The Doris Day Show* on television and by suing her former lawyer, but her film carrer was over.

FILMOGRAPHY
Romance on the High Seas 1948
Young Man with a Horn 1950
On Moonlight Bay 1950
Young at Heart 1955
The Pajama Game 1957
Pillow Talk 1959
Lover Come Back 1962
That Touch of Mink 1962

Doris Day, John Raitt in *The Pajama Game* (1957).

FILMOGRAPHY
The Tragedy of Love 1924
The Blue Angel 1930
Morocco 1930
Dishonoured 1931
Shanghai Express 1932
Blonde Venus 1932
The Scarlet Empress 1934
The Devil is a Woman 1935
Desire 1936
Knight Without Armour 1937
Angel 1937
Destry Rides Again 1939
The Flame of New Orleans 1941
The Lady is Willing 1942
Foreign Affair 1948
Stage Fright 1950
No Highway in the Sky 1951
Rancho Notorious 1952
Witness for the Prosecution 1958
Judgment at Nuremberg 1961
Just a Gigolo 1978

Robert Donat in *The Thirty-Nine Steps* (1935).

Kirk Douglas as Vincent Van Gogh in *Lust for Life* (1956).

DONAT, Robert 1905-1958

Popular and widely admired, this dashing and gifted actor with a superb voice was born in Manchester, England. He studied elocution as a child to rid himself of a stutter and by age 16 had made his stage debut.

Donat played Shakespearian and classical roles, becoming a film actor in 1930. He could have gone to Hollywood but he hated it, and though he appeared in American movies, even winning an Academy Award for Best Actor for *Goodbye Mr Chips* (1939), his home base was always Britain.

Donat was always plagued by severe insecurities and a nearly debilitating case of asthma, yet he created some of film's finest roles. He continued working until his death at the age of 53.

FILMOGRAPHY
The Private Life of Henry VIII 1933
The Count of Monte Cristo 1934
The Thirty-Nine Steps 1935
The Ghost Goes West 1936
The Citadel 1938
Goodbye Mr Chips 1939
The Young Mr Pitt 1942
The Winslow Boy 1948
The Inn of the Sixth Happiness 1958

DORS, Diana 1931-1984

Diana Dors (born Diana Fluck) was often called Britain's answer to Marilyn Monroe. The bosomy blonde Dors gained fame as a sex symbol. Later the identification hurt her career, as she was rarely given parts that allowed her to use her considerable acting talents.

FILMOGRAPHY
Oliver Twist 1948
The Good Time Girl 1948
It's a Grand Life 1953
Yield to the Night 1956
Hannie Caulder 1971
Theatre of Blood 1973
Steaming 1985

DOUGLAS, Kirk 1916-

When Kirk Douglas (born Issur Danielovitch Demsky) first came to Hollywood he looked like a hero from a comic book: strong features, strong body, a toothy smile and a dimple in his chin. Though Kirk Douglas would appear in popular westerns and adventure films as befitted his looks, he also gave intelligent performances in several highly significant movies such

as *Paths of Glory* (1957), which might never have been produced without his help. When it counts he has shown real integrity in his work, both as an actor and producer.

Douglas was born in Amsterdam, New York, to Russian immigrant parents. He worked his way through St Lawrence University, where he was also a wrestling champion. Then he came to New York, wrestled professionally and worked as an usher and bellhop so he could attend The New York Academy of Dramatic Arts.

After his Broadway debut in 1941 he joined the Navy, returning to Broadway after World War II, also appearing on radio in soap operas. Then Douglas was off to Hollywood. His big break came with a low-budget movie about a sexy, immoral boxer, *Champion* (1949). It made him a star. He turned down flashier films to make *Young Man with a Horn* (1950), the life story of trumpet player Bix Beiderbecke. Along with Burt Lancaster and Tony Curtis, he was rapidly establishing himself as one of the new postwar breed of masculine movie idols, successors to John Garfield.

In 1955 Douglas formed his own company, producing movies he appeared in, such as *The Vikings* (1958), and films featuring other stars. Despite his movie success Douglas retained an interest in theater and in 1963 he appeared on Broadway in *One Flew Over the Cuckoo's Nest*. When he failed to get the backing he needed to produce it as a film, he passed the play on to his son Michael, a television and film actor. With his father's backing, Michael Douglas produced the film version of the Ken Kesey novel and it was a major 1975 hit, winning five Oscars.

Though Kirk Douglas's box-office appeal diminished in the 1960s he continued to be a forceful presence in the film industry, turning to directing in the 1970s. He also does television.

FILMOGRAPHY
The Strange Love of Martha Ivers 1946
Out of the Past 1947
Champion 1949
Young Man with a Horn 1950
The Glass Menagerie 1951
Ace in the Hole 1951
Detective Story 1951
Twenty Thousand Leagues Under the Sea 1954
Lust for Life 1956
Gunfight at the OK Corral 1957
Paths of Glory 1957
The Vikings 1958
Spartacus 1960
Lonely Are the Brave 1962
The List of Adrian Messenger 1963
Seven Days in May 1964
There Was a Crooked Man 1970
The Fury 1978
Tough Guys 1986

Right: The young Kirk Douglas.

DOUGLAS, Melvyn 1901-1981

Melvyn Douglas (born Melvyn Edouard Hesselberg) was a leading man first, character actor later, but was always superb. He was born in Macon, Georgia and made his Broadway debut in 1928. He then went to Hollywood, appearing opposite Greta Garbo in *As You Desire Me* (1932). Suave, debonair and intelligent, Douglas was wonderful with Garbo and other great female stars, including Crawford, Dietrich, Colbert, Dunne and Loy.

He won an Academy Award for Best Supporting Actor for *Hud* (1963). Later he did stage and television, winning a Tony and an Emmy Award. His second wife was actress and politician Helen Gahagan.

FILMOGRAPHY
As You Desire Me 1932
Counsellor-at-Law 1933
Dangerous Corner 1934
She Married Her Boss 1935
Theodora Goes Wild 1936
I Met Him in Paris 1937
That Certain Age 1938
Ninotchka 1939
Hud 1963
The Americanization of Emily 1964
I Never Sang for My Father 1970
Being There 1979
Ghost Story 1981

Below: Melvyn Douglas in *Ninotchka* (1939).

DOVE, Billie 1900-

Billie Dove (born Lillian Bohney) was a spectacular beauty who began her career as a Ziegfield showgirl and moved on to become one of the silent screen's loveliest and most popular stars. Billed as 'The American Beauty,' she appeared with Douglas Fairbanks in an important early color film, *The Black Pirate* (1926).

FILMOGRAPHY
Beyond the Rainbow 1922
Polly of the Follies 1922
The Black Pirate 1926

DOWN, Leslie-Anne 1954-

Delicately beautiful, Leslie-Anne Down made a perfect Miss Georgina in the extremely popular television series *Upstairs Downstairs*. The London-born actress went on to star in films but to date her film career has not matched her television fame.

FILMOGRAPHY
The Pink Panther Strikes Again 1976
A Little Night Music 1977
The Betsy 1978
The Great Train Robbery 1979
Hanover Street 1979

DRESSLER, Marie 1869-1934

Marie Dressler (born Leila Marie Koerber) put the lie to the notion that a woman had to be young and beautiful to be a star. This Canadian-born performer was an experienced light-opera singer and actress at age 20. By 1892 she was on Broadway and was a vaudeville star a decade later.

Dressler was fat and homely but possessed a great natural comic talent. She made her screen debut with Charlie Chaplin in *Tillie's Punctured Romance* (1914), following this up with other silent films, but real movie stardom came with talkies. *Anna Christie* (1930) proved her to be a fine serious actress and she won an Academy Award for Best Actress for *Min and Bill* (1930).

FILMOGRAPHY
Tillie's Punctured Romance 1914
Bringing Up Father 1928
Anna Christie 1930
The March of Time 1930
Min and Bill 1930
Emma 1932
Prosperity 1932
Tugboat Annie 1933
Dinner at Eight 1933

Faye Dunaway in *Mommie Dearest* (1981).

A suspicious Marie Dressler in *Tugboat Annie* (1933).

Richard Dreyfuss, *Close Encounters* (1977).

DREYFUSS, Richard 1947-

Energetic, likeable and boyishly charming, Dreyfuss appeared in some of the most popular films of the 1970s, though sometimes, as in *Jaws* (1975), he was overshadowed by the special effects. He received an Academy Award for Best Actor for *The Goodbye Girl* (1976).

FILMOGRAPHY
American Graffiti 1973
The Apprenticeship of Duddy Kravitz 1974
Jaws 1975
Close Encounters of the Third Kind 1977
Whose Life is it Anyway? 1981
Down and Out in Beverly Hills 1985

DUNAWAY, Faye 1941-

High cheek bones, green eyes and chic style make Dunaway one of contemporary Hollywood's loveliest leading ladies. Born in Bascom, Florida, she did *Hogan's Goat* Off Broadway, then went to Hollywood, rising from virtual-unknown to star in a matter of months, thanks to *Bonnie and Clyde* (1967).

Dunaway has appeared in a variety of films. *Little Big Man* (1970) was a western; *Chinatown* (1974) was a tough guy detective story; *Three Days of the Condor* (1975) a suspense movie. Dunaway won an Academy Award for Best Actress for her fine performance as an ambitious neurotic in *Network* (1976). She was chosen to play Joan Crawford in *Mommie Dearest* (1981), achieving an uncanny physical resemblance to the late star.

FILMOGRAPHY
Bonnie and Clyde 1967
Little Big Man 1970
The Three Musketeers 1973
Chinatown 1974
Network 1976
Mommie Dearest 1981
Supergirl 1984

Fairbanks in *The Mark of Zorro* (1920). He was the first in a long line of Zorros.

Alice Faye greets Edward Arnold as Don Ameche looks on – *Lillian Russell* (1940).

FALK, Peter 1927-

One-eyed actor Peter Falk has turned his handicap into an advantage. His squinty style makes him adept at playing cops, hoods and working-class guys. Falk is a highly respected stage actor who was a success on television's *Columbo*. Fine film performances have won him Oscar nominations.

FILMOGRAPHY
Murder, Inc 1960
Pocketful of Miracles 1961
The Great Race 1965
Murder by Death 1976
The In-Laws 1979
All the Marbles 1982

FARROW, Mia 1945-

Frail and delicately beautiful, Farrow is the daughter of actress Maureen O'Sullivan, the ex-wife of Frank Sinatra, and the present wife of Woody Allen. At her best in *Rosemary's Baby* (1968), she was very good as a Mafia moll in *Broadway Danny Rose* (1984).

FILMOGRAPHY
Rosemary's Baby 1968
The Great Gatsby 1974
Death on the Nile 1978
Zelig 1983
Broadway Danny Rose 1984
Supergirl 1984
Hannah and Her Sisters 1986
Radio Days 1987

FAYE, Alice 1912-

Hollywood's leading star of musicals in the 1930s and early 1940s Faye (born Ann Leppert) was blonde and pretty with a charming contralto voice. Often she did her best work when paired with Don Ameche. A professional performer from the age of 14, Faye was plucked from a Broadway chorus line by singer Rudy Vallee to appear on his radio show.

Her feuds with Darryl F Zanuck, head of 20th Century Fox, were legendary. Threatening to ruin her career, he banned her radio appearances. But Faye was a sensitive, vulnerable and lovely talent and audiences always adored her. Married first to singer Tony Martin, she married band leader Phil Harris in 1941.

FILMOGRAPHY
Wake Up and Live 1937
In Old Chicago 1938
Alexander's Ragtime Band 1938
Rose of Washington Square 1939
Lillian Russell 1940
Tin Pan Alley 1940
Hello, Frisco, Hello 1943
Fallen Angel 1945
State Fair 1962
The Magic of Lassie 1978

FIELDS, Dame Gracie 1898-1979

Singer, actress, and comedienne Fields (born Grace Stansfield) was a music hall entertainer at the age of 13. During the 1930s she became Britain's highest-paid actress, a major box-office draw on screen and so popular on radio that Parliament once adjourned early so members could listen to one of her broadcasts. Her bold spirit and Lancashire humor buoyed moviegoers during the dreary years of Depression.

Fields came to America when her second husband, Italian-born Monty Banks, was declared an alien by the British government in World War II.

She was a success in Hollywood, playing opposite Monty Woolley, retiring from films after the War. Gracie Fields returned to Europe and was created Dame Commander of the Order of the British Empire in 1979.

FILMOGRAPHY
Sally in our Alley 1931
Love Life and Laughter 1933
Sing As We Go 1934
Keep Smiling 1938
Holy Matrimony 1943
Molly and Me 1945
Paris Underground 1945

Gracie Fields in 1943.

FIELDS, W C 1879-1946

A great comic genius, Fields (born William Claude Dunkinfield) had a huge bulbous nose, a huge bulbous belly, and a raspy voice. Yet he combined agility and grace with a gift for one liners, so he was brilliant in all media, from vaudeville and theater to films and radio.

The son of a poor cockney immigrant in Philadelphia, Fields's childhood was tragic. He ran away from home at 11, surviving by his wits, but dreamed of being a great juggler and it was this skill which first allowed him to break into show business.

By the time he was 20 he was a comic star in vaudeville, giving a command performance at Buckingham Palace while on a European tour. He had a long string of successes in the Ziegfeld Follies and George White's Scandals and in 1923 was the star of a hit Broadway musical, *Poppy*, retitled for the screen *Sally of the Sawdust* (1925). Fields had been making movies since 1915 and most of them were more popular with the critics than with the public, but by the late silent era he had achieved a modest following of devoted fans. He fared better in talkies.

W C Fields usually played the world's greatest drinker (a role he upheld off-screen as well), the all-time cynic and misanthrope, hen-pecked past endurance, persecuted by authorities of every stripe. He fought back by bragging, griping, avoiding his enemies, especially children, and weakly abandoning himself to pointless fits of temper. When all else failed he resorted to lies and making oily compliments.

Under pseudonyms like Otis J Criblecoblis and Mahatma Kane Jeeves, Fields wrote many of his own film scripts. He became a cult hero as early as the 1930s in part because of his legendary fears and odd behavior. He shone not only in his classic films but when he stepped out of character to play Humpty Dumpty in *Alice in Wonderland* (1933) or Mr Micawber in *David Copperfield* (1934). In *My Little Chickadee* (1940) he appeared with another comic genius, Mae West. Not only have his films survived but today his reputation is greater than it was even at the peak of his long and successful career.

Above: W C Fields and Mae West in *My Little Chickadee* (1940).

Left: Fields in a typical pose as *The Bank Dick* (1940).

FILMOGRAPHY

Pool Sharks 1915
Sally of the Sawdust 1925
It's the Old Army Game 1926
So's Your Old Man 1926
Two Flaming Youths 1927
Tillie's Punctured Romance 1927
Million Dollar Legs 1932
The Fatal Glass of Beer 1932
The Barber Shop 1933
Tillie and Gus 1933
Alice in Wonderland 1933
Mrs Wiggs of the Cabbage Patch 1934
It's a Gift 1934
David Copperfield 1934
The Man on the Flying Trapeze 1935
You Can't Cheat an Honest Man 1939
My Little Chickadee 1940
The Bank Dick 1940
Never Give a Sucker an Even Break 1941

FINCH, Peter 1916-1977

Australia's leading radio actor, Finch (born William Mitchell) came to London in 1949, the protégé of Laurence Olivier. A handsome rugged-looking man, he became a respected stage and film actor who received several British Film Academy Awards and a posthumous Academy Award for *Network* (1976).

FILMOGRAPHY
A Town Like Alice 1956
The Nun's Story 1959
The Trials of Oscar Wilde 1960
No Love for Johnnie 1961
Sunday Bloody Sunday 1971
Network 1976

FINNEY, Albert 1936-

Finney has been called the second Olivier. An illustrious stage actor and brilliant film star, Finney comes as close as anyone to deserving that title. Born in Salford, England, the son of a bookie, Finney was encouraged by his headmaster at a grammar school to apply for a scholarship at the Royal Academy of Dramatic Art. After completing his studies he made his debut in 1956 with the Birmingham Repertory Theatre and for the next four years did chiefly Shakespearian roles.

Fame came with *Billy Liar*, on stage, and the film *Saturday Night and Sunday Morning* (1960). Finney was virile and sensitive as a working-class youth trapped by the circumstances of his life, and the movie was a huge success. So was *Tom Jones* (1963), a bawdy energetic romp. Significantly, though the movie made Finney a millionaire and won him the Best Actor Award at the Venice Film Festival, he did not abandon the stage. On the contrary, he turned down lucrative movie contracts and flashy roles so he could continue in the theater. His most successful play of this era was *Luther*, performed in Britain and America.

In 1965 Finney formed his own production company for films, plays and television, which did not prevent him spending two seasons with Britain's

Albert Finney as Daddy Warbucks, with Aileen Quinn in *Annie* (1982).

FILMOGRAPHY
The Entertainer 1959
Saturday Night and Sunday Morning
  1960
Tom Jones 1963
The Victors 1963
Night Must Fall 1963
Two for the Road 1967
Charlie Bubbles 1967
The Picasso Summer 1969
Scrooge 1970
Gumshoe 1971
Murder on the Orient Express 1974
The Duellists 1977
Wolfen 1981
Looker 1981
Shoot the Moon 1982
Annie 1982
The Dresser 1983
Under the Volcano 1984

Above: Albert Finney as Inspector Poirot in
Murder on the Orient Express (1974).
Left: Finney in his powerful role as Geoffrey
Firmin in *Under the Volcano* (1984).

National Theatre, enhancing his reputation as one of the best actors of his
generation. Though his movies of this
period were not blockbusters he was
always good – as a psychotic murderer
in the remake of the 1940s classic *Night
Must Fall* (1963), and as the self-
absorbed husband in *Two for the Road*
(1967), co-starring Audrey Hepburn.

In 1970 Finney, once married to
actress Jane Wenham, was married a
second time to French film star Anouk
Aimee. In the years that followed,
Finney tackled the premier roles of the
theater like Tamburlaine, Hamlet and
Macbeth. He also showed exceptional
range on screen in a rather eccentric
choice of roles. He has played
Scrooge, Hercule Poirot, Daddy Warbucks, oddballs and neurotics. There
is simply very little that Albert Finney
cannot do.

FLYNN, Errol 1909-1959

Colorful, witty and charming – Errol Flynn, the dashing hero of some of Hollywood's finest adventure films, a talented comedian and a more than competent dramatic actor – was usually underrated by the critics. But fans and critics alike agreed he had few peers when it came to off-screen escapades. Born in Hobart, Tasmania, the son of a distinguished marine biologist, Flynn was sent to various schools in Britain. He was expelled from each. At 15 he became a clerk with a shipping company in Sydney, Australia, and at 16 entered government service in New Guinea.

Finding life tame, Flynn set out on a sailing adventure, which he later wrote about in the first of his autobiographies, *Beam Ends*, published in 1937. His schemes also included searching for gold and managing a plantation. Then it was off to England to become an actor and a contract with Warner Brothers which brought him to Hollywood in 1935.

That same year Flynn married actress Lili Damita. He also found himself a major star, thanks to *Captain Blood* (1935). With Olivia De Havilland he made a series of costume pictures which were immensely popular. Female fans adored him for his wry cynicism, good body and legs that looked great in tights. Much publicized bar-room brawls, three marriages and scores of flamboyant affairs helped build the Errol Flynn 'Don Juan' legend.

In 1942 Flynn was the center of a notorious statutory rape case involving two teenage girls who claimed he'd had his way with them on his yacht. Though Flynn was acquitted, uttering many amusing comments along the way, the case hurt his career. So did being declared 4F during World War II, even though Flynn suffered from a heart defect, tuberculosis and recurring malaria.

In the late 1940s Flynn began using drugs which, added to his alcoholism, began to take a toll on his looks. His career took a plunge and he lost all his money in ill-conceived film production ventures. When Flynn died at 50 his body was old beyond his years. Still, the thunderous good times of his romping youth shine through in movies like *The Adventures of Robin Hood* (1938).

Right: Flynn as Robin Hood.

70

Above: Flynn as General George Armstrong Custer in *They Died with Their Boots On* (1941).

Flynn – *The Adventures of Robin Hood* (1938).

FILMOGRAPHY
Murder at Monte Carlo 1934
Captain Blood 1935
The Charge of the Light Brigade 1936
The Prince and the Pauper 1937
The Perfect Specimen 1937
The Adventures of Robin Hood 1938
The Sisters 1938
The Dawn Patrol 1938
The Sea Hawk 1940
They Died with Their Boots On 1941
Gentleman Jim 1942
Objective Burma 1945
Cry Wolf 1946
That Forsyte Woman 1949
Kim 1951
The Master of Ballantrae 1953
Lilacs in the Spring 1955
King's Rhapsody 1956
The Sun Also Rises 1957
Too Much Too Soon 1958

FONDA, Henry 1905-1983

By the time he died, Henry Fonda had attained mythic proportions in America, the result of a long career spent playing characters embodying the values of the midwestern prairie which was his home. Honesty, sincerity, quiet decency, and reason rather than passion seemed to echo in his flat unaccented voice. He was not the kind of hero to inspire awe but one an audience could like.

Fonda was an office boy at an Omaha, Nebraska credit company when he began acting. He later became a member of the University Players company which included the first of his five wives, Margaret Sullavan. By 1934 he was a respected Broadway performer. Movies followed and the shy unassuming Fonda shot to stardom within a year. The versatile actor appeared in westerns, comedies and melodramas until the greatest role in his career came along, Tom Joad in *The Grapes of Wrath* (1940). Fonda's private life, however, was not as rosy.

In 1936 Fonda married socialite Frances Seymour Brokaw. Mrs Fonda committed suicide in a rest home in 1950. The couple had two children, Jane and Peter, later actors in their own right.

Henry Fonda joined the Navy during World War II, and when he returned his films reflected a new maturity. He longed for the stage and in 1948 had an enormous success in the title role of *Mister Roberts*. He repeated his triumph in the film version of the play (1955). From then on his career alternated between screen and theater. Films like *Twelve Angry Men* (1957), for which he won a British Film Academy Award, *Advise and Consent* (1961) and *The Best Man* (1964), reflected his preference for scripts with political and social content. He also appeared on television, his least favorite medium.

In 1978 Henry Fonda won the Life Achievement Award of the American Film Institute. Then, thanks to a film produced by his daughter Jane, *On Golden Pond* (1982), Fonda was given the opportunity with co-star Katharine Hepburn to score a major acting triumph, and at last he was awarded a much deserved Academy Award for Best Actor. Fonda died soon after.

Henry Fonda and Katharine Hepburn in *On Golden Pond* (1982). Both won Oscars.

FILMOGRAPHY
The Farmer Takes a Wife 1935
The Trail of the Lonesome Pine 1936
The Moon's Our Home 1936
You Only Live Once 1937
Wings of the Morning 1937
Jezebel 1938
The Story of Alexander Graham Bell 1939
Young Mr Lincoln 1939
Drums Along the Mohawk 1939
The Grapes of Wrath 1940
The Lady Eve 1941
The Male Animal 1942
The Ox Bow Incident 1943
My Darling Clementine 1946
Fort Apache 1948
Mister Roberts 1955
The Wrong Man 1956
Twelve Angry Men 1957
Stage Struck 1957
Advise and Consent 1961
The Best Man 1964
Madigan 1968
Rollercoaster 1977
On Golden Pond 1982

Left: Fonda in *The Grapes of Wrath* (1940).

FONDA, Jane 1937-

Though she is the daughter of actor Henry Fonda and the sister of actor Peter Fonda, Jane is a star in her own right, a political presence, an accomplished actress, and one of the most famous women in America. Her childhood was marked by tragedy when her mother, Frances Brokaw, committed suicide in a rest home in 1950.

Fonda showed little interest in acting as a child and while attending Vassar College decided to go to Paris to study art. Upon her return she dabbled in modeling, making the cover of *Vogue* twice. Lee Strasberg of the Actors Studio persuaded her to become an actress. She made both her Broadway and film debuts in 1960, planning a conventional career.

In 1965 she married Roger Vadim, ex-husband of Brigitte Bardot, who tried to turn her into another sex symbol. She was cute in *Cat Ballou* (1965), but there was no way to guess the changes that were about to take place in her life and career.

Fonda became deeply involved in radical, and later feminist, politics during the Vietnam War. With actor Donald Sutherland she formed the Anti-War Troupe, touring military camps despite Pentagon opposition. Nicknamed 'Hanoi Jane,' she became a symbol of the riotous 1960s to her detractors. Still she continued her activities even at the risk of destroying her career. Divorced from Vadim, she married a political militant, Tom Hayden.

Fonda's career not only survived but prospered. She won Academy Awards for Best Actress for *Klute* (1971) and *Coming Home* (1978). Though she's appeared in movies with light comic appeal she refuses to make films which run counter to her political views.

Fonda's interests extend beyond films. Her exercise program has become a national craze and she markets a line of work-out clothes. Perhaps Fonda's finest moment came when in tribute to her father she produced and appeared in *On Golden Pond* (1982). Both knew while filming it that it would be his last movie.

Above right: The talented Jane Fonda, looking not unlike her father, Henry.
Right: Jane Fonda in *Julia* (1977), the story of the relationship between two women in the 1930s.

FILMOGRAPHY
Tall Story 1960
Walk on the Wild Side 1961
Cat Ballou 1965
Barefoot in the Park 1967
They Shoot Horses, Don't They? 1969
Klute 1971
Fun with Dick and Jane 1977
Julia 1977
Coming Home 1978
Comes a Horseman 1979
The China Syndrome 1979
9 to 5 1980
On Golden Pond 1982
Agnes of God 1985
The Morning After 1987

Joan Fontaine in *Suspicion* (1941).

FONTAINE, Joan 1917-

Joan Fontaine was born Joan de Havilland in Tokyo to British parents. She moved to America as a child. Her first pseudonym, used primarily on stage, was Joan Burfield. A year younger than her sister, actress Olivia De Havilland, Fontaine began her film career playing mousy ladylike types and moved on to sophisticated glamorous roles.

It took her years to achieve a success equal to her sister's and their rivalrous feud was notorious. Though Fontaine's finest moment in film came when she played the innocent heroine in Alfred Hitchcock's brilliant *Rebecca* (1940), she took an Academy Award for Best Actress for a movie released the following year, *Suspicion* (1941).

FILMOGRAPHY
A Damsel in Distress 1938
Gunga Din 1939
Rebecca 1940
Suspicion 1941
The Constant Nymph 1943
Jane Eyre 1943
The Affairs of Susan 1945
Letter from an Unknown Woman 1948
Something to Live For 1952
Until They Sail 1957
Tender is the Night 1961
The Devil's Own 1966

FORD, Glenn 1916-

Glenn Ford (born Gwyllyn Ford) got his start playing juveniles on stage in California where his boyish good looks soon won him a movie contract. A stint with the Marines in World War II interrupted his career.

Ford returned from the war mellowed and mature, shedding his little-boy image fast when he played opposite Rita Hayworth in steamy 1940s films. A solid steady actor, Ford appeared in comedies, thrillers, westerns and dramas and by the late 1950s was tops at the box office. His low-key style allowed him to adjust to playing aging characters as the years passed.

FILMOGRAPHY
So Ends Our Night 1941
Destroyer 1943
Gilda 1946
A Stolen Life 1946
The Man From Colorado 1948
Affair In Trinidad 1952
The Big Heat 1953
The Blackboard Jungle 1955
3:10 to Yuma 1957
Cowboy 1958
The Courtship of Eddie's Father 1963
Midway 1976
Superman 1978
The Visitor 1979
Happy Birthday to Me 1981

Below: Glen Ford with the beautiful Rita Hayworth in *Gilda* (1946).

Below: Gable with Jack Holt and Jeanette MacDonald in *San Francisco* (1936).

FILMOGRAPHY

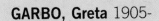
Hollywood has spawned no myth greater than the myth of Greta Garbo. Paradoxically sensual and spiritual, the beautiful and sensitive Garbo was the most magnetic actress in the history of film.

Garbo (born Greta Louisa Gustafson) grew up in poverty in Stockholm, Sweden, attending the Royal Dramatic Theatre School on scholarship. There director Mauritz Stiller discovered her, made her his protégée and turned the photogenic actress into a Swedish film star of some note, even refusing an offer from MGM if Garbo was not given a contract.

Big and clumsy off-screen, with large feet, the unconventionally lovely Garbo was not MGM boss Louis B Mayer's idea of a sex symbol but when her first film for the studio *The Torrent* (1926), was a huge success he saw the light, and she received top promotion.

The moody and elusive or just plain clever Garbo got more publicity than any other star simply by running away from it. She also got an enormous salary from MGM. Garbo generally played fallen women whose sensual beauty drove men mad. Invariably she paid for her sins and men and women alike flocked to the movies to watch Garbo suffer. She often appeared with John Gilbert and gossip columnists were quick to call them lovers.

Garbo's success went beyond anything the film world had ever known. Women everywhere copied her. She mingled with celebrities and aristocrats as she chose. Though Garbo never married her name was linked with director Rouben Mamoulian, conductor Leopold Stokowski and nutrition expert Gaylord Hauser. But since 'The Swedish Sphinx' kept her private life truly private these romances may be merely rumors.

Garbo made the transition to sound easily, making some of her best films during the talkies era, most notably *Ninotchka* (1939), which offered her a rare chance to show off her comic talents. In the early 1940s when some of her box-office appeal had faded and a new wind of puritanism was sweeping Hollywood, Garbo simply quit. But the Garbo legend grew stronger and today, well over 40 years since her last movie was released, she remains the most famous star in the world. In 1954 she was awarded a special Academy Award in honor of her unique career.

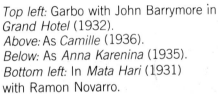

Top left: Garbo with John Barrymore in *Grand Hotel* (1932).
Above: As *Camille* (1936).
Below: As *Anna Karenina* (1935).
Bottom left: In *Mata Hari* (1931) with Ramon Novarro.

One has only to look at a picture of Ava Gardner at the height of her beauty to understand why she was Hollywood's leading sex symbol and glamor queen between the end of World War II and the reign of Marilyn Monroe. She was exotically gorgeous and steamingly sensual.

Gardner was one of six children of a poor tenant farmer from North Carolina. Dreaming only of a job as a secretary, Gardner paid a visit to her married sister in New York. The visit transformed her life. Her brother-in-law was a photographer and a picture he took of her reached the MGM casting office, winning her a screen test. She was just another starlet appearing in bit parts though until a brief marriage to actor Mickey Rooney in 1942 brought her a lot of free publicity. So did a short-term marriage to band leader Artie Shaw in 1945.

It wasn't until *The Killers* (1946) that audiences really zoomed in on Gardner's erotic charisma. She was an exquisitely ravaged Julie in *Show Boat* (1951), angry that they dubbed her voice, although the movie's record album with her voice on it was a success. In 1951 she married Frank Sinatra

Ava Gardner with Grace Kelly in *Mogambo* (1953).

Gardner in *The Naked Maja* (1959) as the model for Goya's painting.

after a headline-making scandal over their affair and his divorce from his first wife. *Mogambo* (1953), a remake of *Red Dust*, won Gardner an Academy Award nomination. She played a wise-cracking showgirl.

In real life, too, Gardner was proving clever, witty and quotable. After her divorce from Sinatra in 1957 she spent a lot of time abroad, and the gossip columnists had a field day over her fondness for matadors and her lavish life amidst the rich and famous. When she did make films she was hauntingly lovely, wonderful in *The Night of the Iguana* (1964) as the earthy hotel owner. She has retained her glamor and mystique as she's grown older and is definitely one of the great movie goddesses of all time.

FILMOGRAPHY
The Killers 1946
The Hucksters 1947
One Touch of Venus 1948
Show Boat 1951
Pandora and the Flying Dutchman 1951
The Snows of Kilimanjaro 1952
Mogambo 1953
The Barefoot Contessa 1954
The Sun Also Rises 1957
The Naked Maja 1959
On the Beach 1959
Seven Days in May 1964
The Night of the Iguana 1964
Mayerling 1968
The Life and Times of Judge Roy Bean 1972
Earthquake 1974
The Cassandra Crossing 1977
The Kidnapping of the President 1980
Priest of Love 1981

GARFIELD, John 1913-1952

John Garfield excelled as the defiant young guy trying to rise from poverty through charm and brute strength yet who is vulnerable beneath the facade. Garfield, born Julius Garfinkle, was the product of a brawling New York City slum childhood, the personification of the street-wise rebel hero he often portrayed on film.

He appeared in the definitive version of *The Postman Always Rings Twice* (1946) and received acclaim for his role as a boxer in *Body and Soul* (1947). Garfield was blacklisted in the 1950s for refusing to give a government committee the names of friends who were Communists. He died of a heart attack shortly afterwards.

FILMOGRAPHY
Four Daughters 1938
They Made Me a Criminal 1939
The Sea Wolf 1941
Pride of the Marines 1945
The Postman Always Rings Twice 1946
Humoresque 1946
Body and Soul 1947
Gentleman's Agreement 1947
Force of Evil 1949
The Breaking Point 1950
He Ran All the Way 1951

John Garfield with Lana Turner in *The Postman Always Rings Twice* (1946).

GARLAND, Judy 1922-1969

She had a great voice – stirring, soulful and wistful. She had lots of nervous energy and a streak of vulnerability. What's more, Garland (born Frances Gumm) could dance and Garland could act. 'The little girl with the great big voice' was born into a vaudeville family, making her stage debut at age three, part of the Gumm Sisters Kiddie Act. Guided by her ambitious mother, the basically shy Judy made her way to Hollywood. She had an MGM contract by the age of 13.

She showed star quality singing her heart out to a picture of Clark Gable in *Broadway Melody of 1938* (1938), and with Mickey Rooney was popular appearing in a string of movies showing the rosy side of teenage life. But it was as Dorothy in *The Wizard of Oz* (1939) that Judy really shone. She won a special Academy Award for best juvenile performer of the year.

Although Judy's career was successful, her personal life was tragic. To combat fatigue and help her keep her weight down, MGM bigwigs had her put on pills. She was to have a drug problem all her life, later compounded by alcohol.

During the 1940s Judy made some of MGM's best technicolor musicals, including *Meet Me in St Louis* (1944). She married the movie's director, Vincente Minnelli, and their daughter Liza grew up to become a star in her own right. Judy later married Sid Luft who arranged an engagement for her at the London Palladium when her film career faltered. Judy was a dazzling stage performer and the show was a great success. She then went on to New York's Palace Theater.

A Star is Born (1954), with James Mason, was a smash hit and is a classic today. Though Judy continued to make fine films and give great concerts her private troubles proved overwhelming. Her marriage to Luft fell apart and there was an ugly custody battle over their two children, one of whom is singer Lorna Luft. There was one more marriage for Judy, suicide attempts, a tour that didn't go well. Still she seemed on her way back when she died of an overdose of sleeping pills. Deeply mourned by both fans and show business people even today, Judy Garland is a unique star.

Judy Garland with Mickey Rooney – everyor

Garland as Dorothy and Margaret Hamilton as the Wicked Witch of the West in *The Wizard of Oz* (1939).

couple.

FILMOGRAPHY
Pigskin Parade 1936
Broadway Melody of 1938 1938
Love Finds Andy Hardy 1938
The Wizard of Oz 1939
Babes in Arms 1939
Ziegfeld Girl 1941
For Me and My Gal 1942
Meet Me in St Louis 1944
The Clock 1945
The Harvey Girls 1946
Easter Parade 1948
In the Good Old Summertime 1949
Summer Stock 1950
A Star is Born 1954
Judgment at Nuremberg 1960
A Child is Waiting 1962
I Could Go On Singing 1963

Left: Garland in *A Star Is Born* (1954).

Judy Garland, again with Fred Astaire, in *Easter Parade* (1948).

Above: With Astaire in *Easter Parade* (1948).

GARNER, James 1928-

This good-looking actor, born James Baumgarner, has successfully combined careers in two media, films and television. He achieved stardom with the TV show *Maverick*, repeating his triumph later with *The Rockford Files*. In movies his style is low-key and he projects a wry charm.

FILMOGRAPHY
Cash McCall 1959
The Great Escape 1963
The Thrill of It All 1963
The Americanization of Emily 1964
Thirty-Six Hours 1964
Support Your Local Sheriff 1970
Victor Victoria 1982
Murphy's Romance 1985

GARSON, Greer 1908-

A lovely red-haired Anglo-Irish leading lady, Greer Garson had class. Her forté was playing strong but gracious and elegant women. Her career reached its peak during World War II when her performance as a brave British housewife in *Mrs Miniver* (1942) won her an Academy Award for Best Actress.

FILMOGRAPHY
Goodbye, Mr Chips 1939
Pride and Prejudice 1940
Mrs Miniver 1942
Random Harvest 1942
That Forsyte Woman 1949
Sunrise at Campobello 1960
The Happiest Millionaire 1967

Mitzi Gaynor as Nellie Forbush in *South Pacific* (1958) – the 'Honey Bun' number.

GAYNOR, Mitzi 1930-

Though Mitzi Gaynor was born in Chicago, this charming actress, dancer and singer, the daughter of a ballerina, was the descendant of Hungarian aristocrats. She was born Franceska Mitzi von Gerber. By age 12 Gaynor was a member of the corps de ballet of the Los Angeles Civil Light Opera.

She began her film career in musicals in 1950 but her bright perky style was often better than the material she was given and her movies did not always fare well at the box office. Dropped by 20th Century Fox in 1954, she married agent Jack Bean who helped her recoup her movie career temporarily. Performing live was her real specialty.

FILMOGRAPHY
Golden Girl 1951
The I Don't Care Girl 1953
Down Among the Sheltering Palms 1953
There's No Business Like Show Business 1954
Anything Goes 1956
The Joker Is Wild 1957
Les Girls 1957
South Pacific 1958
Happy Anniversary 1959
Surprise Package 1960
For Love or Money 1963

GERE, Richard 1949-

Touted as one of Hollywood's new sex symbols, yet also regarded as an actor of impressive talent, Gere scored a

Richard Gere with Lou Gossett Jr in *An Officer and a Gentleman* (1982).

major film success in *An Officer and a Gentleman* (1982). Yet aside from this film his career has been more promise than fulfilment.

Gere dropped out of college to try to make it on Broadway but he got his first real break in the London production of the musical *Grease*. On the strength of that performance he did a season with the Young Vic Company, a rare opportunity for an American actor.

Gere has always been serious about the theater and in 1980 he left Hollywood to go to Broadway and star in *Bent* – a depressing and uncommercial play about homosexuals in Nazi death camps. This was a major risk, particularly for a sex symbol, but Gere got marvellous notices.

FILMOGRAPHY
Report to the Commissioner 1975
Baby Blue Marine 1976
Looking for Mr Goodbar 1977
Days of Heaven 1978
Bloodbrothers 1978
Yanks 1979
American Gigolo 1979
An Officer and a Gentleman 1982
Breathless 1983
Beyond the Limits 1983
The Cotton Club 1984

GIBSON, Edward 'Hoot' 1892-1962

Gibson was a cowboy and rodeo star who got his start in pictures as a stuntman. In 1919, billed as 'The Smiling Whirlwind,' he had his own two-reel series. Bigger action films followed but he achieved his greatest popularity as a star of silent comic westerns.

FILMOGRAPHY
The Hazards of Helen 1915
The Denver Dude 1922
Surefire 1924
Points West 1929
Sunset Range 1935
The Horse Soldiers 1959
Ocean's Eleven 1961

GIELGUD, Sir John 1904-

Sir John Gielgud was known primarily for his illustrious stage career, but this great British Shakespearean actor began appearing in silent films. Critics often accused Gielgud of looking uncomfortable in films, in contrast to his colleague Laurence Olivier, who seemed to move with ease with both theater and movies. Yet from early on Gielgud turned in a number of excellent performances.

Amazingly, Gielgud seems to have improved with age. Now in even small roles on screen he steals the show and he has brought many a gleaming moment to television productions as well.

John Gielgud as Chang in *Lost Horizon* (1973).

FILMOGRAPHY
Who is the Man? 1924
Secret Agent 1936
The Prime Minister 1940
Julius Caesar 1953
Richard III 1956
The Barretts of Wimpole Street 1957
Becket 1964
The Charge of the Light Brigade 1968
Julius Caesar 1970
Murder on the Orient Express 1974
Providence 1977
Murder by Decree 1979
The Elephant Man 1980
Arthur 1981
Chariots of Fire 1981
Gandhi 1982

GILBERT, John 1895-1936

Handsome dark-haired men with passionate eyes were all the rage in the silent era and no one, not even Rudolph Valentino, eclipsed Gilbert (born John Pringle) on screen. This fine silent-movies actor was born into a show-business family in Logan, Utah. From an early age he dreamed of becoming a movie star and in 1916 he broke into films as an extra, using the name Jack Gilbert.

He was soon seen in leads and featured roles through chiefly as 'the other man' or an unsympathetic character because it was generally believed his Latin-type looks gave him a slightly villainous air. During this phase of his career Gilbert often co-wrote scripts for the films he made.

By the early 1920s he was playing dashing heroes in movies like *Monte Cristo* (1922) and *Arabian Love* (1922). From 1921 on he was John Gilbert, shedding Jack forever, and emerging, once he went to MGM, as an extraordinarily popular star. He played a wide range of roles. Gilbert was in the circus drama *He Who Gets Slapped* (1924) with Lon Chaney. In *The Snob* (1924) he played a despicable cad. He made a remarkable silent musical, *The Merry Widow* (1925). King Vidor directed him in *The Big Parade* (1925), a brilliant movie about World War I. It grossed a fortune.

Over the years Gilbert appeared with some of the most famous leading ladies of silent films including Renée Adorée, Billie Dove, Barbara La Marr, Mae Murray, Lillian Gish and Norma Shearer. His reputation as a great lover was established through the movies he made with Greta Garbo, beginning with

85

John Gilbert in *The Big Parade* (1925).

Inset: Gilbert with Greta Garbo in *Romance* (1930).

Flesh and the Devil (1927). Rumors of their affair, real or studio created, fanned the fires and upped the box-office takings.

Gilbert's career went sour during the sound era, presumably because he had a high squeaky voice. Though his voice lacked authority it was adequate and could, with training, have been improved. Actually Gilbert was a victim of changing fashions. He simply couldn't adapt to the low-key style of talkies and tragically died penniless, an alcoholic, at the age of 41.

FILMOGRAPHY

The Princess of the Dark 1916	The Snob 1924
The Millionaire Vagrant 1916	The Merry Widow 1925
White Heather 1919	The Big Parade 1925
The Great Redeemer 1920	La Bohème 1926
Deep Waters 1921	Bardelys the Magnificent 1926
Monte Cristo 1922	Flesh and the Devil 1927
Arabian Love 1922	Love 1927
While Paris Sleeps 1922	A Woman of Affairs 1929
Honor First 1922	His Glorious Night 1929
The Madness of Youth 1923	Redemption 1930
Saint Elmo 1923	Queen Christina 1933
Cameo Kirby 1923	Downstairs 1932
He Who Gets Slapped 1924	The Captain Hates the Sea 1935

GISH, Dorothy 1898-1968

A child actress, as was her sister Lillian, Dorothy Gish began her screen career in 1912 under the guidance of director D W Griffith. Though Lillian is more famous today as a dramatic actress, during the silent era Dorothy Gish was a major star in her own right.

A talented light comedienne and pantomimist, Gish made many movies, and though the Gish sisters appeared together frequently at the beginning of their careers, later they generally went their separate ways. Gish made her last silents in London, then appeared primarily on stage. She remained close to her sister Lillian all her life.

FILMOGRAPHY
An Uneasy Enemy 1912
The Sisters 1914
Susan Rocks the Boat 1916
Hearts of the World 1918
Battling Jane 1918
Remodeling Her Husband 1920
Orphans of the Storm 1922
Romola 1924
Nell Gwyn 1926
Madame Pompadour 1927
Our Hearts Were Young and Gay 1944
The Whistle at Eaton Falls 1951
The Cardinal 1963

Above: A studio shot of Dorothy Gish in the 1930s.

Lillian Gish in *Birth of a Nation* (1914).

GISH, Lillian 1896-

A superb actress, often compared to Bernhardt, Gish was able to convey power and strength on screen despite her fragile appearance. She was, according to actress and critic Louise Brooks, a 'shining symbol of purity,' an image that created problems for her when Victorian sentimental standards faded in the late 1920s. But for many years Gish, a pioneer in film, was the reigning star of silent pictures.

She was born in Springfield, Ohio, making stage appearances billed as 'Baby Lillian' with her mother and sister Dorothy from the age of five. In 1912 Gish was introduced to D W Griffith through an old friend, Gladys Smith, now known as Mary Pickford, and began appearing in his films that same day. Griffith admired Gish's talent and intelligence. She in turn admired his genius. Together they created some of the classics of the silent era, including *Birth of a Nation* (1914), *Broken Blossoms* (1918) and *Orphans of the Storm* (1922).

Gish learned everything there was to know about film technique, directing her sister Dorothy in *Remodeling Her Husband* (1920), and insisting on full script and production control when she made movies for minor companies. Joining MGM in 1925, Gish chose King Vidor and Victor Sjostrom as her directors. Even though she turned in a masterful performance in *The Scarlet Letter* (1926), and the movie was a great commercial success, the growing popularity of Garbo allowed MGM to rid themselves of the independent well-paid Lillian Gish. She went to United Artists briefly. Sound was no problem for this actress who had an excellent stage-trained voice, but changing fashions were catching up with her. No longer a box-office draw, she decided to leave Hollywood and return to the theater rather than continue her film career.

Gish was in a number of Broadway productions including *Hamlet* starring John Gielgud. From the 1940s Gish did character parts in films. She also appeared on television and lectured widely. In 1970 Gish received a special Academy Award for her important film achievements.

FILMOGRAPHY

An Unseen Enemy 1913
The Madonna of the Storm 1913
Birth of a Nation 1914
The Lily and the Rose 1915
An Innocent Magdalene 1915
Intolerance 1916
Broken Blossoms 1918
True Heart Susie 1920
Way Down East 1920
Orphans of the Storm 1922
The White Sister 1923
Romola 1924
La Bohème 1926
The Scarlet Letter 1926
Annie Laurie 1927
The Wind 1928
His Double Life 1934
The Commandos 1943
Strike at Dawn 1943
Miss Susie Slagle's 1946
Duel in the Sun 1946
Portrait of Jennie 1948
The Cobweb 1955
The Night of the Hunter 1955
Orders to Kill 1958
Follow Me Boys 1966
The Comedians 1967
A Wedding 1978
Sweet Liberty 1986
The Whales of August 1987

Lillian Gish in *The Night of the Hunter* (1955).

FILMOGRAPHY

Modern Times 1936	**Nothing But the Truth** 1941
The Young in Heart 1938	**Reap the Wild Wind** 1942
The Cat and the Canary 1939	**So Proudly We Hail** 1943
The Ghost Breakers 1940	**Kitty** 1945
The Great Dictator 1940	**The Stranger Came Home** 1954
	Time of Indifference 1966

A young Paulette Goddard.

GODDARD, Paulette 1911-

Paulette Goddard, born Marion Levy, could be a good comedienne or a sexy siren. Goddard was as witty and intelligent as she was beautiful. A Ziegfeld girl at 14 who tried her luck in Hollywood, she married Charlie Chaplin and appeared in two of his films. But she was busily making it to stardom on her own with co-stars like Bob Hope and Ray Milland.

By the 1940s she was a top star, a favorite of Cecil B De Mille, but her career took a dip in the 1950s. After divorcing Chaplin she married actor Burgess Meredith, then author Erich Maria Remarque, and lived elegantly in Europe.

GOULD, Elliott 1938-

The ex-husband of superstar Barbra Streisand, Elliott Gould, born Elliott Goldstein, has been in turn a Broadway leading man, an out-of-work stage actor, a Hollywood hot property and a performer in search of good scripts. If he were cast in the right movie, the roller coaster could start up again.

FILMOGRAPHY

The Night They Raided Minsky's 1968
Bob and Carol and Ted and Alice 1969
M*A*S*H* 1970
Getting Straight 1970
The Long Goodbye 1972
Capricorn One 1978
The Devil and Max Devlin 1981

GRABLE, Betty 1916-73

GI Joe's favorite pin-up during World War II, Grable was technicolor's brightest blonde in some of Hollywood's most famous musicals. She was just right for her era, a fantasy version of the kind of girl you'd find in a diner or working shifts in a war plant.

Grable was born in St Louis, Missouri. By nature an easy going sort, she was pushed into her career by her ferocious stage mother. Grable took singing and dancing lessons from an early age and by 12 was in Hollywood, trying to break into movies. She had bits in films while still in her early teens, occasionally appearing under the name Frances Dean. A series of leads in B pictures followed.

Grable married Jackie Coogan in 1937. His success boosted her career. They divorced in 1940, the year she caught the eye of Daryl F Zanuck at 20th Century Fox. She'd just scored a big success on Broadway in *Du Barry Was a Lady*. When she replaced Alice Faye in *Down Argentine Way* (1940), audiences sat up and took notice.

Though Grable was good in light comedies, stardom came through films like *Song of the Islands* (1942), *Coney Island* (1943) and *Sweet Rosie O'Grady* (1943). Grable frequently co-starred with Dan Dailey in lavishly costumed musicals set in a nostalgic bygone era. Grable became Hollywood's highest paid star, box-office magic. Her legs were insured with Lloyd's of London for a million dollars.

In 1943 Grable married trumpet player Harry James. They were divorced in 1965. Critical recognition came with *Mother Wore Tights* (1947), and Grable continued to be popular in films until the mid-1950s when movie musicals went into decline. She had a loyal following who came out later to see her in nightclubs and in plays, especially when she appeared on Broadway in the role made famous by Carol Channing in *Hello Dolly*. She died of lung cancer at 56.

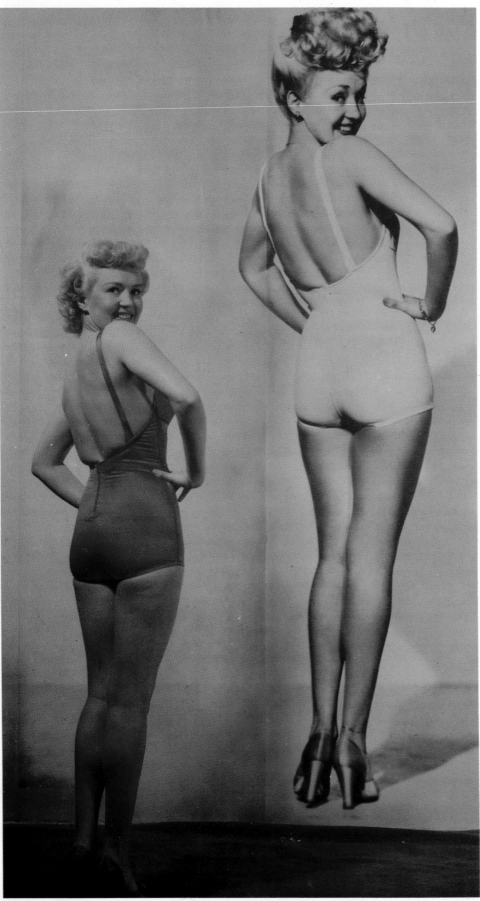

Betty Grable in her pin-up pose from World War II.

FILMOGRAPHY
Whoopee 1930
The Gay Divorcee 1934
Collegiate 1935
Follow the Fleet 1936
Pigskin Parade 1936
College Swing 1938
Million Dollar Legs 1939
Down Argentine Way 1940
Tin Pan Alley 1940
Moon Over Miami 1941
I Wake Up Screaming 1941
Song of the Islands 1942
Springtime in the Rockies 1942
Coney Island 1943
Sweet Rosie O'Grady 1943
Pin Up Girl 1944
The Dolly Sisters 1945
Mother Wore Tights 1947
When My Baby Smiles at Me 1948
Wabash Avenue 1950
My Blue Heaven 1950
How To Marry a Millionaire 1953
How to Be Very Very Popular 1953

Grable and John Payne in *Springtime in the Rockies* (1942).

Betty Grable and June Haver in *The Dolly Sisters* (1945).

The phenomenally handsome and charming Stewart Granger, born James Stewart, was one of Britain's top romantic leads until MGM lured him away to play the hero in swashbuckling Hollywood adventure films. Later he turned to television. From 1950 to 1960 Granger was married to British actress Jean Simmons.

FILMOGRAPHY
The Man in Grey 1943
Waterloo Road 1944
Captain Boycott 1947
King Solomon's Mines 1950
Scaramouche 1952
Beau Brummel 1954
North to Alaska 1960
The Last Safari 1967
The Wild Geese 1977

91

GRANT, Cary 1904-1986

Cary Grant (born Archibald Leach), the extraordinarily handsome British-born star, was one of the most famous screen personalities in the world. He played light romantic comic leads seemingly forever and from a distance at least appeared to lead a charmed life.

Actually Grant's early life was anything but charmed. Born in Bristol, England, into poverty, he ran away from home in his early teens. Joining a travelling acrobatic troupe he came to New York on tour in 1920. Grant scraped along at the lowest level in vaudeville, returning to England in 1923 where he appeared in musical comedies. An accomplished song and dance man, he returned to New York, had a modest success on Broadway, then tried his luck in Hollywood.

He got off to a good start in supporting roles and was given a real boost by Mae West who cast him as her co-star in *She Done Him Wrong* (1933). Soon Grant rivalled Gary Cooper in popularity but it wasn't until the late 1930s, beginning with *The Awful Truth* (1937), that Grant's gift for screwball comedy flowered on the screen.

By the 1940s Grant was the established master of roles requiring a sophisticated man-about-town. What set him apart from other actors of the genre, besides his unique voice with its tinge of Bristol accent, was his air of not taking himself too seriously. He always appeared slightly embarrassed in love scenes and despite his self-assurance was never a snob.

When other leading men of his generation had to turn to aging character roles, Grant still looked great. He was still in top form in *North by Northwest* (1959), and *Charade* (1963). Witty and urbane off screen as well as on, Grant once said 'I play myself to perfection.' Among his ex-wives are heiress Barbara Hutton, actresses Betsy Drake and Dyan Cannon, mother of his only child, a daughter born when he was past 60. In 1970 Cary Grant received a special Academy Award.

Opposite: Cary Grant as Cole Porter with Alexis Smith in *Night and Day* (1945). *Below:* Grant and Hepburn in *Bringing Up Baby* (1938).

FILMOGRAPHY

Blonde Venus 1933
She Done Him Wrong 1933
The Eagle and the Hawk 1933
I'm No Angel 1933
Sylvia Scarlett 1935
The Awful Truth 1937
Topper 1937
Bringing Up Baby 1938
Holiday 1938
Gunga Din 1939
Only Angels Have Wings 1939

My Favorite Wife 1940
The Philadelphia Story 1940
Penny Serenade 1941
Suspicion 1941
Mr Lucky 1943
None But the Lonely Heart 1944
Arsenic and Old Lace 1944
Notorious 1946
The Bachelor and the Bobby Soxer 1947
The Bishop's Wife 1948
Mr Blandings Builds His Dream
  House 1948

I Was a Male War Bride 1949
To Catch a Thief 1955
An Affair to Remember 1957
Indiscreet 1958
North by Northwest 1959
Operation Petticoat 1959
That Touch of Mink 1962
Charade 1963
Father Goose 1964
Walk, Don't Run 1966

FILMOGRAPHY
Evensong 1933
Great Expectations 1946
Oliver Twist 1948
Kind Hearts and Coronets 1949
Last Holiday 1950
The Mudlark 1950
The Lavender Hill Mob 1951
The Man in the White Suit 1951
The Card 1952
The Captain's Paradise 1952
Father Brown 1954
The Ladykillers 1955

The Swan 1956
The Bridge on the River Kwai 1957
The Horse's Mouth 1958
Our Man in Havana 1959
Tunes of Glory 1960
Lawrence of Arabia 1962
The Comedians 1967
Murder by Death 1976
Star Wars 1977
The Empire Strikes Back 1980
Lovesick 1983
Return of the Jedi 1983
A Passage to India 1984

GREENSTREET, Sydney 1879-1954

Usually sinister, and always fat, the British-born Greenstreet became one of Hollywood's most memorable villains. In his best films he was teamed with Humphrey Bogart and/or Peter Lorre.

FILMOGRAPHY
The Maltese Falcon 1941
They Died With Their Boots On 1941
Casablanca 1942
Background to Danger 1943
The Mask of Dimitrios 1944
Three Strangers 1946
The Verdict 1946
The Hucksters 1947
The Woman in White 1948
Flamingo Road 1949

GUINNESS, Sir Alec 1914-

When it comes to film technique, versatility, and an artistic instinct for the understated no actor can rival Guinness. Born in London, this foremost British actor made his screen debut in 1933. It would be years before he would be seen on screen again. Discovered by John Gielgud, Guinness later went to the Old Vic Company, eventually appearing in leading roles.

In 1941 Guinness joined the Royal Navy and after the war returned to the stage. For the most part he continued his career in the theater right through his years as a major screen attraction and beyond. An extraordinary Fagin in *Oliver Twist* (1948), he played eight different characters in *Kinds Hearts and Coronets* (1949), won a Picturegoer Gold Medal as Disraeli in *The Mudlark* (1950), appeared in two of Ealing Studios best comedies, *The Lavender Hill Mob* (1951) and *The Man in the White Suit* (1951). In 1951 Guinness became Britain's top box-office star and the fifth in the world.

He didn't stop making great pictures, charming the public as a mild priest turned sleuth in *Father Brown* (1954) and as a mad mastermind undone by a sweet old lady in *The Ladykillers* (1955). *The Bridge on the River Kwai* (1957), won him a British Film Acad-

Opposite top: Alec Guinness in *The Fall of the Roman Empire* (1964).
Opposite bottom: Guinness in *The Bridge on the River Kwai* (1957).

emy Award and a Academy Award for Best Actor.

Alec Guinness was knighted in 1959 for his achievements, but he was on the threshold of difficult years, when the critics took to sniping at him. Still he had his triumphs. He won a Venice Film Festival Award for *The Horse's Mouth* (1958), for which he wrote the screenplay. He was an excellent Feisal in *Lawrence of Arabia* (1962), magnificent in *Tunes of Glory* (1960) and he was a hit on Broadway in *Dylan* (1964).

Guinness outlasted the sniping, maintaining his reputation through a series of fine supporting roles in films, further serious stage performances, and superb appearances on television. Ironically, he achieved his greatest financial success in *Star Wars* (1977). Owning a small percentage of the film's profits has made him millions.

GWENN, Edmund 1875-1959

This veteran Welsh actor began his London stage career in the early 1900s where he was much admired by playwright George Bernard Shaw. Though Gwenn made his debut in British films in 1916, it was in Hollywood during the 1940s that he became a movie star.

The stocky but elfish Gwenn played lovable avuncular types, receiving an Academy Award for Best Supporting Actor for his performance as Kris Kringle in *Miracle on 34th Street* (1947). He was splendid in Hitchcock's *The Trouble with Harry* (1955), at the ripe old age of 80.

FILMOGRAPHY
The Real Thing at Last 1916
The Skin Game 1932
The Good Companions 1933
Sylvia Scarlett 1935
Pride and Prejudice 1940
Foreign Correspondent 1940
Charlie's Aunt 1941
Lassie Come Home 1943
Between Two Worlds 1944
Miracle on 34th Street 1947
Life With Father 1947
Apartment for Peggy 1948
Mister 880 1950
The Student Prince 1954
The Trouble with Harry 1955
Calabuch 1957

Edmund Gwenn and a young Natalie Wood in *Miracle on 34th Street* (1947).

HACKMAN, Gene 1930-

Hackman can play a villain or a saint. Either way Hackman is one of the finest character actors in Hollywood. Though not handsome or charismatic enough to draw audiences in on the strength of his name alone, he has been turning out fine performances in films for over 20 years.

Born in California, Hackman quit high school to join the Marines, then drifted from one small town to another until deciding to become an actor in his 30s. Success came with *Bonnie and Clyde* (1967) and he won an Academy Award for Best Actor for the role of the eccentric detective Popeye Doyle in *The French Connection* (1971).

FILMOGRAPHY
Lilith 1964
Bonnie and Clyde 1967
I Never Sang for My Father 1969
The French Connection 1971
The Poseidon Adventure 1972
The Conversation 1974
Superman 1978
Superman II 1980
Reds 1982
Under Fire 1983
Twice in a Lifetime 1986
Hoosiers 1986

Gene Hackman as Popeye Doyle in *The French Connection* (1971).

Below: Sir Cedric Hardwicke.

HAMPSHIRE, Susan 1938-

Susan Hampshire, a charming London-born actress, has been on stage since childhood and made her screen debut at the age of six. She began appearing in films again in 1959 but is best known as Fleur in the British television series, *The Forsythe Saga.*

FILMOGRAPHY
Upstairs and Downstairs 1959
The Three Lives of Thomasina 1963
Paris in the Month of August 1966
A Time for Loving 1972
The Lonely Woman 1976

HARDWICKE, Sir Cedric 1893-1964

Admired in both Britain and America this prominent actor was born in Rye, England and made his London stage debut in 1912. A distinguished career in theater and films led to his being knighted in 1934.

Settling in Hollywood in the late 1930s, Hardwicke often appeared in movies which weren't worthy of his talents. He played villains and Nazis until, after World War II, he alternated between stage and screen.

FILMOGRAPHY
Nelson 1926
Dreyfus 1931
Nell Gwyn 1934
Becky Sharp 1935
King Solomon's Mines 1937
On Borrowed Time 1939
Stanley and Livingstone 1939
Tom Brown's Schooldays 1940
Victory 1940
The Commandos Strike at Dawn 1942
The Moon is Down 1943
Ivy 1947
Nicholas Nickleby 1947
I Remember Mama 1948
The Winslow Boy 1948
The Desert Fox 1951
Richard III 1955
The Ten Commandments 1956
Around the World in Eighty Days 1956
Baby Face Nelson 1957
The Pumpkin Eater 1964

HARRIS, Richard 1932-

Night-club battles and on-set brawls have marked the colorful career of this talented actor. Harris has always drawn much of his charisma and strength from his earthy pugnaciousness and rugged 'man's man' image.

Born in Limerick, Ireland, he later attended the London Academy of Music and Dramatic Art, making his stage debut in 1956 and his movie debut in 1958. Stardom came to Harris with his performance as a rugby-playing rebel in *This Sporting Life* (1963). Besides films, he scored a major triumph as Richard Burton's replacement in the stage version of *Camelot*. He also played Arthur in the film and in a successful revival which was televised.

FILMOGRAPHY
The Wreck of the Mary Deare 1959
The Guns of Navarone 1961
Mutiny on the Bounty 1962
The Red Desert 1964
Camelot 1967
The Molly Maguires 1969
A Man Called Horse 1969
Cromwell 1970
Robin and Marian 1975
The Cassandra Crossing 1977
The Wild Geese 1978
Tarzan, The Ape Man 1981

Rex Harrison, as Henry Higgins, mocks Audrey Hepburn in *My Fair Lady* (1964).

HARRISON, Sir Rex 1908-

Sir Rex Harrison, cool and debonair, is a superb British-born star of stage and screen who adds a unique diamond-sharp edge to sophisticated comedy. He appeared in such movie classics as *Major Barbara* (1940) and *Blithe Spirit* (1945).

Harrison took the world by storm during the 1950s as Professor Henry Higgins in *My Fair Lady*. He repeated the role in the 1964 movie version of the Broadway musical, winning an Academy Award. He has remained a sterling performer.

FILMOGRAPHY
Storm in a Teacup 1937
St Martin's Lane 1938
The Citadel 1938
Night Train to Munich 1940
Major Barbara 1940
Blithe Spirit 1945
The Rake's Progress 1946
Anna and the King of Siam 1946
The Ghost and Mrs Muir 1947
Unfaithfully Yours 1948
Escape 1948
The Four Poster 1952
The Reluctant Debutante 1958
Cleopatra 1962
My Fair Lady 1964
The Agony and the Ecstasy 1965
Doctor Doolittle 1967
The Fifth Musketeer 1977
Shalimar 1978

Left: Richard Harris, the brooding King Arthur in *Camelot* (1967).

HART, William S 1870-1946

Under William S Hart's guidance the American western film emerged as a serious realistic genre, something more than a child-like fantasy of shoot-em-up cowboys and Indians in a rosy dream of the West. Actor and director Hart, the son of an itinerant laborer, was born in Newburgh, New York, but spent much of his early years in the West, which he loved.

At the age of 19 Hart moved to New York City, where he became such a prominent Shakespearean actor that it was rumored the initial 'S' in his name stood for Shakespeare. It actually stood for his middle name, Surrey. During the 1890s Hart began appearing in western dramas on Broadway such as *The Squaw Man*, *The Virginian* and *The Trail of the Lonesome Pine*.

In 1914, at the age of 44, Hart started making movies for his friend, producer and director Thomas H Ince. A villain in two-reelers, he soon became a star and went on to direct the films he appeared in and occasionally wrote the scripts. Hart had known real cowboys and Indians in his youth and his vivid memories of the West made him approach Westerns from a new angle. Insisting on realism and careful reconstructions of sets and costumes, Hart westerns were strong on plot and character. He created the villain turned hero, the man who starts out as evil but who is redeemed at the end of the film by a virtuous act.

Unlike most of his contemporaries, Hart refused to romanticize and prettify the West. The towns in his films were dusty and filled with shacks, and Hart was serious and unsmiling riding his pinto pony Fritz. Instead of glamorous adventure films, his movies had the feel of a documentary. There was nothing like them before and there has never really been anything quite like them since.

Hart's popularity dwindled when action heroes strong on stunts, like Tom Mix and Buck Jones, caught the public's fancy. In 1925 Hart sued United Artists because he felt the studio had mishandled the distribution of his last film, *Tumbleweeds* (1925). He won his case and though the movie turned out to be a critical and commercial success, Hart retired and wrote Western novels. His influence on westerns cannot be exaggerated.

Right: William S Hart.

HARVEY, Laurence 1928-1973

[L]aurence Harvey, born Larushka [M]ischa Skikne in Lithuania and raised [in] South Africa, moved to England to [st]udy acting. Though sometimes [ac]cused of being cold and uninspiring, [h]e created several memorable screen [ro]les and was a success as *Henry V* at [th]e Old Vic. He died at only 45 of [ca]ncer.

[FI]LMOGRAPHY
[I] Believe in You 1952
[R]omeo and Juliet 1954
[K]ing Richard and the Crusaders 1954
[I] Am a Camera 1955
[R]oom at the Top 1959
[E]xpresso Bongo 1959
[B]utterfield Eight 1960
[T]he Manchurian Candidate 1963
[D]arling 1965
[N]ight Watch 1973

HAWKINS, Jack 1910-1973

Jack Hawkins, the strong and dominant British actor, began his theater career at the age of 13 and made his debut in films at 20, but had to wait until middle-age before becoming an international star. His first wife was the noted British-born stage actress Jessica Tandy.

A prolific performer, Hawkins was dynamic in either leads or character roles, generally playing tough decisive men of action who retained their charm and sense of humor. In 1966 Hawkins lost his voice following an operation for cancer of the larynx and his subsequent performances in films were dubbed.

Below: Jack Hawkins in TV's *QB VII* (1974).

FILMOGRAPHY
The Lodger 1932
Peg of Old Drury 1935
The Fallen Idol 1948
State Secret 1950
Angels One Five 1952
The Cruel Sea 1952
The Bridge on the River Kwai 1958
The League of Gentlemen 1959
Ben Hur 1959
Lawrence of Arabia 1962
Rampage 1963
Shalako 1968
Nicholas and Alexandra 1971
Tales that Witness Madness 1973

HAWN, Goldie 1945-

Though she often plays dumb blondes Goldie Hawn isn't one, having emerged after her start on television's *Laugh-In* as a fine comedienne, a sensitive actress and a clever producer. Hawn won an Academy Award for Best Supporting Actress for *Cactus Flower* (1969). *Private Benjamin* (1980) is her biggest hit so far.

Goldie Hawn as *Private Benjamin* (1980).

FILMOGRAPHY
Cactus Flower 1969
Shampoo 1975
Foul Play 1978
Private Benjamin 1980
Best Friends 1982
Swing Shift 1983
Protocol 1984
Wild Cats 1986

HAYWARD, Susan 1918-1975

The beautiful husky-voiced, red-haired Susan Hayward, born Edythe Marrener in Brooklyn, New York, was top-box office but she never acquired a star's mystique. A serious actress, she found her niche playing tough aggressive women, often on the skids. Audiences loved *I'll Cry Tomorrow* (1955), about an alcoholic, and Hayward won an Academy Award for Best Actress for her role as a call girl convicted of murder in *I Want to Live* (1958).

In 1955 a court case involving her ex-husband Jess Barker over the custody of their twin sons led to Hayward's attempting suicide. Newspapers had a field day. She died of a brain tumor when only 56.

FILMOGRAPHY

Adam Had Four Sons 1941
The Hairy Ape 1944
Smash-Up 1947
Tulsa 1949
My Foolish Heart 1949
I Can Get It For You Wholesale 1951
With a Song in my Heart 1952
I'll Cry Tomorrow 1955
I Want to Live 1958
Back Street 1961
Valley of the Dolls 1967
The Revengers 1972

Below: Susan Hayward – *Where Love Has Gone* (1964).

HAYWORTH, Rita 1918-

Rita Hayworth was the love goddess of the 1940s, so glamorous, seductive and beautiful that even the camera fell in love with her. Shy and inhibited in private life, she came alive before the camera and it repaid her, making her a lovely vision in black and white and a blaze of ruby glory in Technicolor.

She was born Margarita Carmen Cansino, daughter of Eduardo Cansino, a well-known Latin dancer. A teenager when she began dancing in films, her naturally dark hair and Spanish background led to her being stereotyped at first as a sultry señorita. She slimmed down, took acting lessons, changed her name and her hairline and shed her old persona. A series of 'B' pictures led to *Only Angels Have Wings* (1939) and *The Strawberry Blonde* (1941), where she appeared for the first time (ironically, because the film was shot in black and white) with red hair.

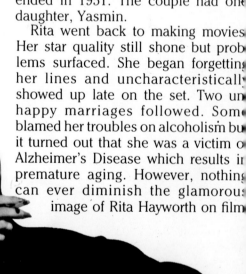

Soon Rita was Columbia Pictures top star, a versatile performer wh could play 'good girls' and temp tresses, appear in straight dramati films and, despite dubbed singing danced her way through a musical ver nicely. During World War II the G loved her.

Off screen Rita made big news whe she married Hollywood's wonder bo and genius, actor and director, Orso Welles. The couple had one child, daughter, Rebecca. Orson and Rit were divorced in 1945. In 1948 Rita me Aly Khan, Europe's reigning playboy the son of the Aga Khan, spiritua leader of the Ismaili Muslims and on of the world's richest men. By then Rit was one of hte world's most desirabl women, having made *Gilda* (1946), co starring Glenn Ford, the smash hi movie which took Hollywood out of the wholesome era forever.

The romance of Rita and Aly mad headline news and their glittering wedding drove fans wild. But Aly re mained a playboy and the marriage ended in 1951. The couple had on daughter, Yasmin.

Rita went back to making movies Her star quality still shone but prob lems surfaced. She began forgetting her lines and uncharacteristically showed up late on the set. Two un happy marriages followed. Som blamed her troubles on alcoholism bu it turned out that she was a victim o Alzheimer's Disease which results in premature aging. However, nothing can ever diminish the glamorou image of Rita Hayworth on film

FILMOGRAPHY

Under the Pampas Moon 1935	The Lady from Shanghai 1948
Human Cargo 1936	The Loves of Carmen 1948
Only Angels Have Wings 1939	Affair in Trinidad 1952
The Lady in Question 1940	Miss Sadie Thompson 1953
Angels Over Broadway 1940	Pal Joey 1957
The Strawberry Blonde 1941	Separate Tables 1948
Blood and Sand 1941	The Story on Page One 1959
You'll Never Get Rich 1941	Circus World 1964
You Were Never Lovelier 1942	The Money Trap 1966
Cover Girl 1944	The Rover 1968
Gilda 1946	The Wrath of God 1972

Above: The beautiful Rita Hayworth.

Left: Hayworth in *The Lady from Shanghai* (1948).

Far left: Hayworth in her pin-up days.

HEMMINGS, David 1941-

David Hemmings' slight build and expressive eyes give him a distinctive appearance. He began his career as a boy soprano, later turned to nightclubs, stage and television. Films followed and he became a star with *Blow Up* (1966). He continued to play leads in movies. He also directs, paints and writes novels.

FILMOGRAPHY
Blow Up 1966
Camelot 1967
The Charge of the Light Brigade 1968
Barbarella 1968
Islands in the Stream 1977
Just a Gigolo 1978
Murder by Decree 1979

Paul Henreid in *Casablanca* (1942).

HENREID, Paul 1908-

Gallant, handsome, elegant and cosmopolitan Paul Henreid, born in Austria, went first to Britain, then to Hollywood when the rise of Hitler made it necessary for him to leave his country. The son of a banker, Henreid went into publishing but became an actor in the Viennese theater, rising to prominence thanks to directors Otto Preminger and Max Reinhardt.

Henreid became a leading man in American films, appearing opposite Bette Davis in *Now Voyager* (1942). His most famous movie is *Casablanca* (1942) in which he played Ingrid Bergman's husband, anti-Nazi leader Victor Laszlo. In the 1950s Henreid began directing movies and television shows.

FILMOGRAPHY
Goodbye Mr Chips 1939
Night Train to Munich 1940
Now Voyager 1942
Casablanca 1942
Devotion 1946
Of Human Bondage 1946
Song of Love 1947
For Men Only 1951
Holiday for Lovers 1959
Operation Crossbow 1965
Exorcist II: The Heretic 1977

HEPBURN, Audrey 1929-

Born of Irish-Dutch parentage, Audrey Hepburn had been trained as a dancer but had only minor movie and stage parts until she got her big break, the title role in the Broadway adaptation of *Gigi*. This brought her to the attention of director William Wyler, who gave her the lead in the film *Roman Holiday* (1953), a smash success that won her an Academy Award for Best Actress and enormous popularity. In an age when the screen was dominated by bosomy sex-goddesses, the elfin Audrey Hepburn was different and she had class.

Hepburn is best known for light comedy, but she also excelled in more serious roles. She was the perfect Natasha in an otherwise overstuffed 1956 version of *War and Peace*. Somehow Hepburn never attained the superstar status for which she once seemed destined. She lives mainly in Europe and though she is still lovely has made very few films since the late 1960s.

FILMOGRAPHY
Roman Holiday 1953
Sabrina 1954
War and Peace 1956
Funny Face 1957
Love in the Afternoon 1957
The Nun's Story 1959
Breakfast at Tiffany's 1961
Charade 1963
My Fair Lady 1964
How to Steal a Million 1966
Two for the Road 1967
Wait Until Dark 1967
Robin and Marian 1976

Audrey Hepburn in *Sabrina* (1944).

HEPBURN, Katharine 1907-

Revered by fans everywhere, Katharine Hepburn occupies a special place in films. She has won a record four Academy Awards for Best Actress, for *Morning Glory* (1933), *Guess Who's Coming to Dinner* (1967), *The Lion in Winter* (1968), which also earned her a British Film Academy Award and *On Golden Pond* (1982). The skinny lady with the upper-class accent and the strong opinions who looks like a New England school teacher and acts like a duchess seems to have been on top forever. Actually, she battled hard for her career and in the late 1930s was actually declared box-office poison. Hepburn was always a star but not always a phenomenon.

She came from a wealthy family, attended a prestigious girl's college, went to Broadway, then to Hollywood. She was an instant success in her first film *A Bill of Divorcement* (1932). Intellectual, independent, attired in unglamorous slacks and refusing to give autographs, Hepburn was distinctly un-Hollywood. Several popular movies

Opposite: Katharine Hepburn.

Above: Hepburn with Spencer Tracy in
Woman of the Year (1942).
Right: Hepburn in *The African Queen* (1942).

followed and a return to the stage in *The Lake*, which failed badly. Then it was more movies, some good, some mediocre, until she hit her stride in a screwball comedy called *Bringing Up Baby* (1938) with Cary Grant.

Hepburn recouped her fortunes on Broadway in *The Philadelphia Story* and starred in the film version of the play, which was a smash hit. The next phase of her career was a series of films with actor Spencer Tracy. A popular couple on screen, they were devoted to each other off screen as well. Columnists kept mum about the affair, though they hadn't hesitated to link Hepburn to billionaire Howard Hughes in the 1930s.

Hepburn and Humphrey Bogart scored a triumph with *The African Queen* (1951). It was one of her better spinster characterizations, a part at which she excelled. She won the Best Actress Award at the Cannes Film Festival for her fine performance as the hopeless drug-addicted mother in *Long Day's Journey into Night* (1962). Another triumph on Broadway in *Coco*, several critically acclaimed television productions and further films enhanced her legendary status. Opposite the dying Henry Fonda in *On Golden Pond* (1982) Hepburn proved she still had that touch of greatness after over 50 years of making films.

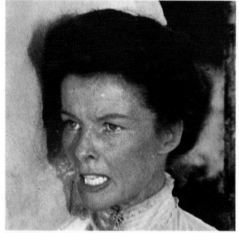

FILMOGRAPHY
A Bill of Divorcement 1932
Morning Glory 1933
Little Women 1933
Alice Adams 1935
Sylvia Scarlett 1935
Stage Door 1937
Bringing Up Baby 1938
Holiday 1938
The Philadelphia Story 1940
Woman of the Year 1942
State of the Union 1948
Adam's Rib 1949
The African Queen 1951
Pat and Mike 1952
The Rainmaker 1956
Suddenly Last Summer 1959
Long Day's Journey into Night 1962
Guess Who's Coming to Dinner 1967
The Lion in Winter 1968
A Delicate Balance 1973
Rooster Cogburn 1975
On Golden Pond 1982

HESTON, Charlton 1923-

Tall, muscular and strong-jawed, Heston looks every inch the hero that he has played throughout most of his film career. He has been Moses, John the Baptist, Michelangelo, Ben Hur, El Cid, Mark Anthony, Andrew Jackson and General 'Chinese' Gordon, among others. Though he has starred in some of the most popular films ever made, he is often overshadowed by hordes of spear-waving extras and spectacular special effects.

Heston was born in a suburb of Chicago and was a speech major in college. He began his professional career as a radio actor in Chicago, and after a stint in the Air Force spent years playing small roles then bigger ones on stage, television and in films.

Cecil B de Mille chose him to play the circus manager in *The Greatest Show on Earth* (1952), a huge box-office success. His real breakthrough to stardom came in another de Mille film, the *Ten Commandments* (1956), in which he played Moses. De Mille said that Heston had been chosen because he looked like Michelangelo's statue. The picture was another enormous financial success. Still another epic success (in both senses of the word) was *Ben Hur*, a 1959 remake of the old silent, which gained Heston an Academy Award for Best Actor.

Right: Charlton Heston in *El Cid* (1961).

Charlton Heston played the title role in *Ben Hur* (1959) and won an Academy Award.

Some of his better performances have come in smaller films, notably *Touch of Evil* (1958) directed by Orson Welles, where he effectively plays a Mexican detective in a seedy little town, without benefit of lavish sets or a cast of thousands.

The popularity of Heston epics declined sharply during the 1960s, but he did score one notable box-office triumph with *Planet of the Apes* (1968) and one of its sequels. The 1970s saw Heston regaining a measure of popularity with disaster films like *Earthquake* (1974).

Off screen he has been active in the politics of Hollywood, serving six terms as president of the Screen Actors' Guild.

Heston in *Number One* (1969), playing an aging football quarterback.

HILLER, Dame Wendy 1912-

Dame Wendy Hiller was a sensation on the London stage at the age of 18 in *Love on the Dole*. Her first major film triumph came in 1938 when she played Liza Doolittle in Shaw's *Pygmalion*. Hiller won an Academy Award for Best Supporting Actress for her moving portrayal of a lonely woman in *Separate Tables* (1958). Throughout her career Hiller has chosen her films with wisdom and care. She was created Dame in 1975.

FILMOGRAPHY
Lancashire Luck 1937
Pygmalion 1938
Major Barbara 1941
I Know Where I'm Going 1945
Outcast of the Islands 1951
Something of Value 1957
Separate Tables 1958
Sons and Lovers 1960
A Man for All Seasons 1966
David Copperfield 1970
Murder on the Orient Express 1974
Voyage of the Damned 1976
The Elephant Man 1981

Dustin Hoffman aged 121 years in *Little Big Man* (1970).

HOFFMAN, Dustin 1937-

Plenty of talent and plenty of brains have made Dustin Hoffman a superstar. He is bold in his choice of roles, a real risk-taker. Hoffman has come up a winner at the box office and as an artist besides.

Born in Los Angeles, California, he dropped out of Santa Monica City College to become an actor. He went to New York and for years worked odd jobs, did bit parts on television and appeared in summer stock. In 1965 he made it as far as Off Broadway. Then at last his luck changed.

Hoffman was chosen by director Mike Nichols to play a young man floundering in a cynical world in his film *The Graduate* (1967). It wasn't Hoffman's first movie. He had done a couple of unmemorable minor roles but despite winning an Obie Award Off-Broadway he was certainly an unknown. *The Graduate* made Hoffman a star.

He proved he wasn't a mere nine days wonder in *Midnight Cowboy* (1969), playing the sad, grotesque Ratso brilliantly. Essentially a character actor, Hoffman opted for versatility and challenging roles rather than personality or charisma in most of his following films. In *Little Big Man* (1970) he aged on screen from adolescence to over 100 years old. He was deliberately eccentric and ugly in *Papillon* (1973), and he worked hard to catch the strange tragic contradictions of comic Lenny Bruce in *Lenny* (1974).

Below: Hoffman in *Little Big Man* (1970).

109

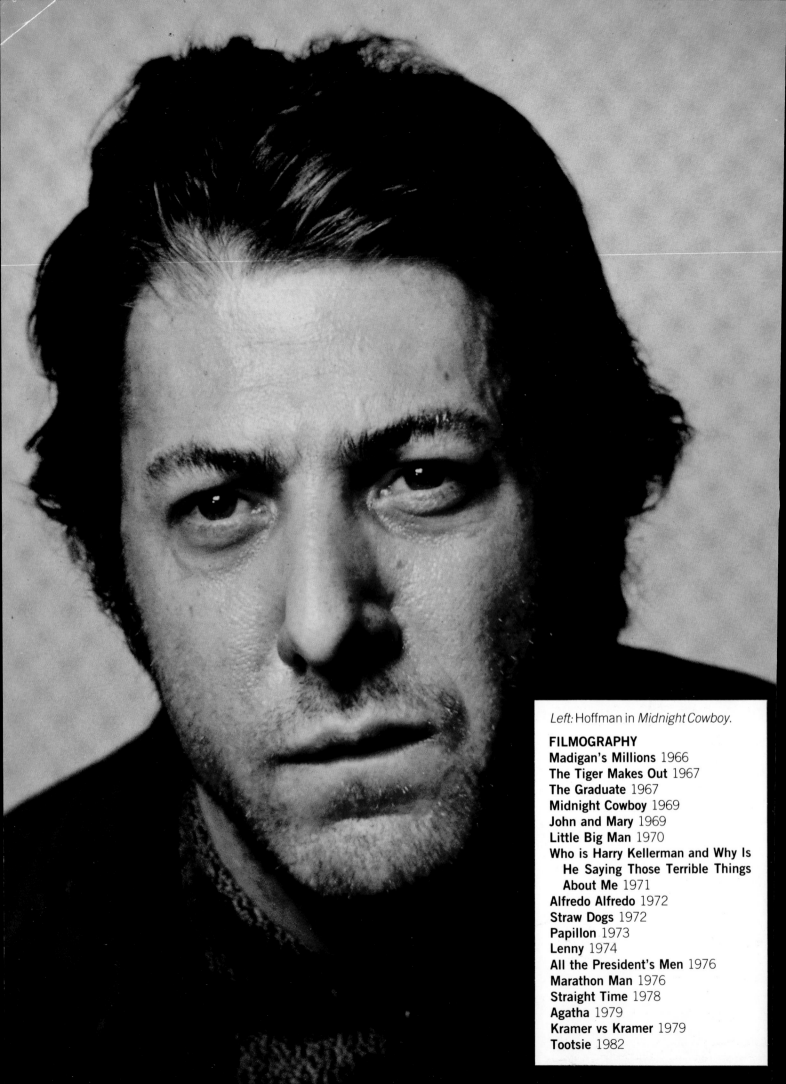

Left: Hoffman in *Midnight Cowboy*.

FILMOGRAPHY
Madigan's Millions 1966
The Tiger Makes Out 1967
The Graduate 1967
Midnight Cowboy 1969
John and Mary 1969
Little Big Man 1970
**Who is Harry Kellerman and Why Is
    He Saying Those Terrible Things
    About Me** 1971
Alfredo Alfredo 1972
Straw Dogs 1972
Papillon 1973
Lenny 1974
All the President's Men 1976
Marathon Man 1976
Straight Time 1978
Agatha 1979
Kramer vs Kramer 1979
Tootsie 1982

Shifting times never caught Hoffman unaware. He was excellent as Carl Bernstein, the reporter who helped break the Watergate story in the film version of the book *All the President's Men* (1976), and he was quick to sense the rise of a new non-macho male image, deftly playing a father who learns to nurture his son in *Kramer vs Kramer* (1979). The movie at last won Hoffman a much deserved Academy Award for Best Actor

Then came his sensitive subtle performance as a man pretending to be a woman in the extraordinarily popular *Tootsie* (1982), a tour de force. The movie never descended into a cheap drag show. Hoffman added to his stature as an actor with a masterful performance as Willie Loman on Broadway in *Death of a Salesman* in 1984.

Hoffman in *Tootsie* (1982) – one of his most brilliant performances.

HOLDEN, William 1918-1981

William Holden's clean-cut good looks were far from dazzling and his low-key restrained acting style wasn't charismatic so it was sometimes easy to overlook what a consummate film actor he was. Though there were times when the public took Holden for granted, a presence in an awful lot of famous movies, he was on the top-ten box-office list from 1954 to 1958 and was top draw in 1956. He was also rewarded for his steady stream of reliably good performances with an enormous income. By the end of his life, Holden, a resident of Geneva, Switzerland, was involved in multimillion dollar business enterprises and was co-owner of the vast Mount Kenya Safari Club. He was by then an ardent conservationist and environmentalist.

Born William Beedle, Jr in O'Fallon, Illinois, he was spotted by a movie talent scout while acting at Pasadena Junior College, and became a star in *Golden Boy* (1939). After that he was Mr Nice Guy in a whole series of films, though he did show an unsuspected flare for comedy in *Dear Ruth* (1947). Then came four important films that broke the mold. He was a psychotic killer in *The Dark Past* (1949), an almost creepy gigolo in the smashing *Sunset Boulevard* (1950) with Gloria Swanson, Judy Holliday's tutor in the funny *Born Yesterday* (1950) and the

Right: William Holden in *The Wild Bunch* (1969) – a controversial landmark western.

Left: Holden in *The Country Girl* (1954).

HOLLOWAY, Stanley 1890-1982

Stanley Holloway was a British music hall performer who also appeared on the legitimate stage. In 1921 he began playing comic roles in films.

Holloway was memorable as Mr Crummles in *Nicholas Nickleby* (1947) and in the brilliantly funny *The Lavender Hill Mob* (1951). He was magnificent as the gravedigger in *Hamlet* (1948). But he is most famous for his dynamic performance as Alfred Doolittle in both the stage and screen versions of the musical *My Fair Lady*. In 1962 Holloway did a television series *Our Man Higgins*.

FILMOGRAPHY
The Co-Optimists 1930
Squibs 1935
The Vicar of Bray 1936
Salute John Citizen 1942
Champagne Charlie 1944
This Happy Breed 1944
Brief Encounter 1945
Nicholas Nickleby 1947
Hamlet 1948
The Lavender Hill Mob 1951
The Titfield Thunderbolt 1952
The Beggar's Opera 1953
No Love for Johnnie 1961
My Fair Lady 1964
The Private Life of Sherlock Holmes 1970
Journey into Fear 1976

Below: Dorothy Lamour, Bing Crosby and Bob Hope in the 'Road' trio.

unheroic hero of *Stalag 17* (1953), which won him an Academy Award for Best Actor.

Holden was the drifter and Kim Novak the beauty queen in the very popular *Picnic* (1955), which allowed the actor a rare shot at being sexy. *The Bridge on the River Kwai* (1957) was an artistic triumph for Holden and his percentage of the take alone set him up with a tidy annual income for life. Further good movies followed.

His personal life had its share of problems. His marriage to actress Brenda Marshall ended in 1970, about the time their son Scott Holden began making movies. Holden's bouts with alcohol were well-known in Hollywood. But he was a man of integrity, as movies like *Network* (1976), *S.O.B.* (1981), and the *Earthling* (1981) show.

FILMOGRAPHY
Golden Boy 1939
I Wanted Wings 1941
Dear Ruth 1947
Rachel and the Stranger 1948
The Dark Past 1949
Sunset Boulevard 1950
Born Yesterday 1950
Stalag 17 1953
Executive Suite 1954
The Country Girl 1954
Love is a Many-Splendored Thing 1955
Picnic 1955
The Bridge on the River Kwai 1957
The Counterfeit Traitor 1962
The Wild Bunch 1969
The Towering Inferno 1974
Network 1976
Fedora 1978
S.O.B. 1981
The Earthling 1981

HOPE, Bob 1904-

Bob Hope gained his greatest fame as a radio comedian, and his first film was *The Big Broadcast of 1938* (1938) a variety-show film. Hope's wise-cracking humor, sharpened by years of vaudeville and Broadway shows, transferred well to the screen.

Hope's real film popularity came with the series of 'Road' pictures made with singer Bing Crosby and co-starring Dorothy Lamour. Though they pursued separate careers, the Crosby-Hope duo was one of the better screen comedy teams. Hope was always the same, brash yet cowardly, a smart aleck, manipulated by Crosby, and always losing Lamour to him. Until the mid-1950s Hope was among the top box-office draws.

Though one of the wealthiest men in show business, Hope has continued to work on stage, television and in the occasional film.

FILMOGRAPHY
The Big Broadcast of 1938 1938
Thanks for the Memory 1938
The Cat and the Canary 1939
Road to Singapore 1940
Ghost Breakers 1940
Road to Zanzibar 1941
Road to Morocco 1942
Road to Rio 1948
The Paleface 1948
Fancy Pants 1950
Road to Hong Kong 1962
Cancel My Reservation 1972
The Muppet Movie 1979

Carmen Miranda wants Horton to dance – *The Gang's All Here* (1943).

Edward Everett Horton was the master of the double take, a lanky comedian who twittered his nervous way through many an embarrassing situation. Always befuddled and confused, he added a bright spot to every movie he was in, a true professional for decades.

Horton was born in Brooklyn, New York, and made his theater debut in 1908 while a student at Columbia University. He moved from singing in the chorus on stage to playing leads and character parts in 150 films, beginning in the early 1920s. He is especially remembered as Fred Astaire's chum in 1930s musicals.

FILMOGRAPHY
Ruggles of Red Gap 1922
The Sap 1929
Holiday 1930
Trouble in Paradise 1932
Alice in Wonderland 1933
It's a Boy 1934
The Gay Divorcee 1935
Top Hat 1935
Lost Horizon 1937
Bluebeard's Eighth Wife 1938
Holiday 1938
Here Comes Mr Jordan 1941
Thank Your Lucky Stars 1943
Summer Storm 1944
Down to Earth 1947
Pocketful of Miracles 1961
Cold Turkey 1970

Leslie Howard as Ashley Wilkes with Vivian Leigh in *Gone With the Wind* (1939)

HOWARD, Leslie 1890-1943

Sensitive, intellectual, with a dreamy air, Leslie Howard was America's idea of the model Englishman. Actually Howard's parents were Hungarian immigrants (his real name was Leslie Stainer) and London was his birthplace almost by chance. Still, there is no arguing with Howard's deep attachment to Britain. He was to become a major force in the British film industry as a director and producer as well as an actor. He abandoned the comforts of Hollywood to live in London during World War II where he was actively engaged in the war effort.

Howard attended Dulwich College and took up acting only because he was shell shocked in World War I and acting was recommended to him as a form of therapy. Blonde, blue-eyed and utterly charming, he rapidly established himself as a leading man on both sides of the Atlantic. He became a major star when Warner Brothers cast

Howard with Norma Shearer as *Romeo and Juliet* (1936) – a triumph for both of them.

im in the film version of his hit play *Outward Bound* (1930), a fascinating drama about a shipload of passengers who slowly come to realize that they're dead.

Beginning with Norma Shearer in *A Free Soul* (1931), he appeared opposite many of Hollywood's most glamorous leading ladies, wooing them skillfully on-screen and off. Despite his delicate appearance, his look of being a poet in need of mothering, Leslie Howard's conquests were the talk of Hollywood, as was his business acumen. Actor David Niven once described him as being 'about as naive as General Motors.'

Howard generally considered Hollywood movies rather silly but he worked wonders with even the most cardboard characters. He shone in *Berkeley Square* (1933), a haunting story of a man sent back in time to the eighteenth century, *Of Human Bondage* (1934), co-starring Bette Davis, and *The Scarlet Pimpernel* (1935), a costume drama that rang gold at the box office and brought Howard a Picturegoer Gold Medal.

The chemistry was right opposite brassy Joan Blondell in *Stand-In* (1937), and his performance as Henry Higgins in *Pygmalion* (1938), which he co-directed, was brilliant. He played Ashley Wilkes in *Gone with the Wind* (1939), only under pressure, and he far preferred *Intermezzo* (1939), which he co-produced, co-starring with Ingrid Bergman. Leslie Howard went right on making fine films until 1943 when, while flying back to London from a secret mission to Lisbon, his plane was shot down by the Nazis.

FILMOGRAPHY

Outward Bound 1930
A Free Soul 1931
Five and Ten 1931
Devotion 1931
Service for Ladies 1932
Smilin' Through 1932
The Animal Kingdom 1932
Captured 1933
Berkeley Square 1933
Of Human Bondage 1934
British Agent 1934
The Scarlet Pimpernel 1935
The Petrified Forest 1936
Stand-In 1937
Pygmalion 1938
Gone with the Wind 1939
Intermezzo 1939
The 49th Parallel 1941
The First of the Few 1942

HOWARD, Trevor 1916-

Trevor Howard isn't one of the glamorous stars, the kind that hit the gossip columns or win all the awards. Yet he's a total perfectionist who is invariably good and at times flawless. His performance in *Brief Encounter* (1946), opposite Celia Johnson, places him in the first rank of movie actors.

Born in Cliftonville, England, Howard was educated at Clifton College and made his London stage debut in 1934 while studying at the Royal Academy of Dramatic Art. After he was invalided out of the Royal Artillery in 1943 he played Captain Plume in *The Recruiting Officer*. Next he starred in *A Soldier for Christmas*. Appearing in the cast was actress Helen Cherry, who became his wife.

Howard made his film debut in 1944 and quickly established a reputation as a polished actor of understated style who could be gentle or cynical, able to express anguish behind a bleak stare. Though Howard began his movie career playing romantic leads, he moved on to heroic roles and character parts, tackling all with equal skill.

I See a Dark Stranger (1946), was a tension-packed thriller. Howard was the other man in the sparkling romance *The Passionate Friends* (1948) and he helped make *The Third Man* (1949) a superb spy film.

Unlike many actors who commute regularly between theater and film, Trevor Howard devoted an increasing amount of his time and energy to movies from the late 1940s on. From

Trevor Howard, as Captain Bligh, faces Fletcher Christian (Marlon Brando) in *Mutiny on the Bounty* (1962).

Persistence was the key ingredient in the success of this big handsome leading man who began his career as a male sex object and matured into a solid competent actor. Born Roy Scherer in Winetka, Illinois, Hudson had no formal acting training when he began appearing in films but he learned on the job and by the mid-1950s was a top star.

He won an Oscar nomination for *Giant* (1956). In the 1960s he moved from adventure films and weepy soap opera-type movies to sophisticated comedies, often co-starring Doris Day. His death from AIDS focused public attention on the disease.

FILMOGRAPHY
Winchester 73 1950
Bend of the River 1952
Magnificent Obsession 1953
One Desire 1955
All that Heaven Allows 1955
Giant 1956
Written on the Wind 1956
Something of Value 1957
The Tarnished Angels 1957
Pillow Talk 1959
Lover Come Back 1961
Seconds 1966
Pretty Maids All in a Row 1971
Embryo 1976
The Mirror Crack'd 1980

Far left: Trevor Howard in *Von Ryan's Express* (1965).
Below: Rock Hudson.

the mid-1950s he was seen frequently in American as well as British films, developing into an actor of international stature.

The Key (1958) brought Howard a British Film Academy Award and *Sons and Lovers* (1960) an Academy Award nomination. As Captain Bligh he stole *Mutiny on the Bounty* (1962) away from Marlon Brandon. He was magnificent as a fiery British general in *The Charge of the Light Brigade* (1968), as a priest in *Ryan's Daughter* (1970), and as the man describing Glenda Jackson as the poet in *Stevie* (1977). He's also performed brilliantly on television, notably when reunited with Celia Johnson in *Staying On*, set in India.

FILMOGRAPHY
The Way Ahead 1944
Brief Encounter 1946
I See a Dark Stranger 1946
Green for Danger 1946
They Made Me a Fugitive 1947
The Passionate Friends 1948
The Third Man 1949
An Outcast of the Islands 1952
The Heart of the Matter 1953
The Key 1958
Roots of Heaven 1959
Sons and Lovers 1960
Mutiny on the Bounty 1962
The Charge of the Light Brigade 1968
Ryan's Daughter 1970
The Night Visitor 1971
11 Harrowhouse 1974
Stevie 1977
The Missionary 1982

John Hurt (*right*), with Richard Burton in the remake of *1984* (1984).

HUNT, Linda 1947-

Linda Hunt is tiny, only 4 feet 9 inches and weighs barely 80 pounds; her face is old beyond its years. But she created a sensation playing Billy Kwan, a Chinese Australian dwarf in *The Year of Living Dangerously* (1982) and took an Oscar for Best Supporting Actress for the part. Prior to *Year* she had only one bit part in a film and had appeared primarily in off Broadway productions.

FILMOGRAPHY
The Year of Living Dangerously 1982
The Bostonians 1984
Silverado 1985

HURT, John 1940-

This slightly-built, highly talented and versatile British actor received critical acclaim as the monstrously deformed but sympathetic character in *The Elephant Man* (1980). He received high marks again for his appearances in two remarkable television productions, *I, Claudius* (as Caligula) and *The Naked Civil Servant*.

FILMOGRAPHY
A Man for All Seasons 1966
10 Rillington Place 1971
Midnight Express 1978
Alien 1979
The Elephant Man 1980
Night Crossing 1981
Champion 1982
1984 1984

HUSTON, Walter 1884-1950

Walter Huston came to films when he was already in his mid-40s with a long career in vaudeville and serious drama behind him, and he quickly showed Hollywood that he could be just about the best film actor ever.

Born Walter Houghston in Toronto, Canada, he had originally studied engineering before he joined a road show. After the birth of his son (director-to-be John Huston) he went back to engineering, but he returned to the stage in a few years.

Even in small roles he could outshine the greatest stars. Huston was the best thing about *Rain* (1932), though the lead was the formidable Joan Crawford. He was more memorable than Bogart in *The Treasure of the Sierra Madre* (1948), a part which gained him a long overdue Oscar.

FILMOGRAPHY
Gentlemen of the Press 1929
The Virginian 1929
Abraham Lincoln 1930
The Criminal Code 1931
Law and Order 1932
Rain 1932
The Prizefighter and the Lady 1933
The Tunnel 1935
Dodsworth 1936
All That Money Can Buy 1941
The Shanghai Gesture 1942
The Outlaw 1943
And Then There Were None 1945
Duel in the Sun 1947
The Treasure of the Sierra Madre 1948
The Furies 1950

IRONS, Jeremy 1948-

Uncommonly handsome and a fine low-key actor, Jeremy Irons, born in Cowes on the Isle of Wight, has the potential to be a major star. He has appeared on stage, winning critical acclaim, and he made a splash in the television production, *Brideshead Revisited*, as Charles Ryder. Recent film appearances have added luster to his career.

FILMOGRAPHY
The French Lieutenant's Woman 1981
Moonlighting 1982
Betrayal 1983
Swann in Love 1984
The Mission 1986

Jeremy Irons in *Moonlighting* (1982).

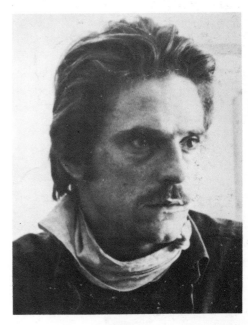

117

JACKSON, Glenda 1936-

Cool strength and keen intelligence are the hallmarks of Glenda Jackson's performances. The British actress spent years supporting herself in odd jobs and struggling to find acting roles. Her luck changed when she appeared in Peter Brook's 1964 stage production of 'Marat/Sade' turning in an unforgettable performance as Charlotte Corday.

She went on to films, winning Academy Awards for Best Actress for *Women in Love* (1969) and *A Touch of Class* (1972), and excelled in the BBC television series *Elizabeth I*. Despite exceptional talent, Jackson sometimes squanders her gifts in unworthy films. However she was in top form as the poet *Stevie* (1978).

FILMOGRAPHY
The Marat/Sade 1966
Negatives 1968
Women in Love 1969
Sunday, Bloody Sunday 1971
Mary Queen of Scots 1971
A Touch of Class 1972
The Maids 1973
The Romantic Englishwoman 1975
Hedda 1976
The Incredible Sarah 1976
Nasty Habits 1976
House Calls 1977
Stevie 1978
Health 1979
Hopscotch 1980
Turtle Diary 1986

Glenda Jackson in *Sunday Bloody Sunday* (1971).

JANNINGS, Emil 1886-1950

Before talkies Emil Jannings had a peerless international reputation. He was born Theodor Friedrich Emil Janenz in Switzerland to a German mother and an American father. Jannings was raised in Gorlitz, Germany, leaving home at 16 to become a sailor. It was the stage, not the sea, which would become his true love and he became an actor at 18.

In 1906 Jannings joined Max Reinhardt's famous theater, considered by many to be the finest in the world, and by the time he made his film debut in 1914 he was a widely admired actor. Though he would emerge as a major force in the brilliant experimental film industry of Germany in the 1920s, ultimately abandoning the stage altogether, Jannings's techniques remained theatrical rather than cinematic. Seen today, many of his highly praised performances seem overdone and overblown.

Jannings found the ideal director in Ernst Lubitsch, an old theater chum. They built their great film careers together when beginning in 1919, Jannings, a strong, heavy-set, powerful man, played a series of historical characters on screen, including Henry VIII and Peter the Great. These were remarkably well received, as was his *Othello* (1923) and his Mephisto in *Faust* (1926).

Jannings came to Hollywood in 1927 and in the first Academy Award ceremony ever he was voted Best Actor for performances in two films, *The Way of All Flesh* (1927) and *The Last Command* (1928). In America, Jannings generally played tragic characters, respectable citizens humiliated and destroyed by the cruelty of society and their own weaknesses. He had played such roles in Germany, too, with remarkable force and characterization and would do so again in the brilliant *The Blue Angel* (1930), which made a star of Marlene Dietrich. Unfortunately, despite his remarkable performance, the movie did not enhance Janning's career in America, and partly because of his thick German accent he never made a successful transition to talking pictures in Hollywood.

In 1933 Jannings, a strong supporter of the Nazis, began making anti-British propaganda films in Germany and in 1938 was appointed the head of Tobis, a large film company. In 1941 he was created an 'Artist of the State' but with the defeat of Hitler his career came to an end.

FILMOGRAPHY
The Brothers Karamazov 1918
Madame Dubarry 1919
Anne Boleyn 1920
Danton 1921
Othello 1923
Peter the Great 1924
Quo Vadis 1924
The Last Laugh 1924
Tartuffe 1925
Faust 1926
Variety 1926
The Way of All Flesh 1927
The Last Command 1928
The Patriot 1928
The Sins of the Fathers 1929
The Blue Angel 1930
The Old and the Young King 1935
Robert Koch 1939
Ohm Kruger 1940
Die Entlassing 1942

Above: Emil Jannings.
Below: Jannings in *Ohm Kruger* (1940).

FILMOGRAPHY
The Jazz Singer 1927
The Singing Fool 1928
Sonny Boy 1929
Say It with Songs 1929
Mammy 1930
Big Boy 1930
Halleluja I'm a Bum 1933
Wonder Bar 1934
Go into Your Dance 1935
The Singing Kid 1936
Rose of Washington Square 1939
Hollywood Cavalcade 1939
Swanee River 1939
Rhapsody in Blue 1945
The Jolson Story (voice only) 1946
Jolson Sings Again (voice only) 1949

Left: Al Jolson, *The Singing Fool* (1928).
Below: A publicity poster of Jolson.

JOLSON, Al 1886-1950

...nergy and dynamism made Al Jolson ...superstar in every branch of show ...usiness. America's first pop recording ...ar, he was a legend in vaudeville, on ...roadway, in films and in radio. ...nough occasionally down career-...ise, he was never out, rising to the top ...ain even in old age. He is considered ...y many to be the greatest and most ...opular entertainer in American ...istory.

Born Asa Yoelson in Russia, Jolson ...ame to America as a child. He began ...nging in a synagogue where his father ...as cantor but he ran away from home ...o join a circus. By 1906 he was singing ...blackface in a minstrel show and by ...909 was a major attraction at New ...ork's Winter Garden Theater, electri-...ing audiences with his mere ...resence.

In 1923 D W Griffith signed Jolson to ...ar in *Mammy's Boy* but the film was

Below: Jolson in *The Singing Fool* (1928), a ...ildly successful movie.

never completed and three years later he sang in an experimental short. Then came movie history. George Jessel had appeared in *The Jazz Singer* on Broadway, the story of a Jewish boy who didn't want to be a cantor and wound up a huge success in vaude-ville. Warner Brothers decided to make the film version of the play into the first real talkie. Jessel demanded too high a salary so Jolson got the role. The sound consisted mostly of background music but Jolson sang a song and spoke a few sentences, including the immortal words, 'You ain't heard nothin' yet.' Movies were never the same again.

Jolson appeared in more films, in-cluding *The Singing Fool* (1928), a part-talkie that grossed more money than any movie until *Gone With the Wind* (1939). Gradually his popularity declined as fashions changed but he recouped success singing for the troops in World War II. A romanticized version of his life, *The Jolson Story* (1946), starring Larry Parks, was an immense hit as was the sequel *Jolson Sings Again* (1949), in which Jolson appears briefly. In both movies the singing was dubbed by Jolson. The

films rejuvenated his radio and record career.

Married four times, Jolson's third wife was dance and film star Ruby Keeler. Jolson died of a heart attack shortly after entertaining US troops in Korea. A man who gave his all to his public he was a one-of-a-kind phenomenon.

JONES, Jennifer 1919-

Jennifer Jones (born Phyllis Isley), could be ethereal or sensual as the role required. Married first to actor Robert Walker, then to producer David Selz-nick who carefully guided her career, she won an Academy Award for Best Actress for *Song of Bernadette* (1943).

FILMOGRAPHY
Song of Bernadette 1943
Duel in the Sun 1946
Portrait of Jennie 1948
Beat the Devil 1954
Love Is a Many-Splendored Thing 1955
The Barretts of Wimpole Street 1957
The Towering Inferno 1974

KARLOFF, Boris 1887-1969

Boris Karloff (born William Henry Pratt) was the reigning king of horror during the 1930s, and for decades his face and voice were instantly recognizable as symbols of terror, though in his later years it was often mock terror. Boris Karloff was an actor of sensitivity and skill, yet because of his identification with the horror genre, he was rarely given a chance to play in other kinds of films.

Born in England, Karloff went to Canada, took up acting and landed a position with a touring stock company. Karloff was a quick study and would play as many as a hundred different roles in a year.

Like other touring actors, Karloff faced hard times because of competition from the growing film industry. In 1918 he went to Hollywood where for years he struggled, working his way up from extra to bit part and occasionally featured player. Because of his sinister appearance he usually got the part of a villain. His wonderfully well-developed voice was a great asset when sound came in.

He was picked by director James Whale for the part of the monster in *Frankenstein* (1931). Karloff, an average-sized man, was given a padded costume and big boots to make him look larger, and a sensational makeup job by Universal's makeup wizard Jack Pierce. Since he didn't wear a mask, one could always see his expression beneath the makeup.

Frankenstein was a sensation and made Karloff a star. He was always identified with the role of the monster, though he only played it three time He also created the character of th Mummy in *The Mummy* (1932). Karlo played Indians, Orientals, gangste and mad scientists – an impressiv number of mad scientists. Though th quality of the films in which he appea ed declined, Karloff always gave throughly professional performanc *Targets* (1968) was one of his last film and one of his best.

Karloff never abandoned the stag He was enormously successful a Captain Hook in *Peter Pan*, but his be role was in the stage version of *Arsen and Old Lace*, where he played madman who killed every time some one told him he looked like Karloff.

Opposite: Karloff as Frankenstein's monste *Below:* Karloff and Lugosi – *The Black Cat* (1934).

FILMOGRAPHY
His Majesty the American 1919
The Prisoner 1923
Frankenstein 1931
The Old Dark House 1932
The Mummy 1932
The Bride of Frankenstein 1935
Son of Frankenstein 1939
Tower of London 1939
The Body Snatcher 1945
The Secret Life of Walter Mitty 1947
The Raven 1963
Targets 1968

KAYE, Danny 1913-1987

A likable comedian whose trademark was the fast patter song, Kaye rocketed to fame in his first few films, but his career faltered and he became better known for his charity work.

Born Daniel Kaminsky in Brooklyn, New York, he started singing and dancing for audiences while still in school. It was his show-stopping patter song 'Tchaikovsky' in Broadway's *Lady in The Dark* that got him a movie contract. His first film, a lavish army comedy *Up in Arms* (1944), was an instant success. It was followed by several similar, and nearly as successful, films, but then there were contract disputes and a poor choice of scripts.

Hans Christian Andersen (1952) was a big hit, though critics thought it excessively sentimental and *White Christmas* (1954) opposite Bing Crosby was another box-office, though not critical, success. His television series ran for three seasons from 1963.

FILMOGRAPHY
Up in Arms 1944
The Kid from Brooklyn 1946
The Secret Life of Walter Mitty 1947
A Song is Born 1948
Hans Christian Andersen 1952
Knock on Wood 1953
White Christmas 1954
The Court Jester 1956
The Man from the Diner's Club 1963
The Madwoman of Chaillot 1969

KEATON, Buster 1895-1966

Buster Keaton was an accomplishe acrobat when little more than a baby, gentle genius, the most innovativ clown of the silent era. Though his is success story that turned to tragedy, had a happy ending after all.

He was born Joseph Francis Keato His parents performed in medicir shows, later moving up to vaudeville and in early childhood Keaton learne all there is to know about comedy fro pratfalls to timing. A vaudeville star c the verge of Broadway, he abandone the stage to make a series of com short films with Fatty Arbuckle. Keato then co-wrote, co-directed and starre in shorts on his own.

Keaton's screen persona was as dignified, handsome and infinitel resourceful young man whose dea pan 'stone face' showed emotion wit brilliant subtlety. His lithe acrobati body expressed whirlwind motion an activity with complete originality as h was caught in the clutch of machiner or dogged by confusion and misunde standings. Keaton was a bridegroor trying to put together a portable hom in *One Week* (1920). *The Playhous* (1922) is dreamy and surrealistic wit amazing photographic illusions. *Th Boat* (1922), which pulls down ever thing around it, has hints of blac fatalism behind the humor.

In 1923 Keaton began making fe ture-length comedies. *Sherlock Junic* (1924) about a movie projectionist los between reality and the dreams on th screen, *The General* (1927), a Civil Wa story, and *Our Hospitality* (1923) ar among his greatest long films. It wa after Keaton gave up his own studi that his troubles began. A trusting sou he was devoured by studio bosses, los control of his movies and was hit b sound. His marriage to Natalie Ta madge dissolved and he drank heavily

For years a neglected artist, Keato survived in films as an actor, assistar director and gag writer. Beginning wit a series of live appearances in Paris his reputation was fully restored Keaton won a special Academy Awar in 1959 and in 1965, shortly before h died of cancer, he received the greates ovation ever given at the Venice Film Festival.

Left: Kaye – *The Secret Life of Walter Mitty* (1947).
Above right: Buster Keaton, the great comic
Right: Keaton in *The General* (1927).

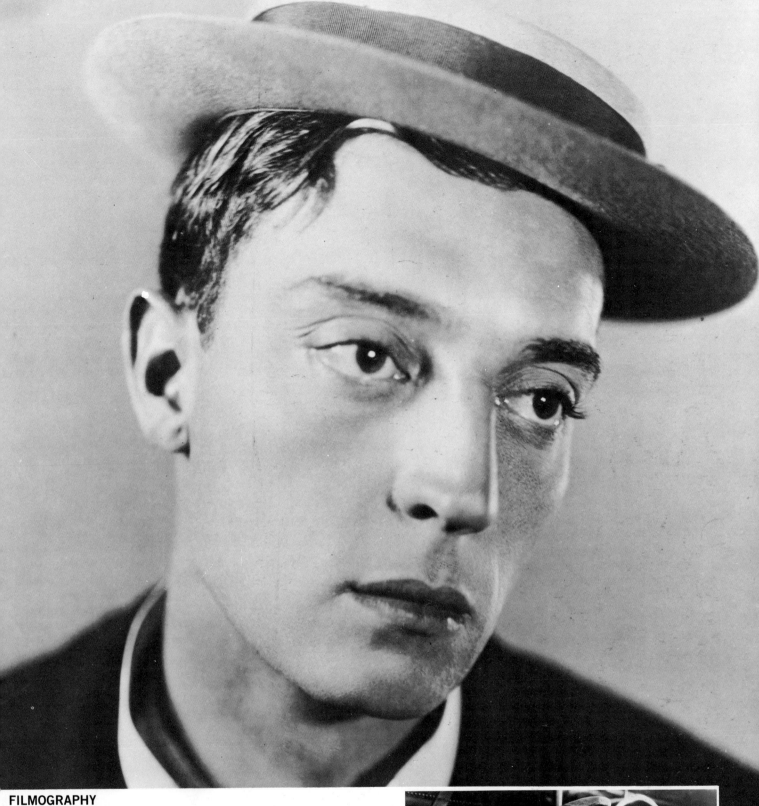

FILMOGRAPHY

The Butcher Boy 1917
Good Night Nurse 1918
The Hayseed 1919
The Saphead 1920
One Week 1920
The Playhouse 1922
The Boat 1922
The Paleface 1922
Cops 1922
Balloonatics 1922
Our Hospitality 1923
Sherlock Junior 1924
The Navigator 1924
The General 1927
The Cameraman 1928

Spite Marriage 1929
Doughboys 1930
The Jones Family in Hollywood 1939
Quick Millions 1939
San Diego I Love You 1944
You're My Everything 1949
The Loveable Cheat 1950
Sunset Boulevard 1950
Limelight 1952
Around the World in Eighty Days 1956
It's a Mad Mad Mad World 1963
Railrodder 1965
Film 1965
A Funny Thing Happened on the Way
    to the Forum 1966

KEATON, Diane 1949-

Diane Keaton was born Diane Hall in Los Angeles, but moved to New York to study acting, appearing in the musical *Hair*. She then worked with Woody Allen, becoming a film star under his direction. She won an Academy Award for Best Actress for *Annie Hall* (1977) and played Bryant in Warren Beatty's film *Reds* (1981).

FILMOGRAPHY
The Godfather 1972
Play it Again Sam 1972
Annie Hall 1977
Manhattan 1979
Reds 1981
Shoot the Moon 1982
Hannah and her Sisters 1986
Crimes of the Heart 1986

KEELER, Ruby 1909-

Ruby Keeler was the perfect ingenue in musicals, a pert little thing with big eyes and big tap shoes whose funny cracked voice and baby face endeared her to audiences. She was at her best opposite fellow innocent Dick Powell as guided by choreographer Busby Berkeley.

Born in Halifax, Nova Scotia, Canada, Keeler came to New York as a child. Though her family was poor she took dancing lessons and made it into chorus lines on Broadway at only 14. Nightclubs followed and soon she was a featured attraction in Broadway musicals where Flo Ziegfeld spotted her, offering her a solid role in *Whoopee* with Eddie Cantor.

Al Jolson swooped up Keeler when she went to the West Coast for a br stage engagement. She married Jols in 1928, left *Whoopee*, and though s got star billing in *Show Girl* on Broa way in 1929, went west with her hu band, quitting the show.

During the 1930s Ruby Keeler a peared in some of the best and mc popular musicals ever made in th great age of musicals. *42nd Stre* (1933), cast her as the kid pluck from the chorus to save the sho heading out to the footlights as a swe little nothing and coming back a star is one of the film classics of all tir and decades later was re-created as colorful musical spoof on Broadwa

More froth followed with Berkele wonderful geometrically patterned d

Below: Ruby Keeler in a number from *Go Into Your Dance* (1934).

FILMOGRAPHY
42nd Street 1933
Gold Diggers of 1933 1933
Footlight Parade 1933
Dames 1934
Flirtation Walk 1935
Go Into Your Dance 1935
Shipmates Forever 1935
Colleen 1936
Ready Willing and Able 1937
Sweetheart of the Campus 1941
The Phynx 1970

Above: Keeler and Jolson – *Go Into Your Dance*.

Top: Keeler and Dick Powell in *Flirtation Walk* (1935).

plays of girls forming a backdrop to the simple plots and tuneful songs of Keeler's films. She was good opposite James Cagney in *Footlight Parade* (1933), and the film grossed a fortune. She made one movie with Jolson, *Go Into Your Dance* (1935). In 1937 she left Warner Brothers reluctantly in Jolson's wake after he quarreled with the top brass.

Despite her popularity and four-figure salary Keeler was always modest about her talents. After her divorce from Jolson in 1940 she pursued her movie career half-heartedly for a while; she married a real estate broker and had four children. In 1970 Keeler appeared in a very successful revival of the 1925 musical *No No Nanette* on Broadway.

KELLERMAN, Sally 1941-

For years only small parts fell Sally Kellerman's way until she hit stardom as Major 'Hot Lips' Houlihan, an Army nurse, in *M*A*S*H* (1969), for which she received an Academy Award nomination. The tall blonde Kellerman can play either comic or dramatic roles deftly.

FILMOGRAPHY
M*A*S*H* 1969
Brewster McCloud 1970
Last of the Red Hot Lovers 1972
Slither 1973
Rafferty and the Gold Dust Twins 1975
Welcome to LA 1977
A Little Romance 1979

Gene Kelly's dance style is strong masculine, open, expansive and eve earthy. As a choreographer he revol tionized movie musicals during th 1940s and 1950s, creating dance s quences that told a story and tha formed an integral part of the whol film, a big change from the 1930s whe movie musicals featured mere son and dance men and lines of prett chorus girls in filmed revues.

Charming, a more than competer actor and a director besides, Kelly one of the main reasons MGM becam Hollywood's showplace for the makin of musicals. Born in Pittsburgh, Peni sylvania, Kelly started studying danc as a child. He was in the chorus c *Leave It to Me* on Broadway in 1938 Two years later he choreographed *Bill Rose's Diamond Horseshoe*, starred i *Pal Joey* in 1941 playing a no-good hee and choreographed another Broadwa Hit, *Best Foot Forward*.

Well-established as a major Broad way talent, his next step was Holl wood. Kelly made his debut on scree in *For Me and My Gal* (1942) with Jud Garland. Audiences soon fell in lov with the guy with the husky pleasar singing voice and though the popula Kelly never achieved Fred Astaire elegance, he was a master entertainer Verve and style marked his perform ance opposite Rita Hayworth in *Cove Girl* (1944), and he received an Osca nomination for *Anchors Aweig.* (1945), delighting fans by dancing wit a cartoon mouse. He and Vera-Elle made the screen sizzle dancin 'Slaughter on Tenth Avenue' in *Word and Music* (1948). It's still a classic, a is *An American in Paris* (1951), with it 20-minute ballet to Gershwin's music

On the Town (1949), shot on loca tion in New York, broke new groun and Kelly made the best movie musica ever when he did *Singin' in the Rai* (1952). His *Invitation to the Danc* (1956), a musical without dialogue won the Grand Prize at the West Berli Film Festival.

Kelly has also appeared in non musical films and on television. I 1951 he received a special Academ Award in honor of his versatility and hi 'brilliant achievements in the art c choreography on film.'

Top: Gene Kelly – *Singin' in the Rain* (1952
Left: Kelly (*right*) – *The Three Musketeers* (1948).

Above: Kelly in *Words and Music* (1948).
Right: With Caron – *An American in Paris* (1951).

FILMOGRAPHY

For Me and My Gal 1942
The Cross of Lorraine 1943
Cover Girl 1944
Christmas Holiday 1944
Anchors Aweigh 1945
Ziegfeld Follies 1946
The Pirate 1948
The Three Musketeers 1948
Words and Music 1948
Take Me Out to the Ball Game 1949
On the Town 1949
Summer Stock 1950
An American in Paris 1951
Singin' in the Rain 1952
Brigadoon 1954
Invitation to the Dance 1956
Les Girls 1957
Marjorie Morningstar 1958
Inherit the Wind 1960
What a Way to Go 1964
Forty Carats 1973
Xanadu 1980

KELLY, Grace 1928-1982

Cool, blonde and beautiful, Grace Kelly was fire under ice. Hitchcock used her to perfection in his thrillers and she showed a flare for serious acting which won her an Academy Award for Best Actress for *The Country Girl* (1954). Later, as Princess Grace of Monaco, she was a widely admired celebrity.

Born into a wealthy Philadelphia family Grace Kelly became a model and actress, appearing in a revival of Strindberg's *The Father* on Broadway. She began her movie career in the early 1950s, rapidly achieving stardom. In 1956 she married Prince Ranier of Monaco in a fairy-tale wedding and retired from the screen. The world was stunned when she died in a car crash.

FILMOGRAPHY
High Noon 1952
Mogambo 1953
Dial M for Murder 1954
Rear Window 1954
The Country Girl 1954
Green Fire 1954
The Bridges at Toko-Ri 1955
To Catch a Thief 1955
High Society 1956
The Swan 1956

Left: Grace Kelly in *High Society* (1956).

KERR, Deborah 1921-

[O]ne of America's favorite leading [la]dies, British actress Deborah Kerr [w]as popular for her cool beauty, well-[br]ed air of reserve and versatility. Born [in] Scotland, she began her career as a [ba]llet dancer, then switched to acting.

After a series of stage and film roles [in] Britain she went to Hollywood, play-[in]g in a variety of movies. Her leading [m]en were stars like Clark Gable, [Sp]encer Tracy and Cary Grant. She was [n]oted for her lady-like image until she [pl]ayed a sexy role in *From Here to [E]ternity* (1953).

FILMOGRAPHY
[H]atter's Castle 1941
[T]he Life and Death of Colonel Blimp 1943
[B]lack Narcissus 1947
[T]he Hucksters 1947
[E]dward, My Son 1949
[K]ing Solomon's Mines 1950
[Q]uo Vadis 1951
[D]ream Wife 1953
[F]rom Here to Eternity 1953
[T]he King and I 1956
[A]n Affair to Remember 1957
[S]eparate Tables 1958
[T]he Night of the Iguana 1964
[T]he Arrangement 1969
[T]he Assam Garden 1986

[K]err, Brynner – *The King and I* (1956).

Ben Kingsley in his memorable role as *Gandhi* (1981).

KINGSLEY, Ben 1943-

Ben Kingsley emerged from nowhere sweeping all before him in *Gandhi* (1981), taking an Academy Award for Best Actor as a prize for his stunning debut film performance. Born Krisha Bhanji in Yorkshire, England, Kingsley's father was an Indian doctor and his mother an English model. His love of Shakespeare led him to an acting career.

Kingsley was spotted by Richard Attenborough when he appeared on stage in *Nicholas Nickleby* and was invited to test for the lead in *Gandhi*. Kingsley had done classical and Shakespearian roles as well as television. Following his tour de force in the role of Gandhi he showed his versatility by appearing in *Betrayal* (1982), a Harold Pinter drama.

FILMOGRAPHY
Gandhi 1981
Betrayal 1982
Turtle Diary 1986

KRISTOFFERSON, Kris 1936-

Kris Kristofferson, the Texas-born Rhodes scholar, is a country and western singer and song writer whose low-key acting style is pleasant and warm. With his beard and rugged ap-pearance, he projects a sexuality that creates sparks when he appears oppo-site strong leading ladies, like Barbra Streisand and Jane Fonda.

FILMOGRAPHY
Cisco Pike 1972
Pat Garrett and Billy the Kid 1973
Alice Doesn't Live Here Anymore 1975
A Star is Born 1976
Semi-Tough 1977
Convoy 1978
Flashpoint 1984
Songwriter 1984
Trouble in Mind 1986

KRUGER, Hardy 1928-

Hardy Kruger was born Eberhard Kruger in Berlin. This blonde leading man is a popular star of German theater and films. He is often seen in international screen productions and directs television documentaries.

FILMOGRAPHY
Alibi 1955
The One That Got Away 1957
The Rest is Silence 1959
Sundays and Cybele 1962
The Flight of the Phoenix 1965
The Secret of Santa Vittoria 1969
Barry Lyndon 1975
A Bridge Too Far 1977
Wild Geese 1978
Blue Fin 1979

LADD, Alan 1913-1964

No one ever said that Alan Ladd could act. Indeed, total lack of expression was one of the hallmarks of an Alan Ladd performance. But he had icy good looks and a fine resonant voice which made him one of the top stars of the 1940s and early 1950s.

His star potential was recognized by Sue Carol, a former actress turned agent, who married him and devoted herself to his career. After a series of small parts, Ladd turned in a highly effective performance as the cold-eyed killer in *This Gun for Hire* (1942). His co-star was Veronica Lake and the two soon became a recognized team. Ladd's most successful performance both critically and at the box office was in *Shane* (1953), a western where he played an enigmatic gunman who helps a farmer's family.

Ladd was a sensitive and insecure man and by the 1960s his drinking had become a severe problem. He died in 1964 apparently because of a lethal combination of alcoholic drinks and sedatives.

FILMOGRAPHY
Once in a Lifetime 1932
Citizen Kane 1941
This Gun for Hire 1942
The Glass Key 1942
The Blue Dahlia 1946
Two Years Before the Mast 1946
The Great Gatsby 1949
Chicago Deadline 1949
Shane 1953
The McConnell Story 1955
Boy on a Dolphin 1957
The Proud Rebel 1958
The Carpetbaggers 1964

Alan Ladd as a paid gunman seeking revenge in *This Gun For Hire* (1942).

Stan Laurel and Oliver Hardy played toymakers in *Babes in Toyland* (1934).

LAUREL, Stan 1890-1965
HARDY, Oliver 1892-1957

Stan Laurel (the thin one) was born into a theatrical family in England. He joined Fred Karno's Company which also employed Charles Chaplin. Laurel toured America with Chaplin, sometimes understudied him, and later imitated him. He made his first film short in 1918, and made over 50 shorts, mostly for producer Hal Roach, before he teamed up with Hardy.

Oliver Hardy was born in Harlem, Georgia and was making films as early as 1913. Laurel was the more successful. He had his own series, whereas Hardy had only small and occasional roles. He too was working for Hal Roach. The pair actually appeared together in some 10 short films before Roach decided to team them up permanently in 1927.

Over the next three years they were turning out one short feature per month. Sound was introduced, but it caused hardly a ripple in their careers,

for their best gags didn't rely on dialogue. The archetypical Laurel and Hardy scene in one in which the pair engage in a orgy of mutual destruction with some representative of authority. Several of their films ended with massive pie-throwing sequences. The transition from shorts to full length features was also made smoothly.

While Laurel and Hardy worked for a number of different directors, it was always acknowledged that Laurel was the real creative force behind the films. Personally, Laurel and Hardy remained good friends, but Laurel had his disputes with Roach and the team broke up. They were together again in the 1940s, but were never given the necessary creative freedom, so the quality of their work suffered. Neither man became wealthy, indeed Laurel died in poverty, but he lived long enough to receive a special Oscar in 1960, and to see a revival of interest in Laurel and Hardy comedies.

FILMOGRAPHY
Putting Pants on Philip 1927
Battle of the Century 1927
Double Whoopie 1929
Bacon Grabbers 1929
The Hoosegow 1929
Hog Wild 1930
Laughing Gravy 1931
Helpmates 1931
Sons of the Desert 1933
Babes in Toyland 1934
Way Out West 1936
Blockheads 1938
Flying Duces 1939
The Bullfighters 1945
Robinson Crusoeland (Atoll K) 1952
The Golden Age of Comedy 1958
The Best of Laurel and Hardy 1974

LEE, Christopher 1922-

Gaunt and sinister looking, Christopher Lee made his mark in a series of remakes of classic horror films produced by Britain's Hammer Studios. He was particularly effective as Dracula, a part he played in several films. He has also played the Frankenstein monster, the Mummy, Dr Fu Manchu and Sherlock Holmes.

FILMOGRAPHY
The Curse of Frankenstein 1957
Horror of Dracula 1958
The Hound of the Baskervilles 1959
The Mummy 1959
The Hands of Orlac 1961
The Face of Fu Manchu 1965
Rasputin, The Mad Monk 1966
Dracula Has Risen From the Grave 1968
The Man with the Golden Gun 1974
Return to Witch Mountain 1978

Right: Christopher Lee as the infamous vampire in *Dracula Prince of Darkness* (1965).

Below: Laurel and Hardy with Edgar Kennedy as the bemused policeman.

LEIGH, Janet 1927-

Born Jeanette Morrison, Janet Leigh was a California college student with no previous experience when she signed her first movie contract. A fresh-faced beauty, Leigh was cast mainly as an ingénue but has learned her craft and has performed well in more demanding parts. She will always be remembered as the victim in the shower in Alfred Hitchcock's *Psycho* (1960).

FILMOGRAPHY
The Romance of Rosy Ridge 1947
Words and Music 1949
That Forsyte Woman 1949
Houdini 1953
The Black Shield of Falworth 1954
Touch of Evil 1958
Psycho 1960
Harper 1966
One is a Lonely Number 1972
The Fog 1979

LEIGH, Vivien 1913-1967

Delicate and graceful Vivien Leigh was a talented stage and screen actress, a complex and ambitious performer who won Hollywood's plum role, Scarlett O'Hara in *Gone With the Wind* (1939). Though she was British she played the part of a southern belle to perfection, a feat she achieved again at a later date and in a different role, as Blanche du Bois in *A Streetcar Named Desire* (1951). These two sterling performances alone would qualify her for film immortality.

Born Vivien Mary Hartley in Darjeeling, India, she was educated in convent schools in England and on the continent, making her film debut in 1934. A scant four months after her 1935 stage debut, Leigh appeared in the play *The Mask of Virtue*, and became an instant star. Good film offers followed.

Fire Over England (1936), a costume drama, co-starred Laurence Olivier. Their off-screen romance created a stir. Leigh had married a barrister at the beginning of her career and Olivier, too, was married. Not until 1940, when both divorces were sorted out, were Leigh and Olivier free to wed.

In 1938 Leigh flew to Hollywood to visit Olivier. *Gone With the Wind* had

Right: Vivien Leigh as Scarlett O'Hara, with Clark Gable – *Gone With the Wind* (1939).

gone into production without a Scarlett. Legend has it that Leigh was introduced on the set during the burning of Atlanta, and producer David O Selznick saw at once that he'd found his ideal Scarlett. The role won Leigh an Academy Award for Best Actress.

Her movie career should have gone smoothly from then on and *Lady Hamilton* (1941), with Olivier proved popular. Leigh was charming in *Caesar and Cleopatra* (1945). But there were complications. Always frail Leigh saved her limited stamina for her frequent stage appearances, including Shakespearian and classical roles opposite Olivier. Bouts of physical illness and mental breakdowns also slowed Leigh down and cast a tragic shadow over the brightness of her many achievements.

In 1949 Vivien Leigh played Blanche du Bois on stage in London. Her shimmering interpretation of the character in the film won her another Academy Award for Best Actress and the British Film Academy voted her Best British Actress. Though she died of tuberculosis in 1967 her exquisite film portraits remain.

FILMOGRAPHY
Things are Looking Up 1934
The Village Squire 1935
Gentleman's Agreement 1935
Look Up and Laugh 1935
Fire Over England 1936
Dark Journey 1937
Storm in a Teacup 1937
St Martin's Lane 1938
Twenty-One Days 1938
A Yank at Oxford 1938
Gone With the Wind 1939
Waterloo Bridge 1940
Lady Hamilton 1941
Caesar and Cleopatra 1945
Anna Karenina 1948
A Streetcar Named Desire 1951
The Deep Blue Sea 1955
The Roman Spring of Mrs Stone 1961
Ship of Fools 1965

LEMMON, Jack 1925-

Like good wine, Jack Lemmon just seems to get better and better though he has never really been bad. He's been lucky to appear in some of director Billy Wilder and playwright Neil Simon's best efforts and fortunate in his choice of co-stars from Walter Matthau to Marilyn Monroe. But mostly Lemmon's success has been due to his own talent and dedication to his craft.

He was born into a well-to-do Boston family and was educated at prep schools and Harvard University. After a stint in the Navy he worked as a piano player, radio actor and in off-Broadway productions. He got most of his steady work in television – over 400 shows in a five-year period. Lemmon's film debut was in *It Should Happen to You* (1954) opposite popular comedienne Judy Holliday. His portrayal of Ensign Pulver in the film version of *Mr Roberts* (1955) brought him star status and an Academy Award for Best Supporting Actor.

Lemmon's next big success was Wilder's *Some Like it Hot* (1959), now acknowledged to be one of Hollywood's finest comedies ever, but at the time the film was a risky career move for Lemmon since he had to play much of it in drag. *The Apartment* (1960), another downbeat Wilder comedy, was another triumph for Lemmon – who was being hailed as the best young comedian in Hollywood.

His talents weren't limited to comedy, as he proved spectacularly in *The Days of Wine and Roses* (1962), a grim and touching story of an alcoholic couple.

Teamed with Walter Matthau, he appeared in *The Fortune Cookie* (1966), an excellent Wilder-directed film that got poor notices. *The Odd Couple* (1968), adapted from the Neil Simon play, was a good film that got good notices and put Lemmon back amon the top-ten box-office draws.

Though comedy has always bee Lemmon's mainstay, he took a Academy Award for Best Actor for straight role in *Save the Tiger* (1973) He was impressive in a TV version *The Entertainer* (1976) – show theatrically in some countries. Thi was another risky move since th character had been created by Si Laurence Olivier and Lemmon's per formance invited comparisons, mostl favorable. There were no laughs i *Missing* (1982) either, just anothe superb Jack Lemmon performance.

FILMOGRAPHY
It Should Happen to You 1954
Mr Roberts 1955
Bell, Book and Candle 1958
Some Like it Hot 1959
The Apartment 1960
The Days of Wine and Roses 1962
Irma La Douce 1963
The Fortune Cookie 1966
The Odd Couple 1968
Save the Tiger 1973
The Prisoner of Second Avenue 1975
The Entertainer 1976
The China Syndrome 1979
Missing 1982
Mass Appeal 1984
That's Life 1986

Right: Lemmon – still a star after 30 years. *Below:* Lemmon with Tony Curtis in *Some Like It Hot* (1959).

LEWIS, Jerry 1926-

Jerry Lewis – you either love him or hate him. Many French critics revere his comedy, while most American critics think their French colleagues are crazy. Not that the content of Lewis' comedy is controversial – it's basic mugging and clowning – the disagreement is over quality.

Born Joseph Levich, the son of show people, he occasionally joined their act. By age 20 he was a seasoned if not successful performer. Success came when he teamed up with baritone Dean Martin, and they became the most popular comedy team on stage, TV and in clubs. Films soon followed and the pair made a series of box office winners during the 1950s. The pair split with well-publicized bitterness in 1956.

Since the breakup, Lewis has had a few successes, the biggest being *The Nutty Professor* (1963), but generally the films, many of which Lewis directed and produced himself, have been panned by critics and avoided by audiences, at least in America. His appearance as a TV talk-show host in Martin Scorsese's *King of Comedy* 1983 gained him the first good US notices he has had in years.

FILMOGRAPHY
My Friend Irma 1949
At War with the Army 1951
Jumping Jacks 1952
Artists and Models 1955
Hollywood or Bust 1956
The Delicate Delinquent 1957
The Geisha Boy 1958
The Nutty Professor 1963
The Disorderly Orderly 1964
Boeing-Boeing 1965
Hardly Working 1979
King of Comedy 1983

LISI, Virna 1937-

Virna Lisi, an exquisitely beautiful a voluptuous actress, was born Vir Pieralisi in Ancona, Italy. Lisi appear mainly in decorative roles in a lar number of Italian melodramas a quickie epics before becoming glamorous leading lady in inte national productions, particula romantic comedies.

FILMOGRAPHY
Lost Souls 1958
Duel of the Titans 1961
The Black Tulip 1963
How to Murder Your Wife 1965
Assault on a Queen 1966
Not With My Wife You Don't 1966
The Secret of Santa Vittoria 1969
Bluebeard 1972
Cocktails for Three 1978

Jerry Lewis with Dean Martin (*right*) in *At War with the Army* (1951). At left, Mike Kellin.

Lloyd in *Safety Last* (1923).

LLOYD, Harold 1893-1971

At one time the most popular of the great Hollywood trio of silent clowns, Chaplin, Keaton, and Lloyd, Harold Lloyd was a mixture of bold daredevil and ordinary American optimist. Lloyd was usually dressed blandly in everyday clothes and peered at the world through horn-rimmed spectacles. His great comic gift allowed him to express humor with his whole body, even his teeth.

There was nothing subtle about his gift for great stunts, however. His athletic prowess and feats of daring were amazing. Despite an accident in 1920 when a prop turned out to be a live bomb and exploded, severing his right thumb and forefinger and leaving his hand partially paralyzed, Lloyd bravely performed incredible stunts

and never used a double. In movies like *Safety Last* (1923), when he dangled atop a skyscraper hanging onto the hand of a clock, he had audiences screaming with laughter and terror.

The son of an unsuccessful photographer turned pool hall owner, Lloyd was born in Burchard, Nebraska, but grew up in San Diego, California. He broke into films as a bit player and extra in 1912. When fellow extra Hal Roach set up his own studio in 1912, Lloyd went to work for him, developing a character named Willie Work, but the one-reel comedy series went nowhere.

Roach reorganized under Pathé and, after a stint with Mack Sennett, Lloyd returned to Roach and created a new character, Lonesome Luke. Modeled on Chaplin, Lonesome Luke became popular but it was the wild chase scenes that made the series a success

and Lloyd was only too glad to dump Luke for a new original persona, the colorless average man who triumphs over life's obstacles with inventiveness, pluck and a positive spirit. Within a few years Lloyd was a huge star.

Lloyd was the idealistic but essentially conventional American in private life, too. In 1923 he married his leading lady, Mildred Davis. The marriage lasted until his death. He was active in charitable and service organizations.

Lloyd's career declined after the arrival of the talkies but by then he was a very rich man. In 1952 he received a special Academy Award for being a 'master comedian and good citizen.' He issued compilations of scenes from his works in 1962 and 1963. Lloyd died of cancer at the age of 77.

FILMOGRAPHY
Just Nuts 1915
Luke's Movie Muddle 1916
Over the Fence 1917
Bumping into Broadway 1919
Haunted Spooks 1920
A Sailor-Made Man 1921
Grandma's Boy 1922
Safety Last 1923
Girl Shy 1924
The Freshman 1925
For Heaven's Sake 1926
The Kid Brother 1927
Speedy 1928
Welcome Danger 1929
Feet First 1930
Movie Crazy 1932
The Cats Paw 1934
The Milky Way 1936
Professor Beware 1938
Mad Wednesday 1947

LOLLOBRIGIDA, Gina 1927-

Voluptuous and gorgeous Gina Lollobrigida emerged during the great post-World War II boom in Italian film making. A model and beauty contest winner who hoped originally to become a commercial artist, she made her screen debut in 1947 and by the early 1950s was a famous European star, called affectionately 'La Lollo.'

Trapeze (1956) established her as a Hollywood star and she became very popular with American audiences. Hollywood altered her image, coating her natural sexiness with a laquered glamor. In the 1970s Lollobrigida retired from films to become a professional photographer.

Above left: Gina Lollobrigida.
Below left: Carole Lombard, a fine actress who gained stardom in the 1930s.
Opposite: Harold Lloyd.

LOMBARD, Carole 1908-1942

Carole Lombard was special. She had all the beauty and glamor a star should have but she was also a brilliant comedienne and a fine actress. Witty, high-spirited, earthy and zany, she made friends wherever she went and was admired throughout Hollywood for her sense of humor and sense of style. She was a smart enough businesswoman to beat the Hollywood studio system, eventually freelancing her way into the big money.

Born Jane Peters in Fort Wayne, Indiana, she moved to California at the age of six and made her screen debut at 12 in *A Perfect Crime* (1921). She had a movie contract while still in her teens. A serious automobile accident cut short this budding career but Lombard had courage. After much physical pain she recovered and resumed acting, appearing in a series of Mack Sennett slapstick comedies. She made the transition to talkies beautifully, appearing with her husband-to-be, William Powell in *Man of the World* (1931). She appeared with Clark Gable, later her second husband, in *No Man of Her Own* (1932).

Lombard really emerged as a first-rank star in *Twentieth Century* (1934), where she revealed her highly original comic flair. Nobody would prove better at screwball comedy. Co-star John Barrymore described her as 'perhaps the greatest actress I have ever worked with.' *My Man Godfrey* (1936), *Nothing Sacred* (1937) and *To Be or Not to Be* (1942) attest to her ability.

Lombard's marriage to Clark Gable

145

in 1939 was big news in Hollywood. They looked like the perfect couple. In 1942 Lombard was killed in a plane crash returning from a war bond drive in the Midwest. Gable went into deep mourning. Perhaps the fan-magazine image of them as great lovers was true.

Carole Lombard was missed by fans and critics alike, not only because of her film appearances but because of her unique, generous, madcap personality.

FILMOGRAPHY
A Perfect Crime 1921
Hearts and Spurs 1925
Me Gangster 1928
High Voltage 1929
Fast and Loose 1930
It Pays to Advertise 1931
Man of the World 1931
Ladies' Man 1931
No Man of Her Own 1932
Bolero 1934
We're Not Dressing 1934
Twentieth Century 1934
Now and Forever 1934
Rhumba 1935
Hands Across the Table 1935
Love Before Breakfast 1936
My Man Godfrey 1936
The Princess Comes Across 1936
True Confession 1937
Nothing Sacred 1937
Made for Each Other 1938
They Knew What They Wanted 1940
Mr and Mrs Smith 1941
To Be or Not To Be 1942

LOREN, Sophia 1934-

Sensual beauty got Sophia Loren (born Sophia Scicoloni in Rome) a boost in the world but talent, intelligence and good sense have kept her a superstar. An illegitimate child, she grew up in poverty in a Naples slum. At 14 she won a beauty contest and went to Rome where she met producer Carlo Ponti. He aided her career and eventually married her.

Loren went to Hollywood in 1958 but was often miscast in American pictures. She returned to Italy to appear in *Two Women* (1961), winning an Academy Award for Best Actress. She turned in several other fine performances in later Italian films.

FILMOGRAPHY
The Gold of Naples 1954
Woman of the River 1955
Boy on a Dolphin 1957
The Key 1958
Houseboat 1958
The Black Orchid 1959
Two Women 1961
Yesterday, Today and Tomorrow 1963
Marriage Italian Style 1964
Sunflower 1970
A Special Day 1977
Revenge 1979
Oopsie Poopsie 1981

Left: Loren in a TV film, *Sophia Loren — Her Own Story* (1980).

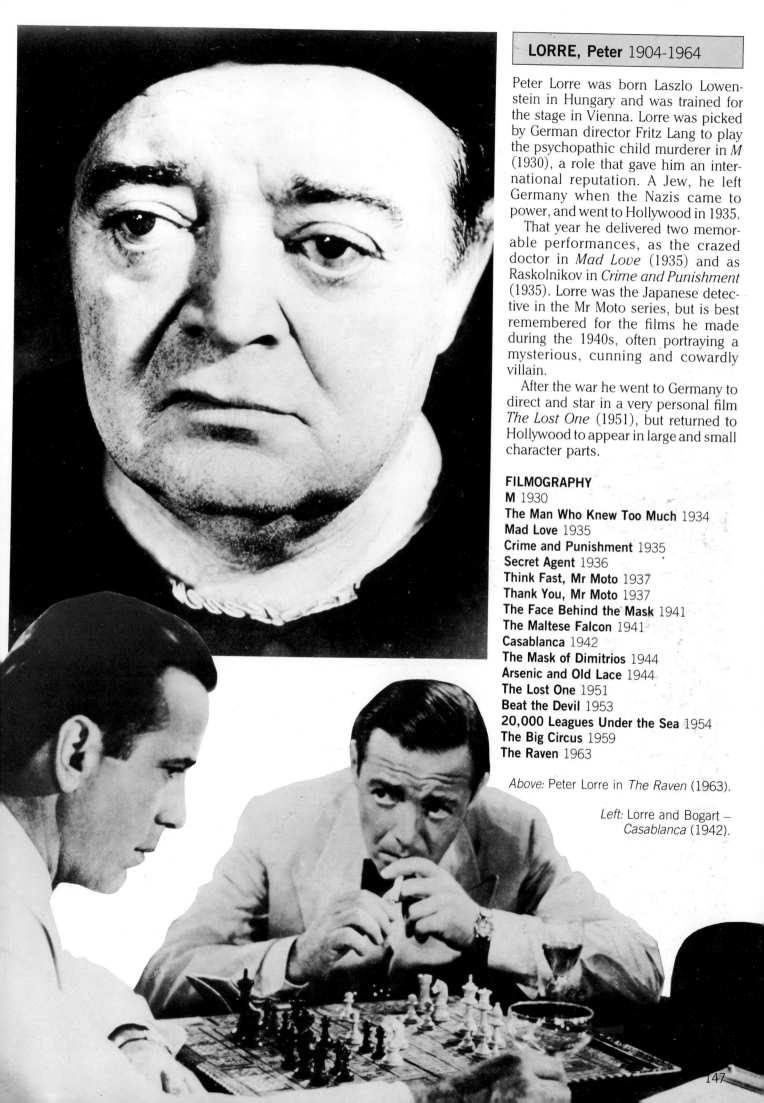

LORRE, Peter 1904-1964

Peter Lorre was born Laszlo Lowenstein in Hungary and was trained for the stage in Vienna. Lorre was picked by German director Fritz Lang to play the psychopathic child murderer in *M* (1930), a role that gave him an international reputation. A Jew, he left Germany when the Nazis came to power, and went to Hollywood in 1935.

That year he delivered two memorable performances, as the crazed doctor in *Mad Love* (1935) and as Raskolnikov in *Crime and Punishment* (1935). Lorre was the Japanese detective in the Mr Moto series, but is best remembered for the films he made during the 1940s, often portraying a mysterious, cunning and cowardly villain.

After the war he went to Germany to direct and star in a very personal film *The Lost One* (1951), but returned to Hollywood to appear in large and small character parts.

FILMOGRAPHY

M 1930
The Man Who Knew Too Much 1934
Mad Love 1935
Crime and Punishment 1935
Secret Agent 1936
Think Fast, Mr Moto 1937
Thank You, Mr Moto 1937
The Face Behind the Mask 1941
The Maltese Falcon 1941
Casablanca 1942
The Mask of Dimitrios 1944
Arsenic and Old Lace 1944
The Lost One 1951
Beat the Devil 1953
20,000 Leagues Under the Sea 1954
The Big Circus 1959
The Raven 1963

Above: Peter Lorre in *The Raven* (1963).

Left: Lorre and Bogart – *Casablanca* (1942).

147

LOVE, Bessie 1898-1986

Bessie Love, born Juanita Horton in Midland, Texas, began making films while she was still in high school. Petite, spirited and extremely versatile in everything from serious drama to musical comedy, she never quite attained the stardom for which she once seemed destined. Love lived and worked in England from the mid-1930s.

FILMOGRAPHY
Intolerance 1915
The Aryan 1916
The Purple Dawn 1920
Dynamite Smith 1924
The Lost World 1925
The Broadway Melody 1928
Chasing Rainbows 1930
Conspiracy 1932
The Barefoot Contessa 1954

The Roman Spring of Mrs Stone 1961
The Loves of Isadora 1969
On Her Majesty's Secret Service 1969
Sunday, Bloody Sunday 1971
The Ritz 1976
Reds 1982

LOY, Myrna 1905-

For years Myrna Loy was Hollywood's perfect wife – witty, charming and altogether likeable. But Loy, born Myrna Williams in Raidersburg, Montana, spent almost her entire first decade in films typecast as a vamp.

Playing the bubbling yet sophisticated Norah Charles in *The Thin Man* (1934) opposite William Powell changed her image and within two years she was Hollywood's top box-office female star. Fans voted her 'Queen of the Movies' to Clark Gable's 'King.' Loy switched from leads to character roles in the mid-1950s.

FILMOGRAPHY
Don Juan 1926
The Desert Song 1929
Arrowsmith 1931
The Mask of Fu Manchu 1932
When Ladies Meet 1933
The Thin Man 1934
Wife vs Secretary 1936
Double Wedding 1937
Too Hot to Handle 1938
The Best Years of Our Lives 1946
Mr Blandings Builds His Dream House 1948
Cheaper by the Dozen 1950
From the Terrace 1960
Airport 1975 1975
Just Tell Me What You Want 1979

Below: Loy and William Powell – *The Great Ziegfeld* (1936).

LUGOSI, Bela 1882-1956

Born Bela Balasko, this Hungarian-born actor is known mainly for one part – Dracula – a role he created on stage and in the classic 1930 film. Lugosi appeared in other superior horror films such as *The Black Cat* (1934), *Son of Frankenstein* (1940) and *The Body Snatcher* (1945), often playing opposite Boris Karloff. He also occasionally appeared in non-horror films, notably *Ninotchka* (1939), with Greta Garbo.

His highly stylized acting and heavily accented English limited his opportunities, and after rocketing to fame in *Dracula* (1930) his career ran steadily downhill until he wound up working in films with names like *Zombies on Broadway* (1946) and *Mother Riley Meets the Vampire* (1952). When he died he was buried in his Dracula cloak.

Right: Ida Lupino in *In Our Time* (1944).
Below: Bela Lugosi *was* Count Dracula.

FILMOGRAPHY
Dracula 1930
Murders in the Rue Morgue 1932
White Zombie 1932
The Black Cat 1934
Mark of the Vampire 1935
Ninotchka 1939
The Body Snatcher 1945
Abbott and Costello Meet Frankenstein 1948

LUPINO, Ida 1914-

Tough and talented Ida Lupino achieved what few women have yet to achieve in films: a career which combines acting, screen writing, directing and producing. Daughter of British comedian Stanley Lupino, she was born in London and began her film career in Britain.

After going to Hollywood, she appeared in minor films until a strong performance in *The Light That Failed* (1940) brought her recognition. She frequently played strong ambitious women before turning to directing in the 1950s. It was in the 1950s, too, that she appeared with her husband actor Howard Duff in a television series, *Mr Adams and Eve.*

FILMOGRAPHY
Her First Affaire 1933
Artists and Models 1937
The Light that Failed 1940
They Drive by Night 1940
High Sierra 1941
Ladies in Retirement 1941
The Hard Way 1942
Devotion 1946
Roadhouse 1948
On Dangerous Ground 1951
The Bigamist 1953
The Big Knife 1955
Junior Bonner 1972
The Food of the Gods 1976

149

MACDONALD, Jeanette 1903-1965
and
EDDY, Nelson 1901-1967

Jeanette MacDonald and Nelson Eddy were the most popular singing duo in the history of films. In the 1930s audiences flocked to see them in screen versions of operettas. They were dubbed 'America's Sweethearts.'

Though pure gold at the box office for MGM, modern critics find the team's movies dated, naive and even silly. But films like *Naughty Marietta* (1935), *Rose Marie* (1936) and *Maytime* (1937) evoke a more romantic era when the public's taste ran to pretty costumes, fluid melodies and happy endings. The era may not have faded entirely because revivals of the films have done quite well, though granted they have a certain cult following. Despite the on-screen tenderness, MacDonald and Eddy were rumored to be enemies, each bent on outshining the other. If so, as far as posterity is concerned MacDonald won the war.

Jeanette MacDonald, born in Philadelphia, Pennsylvania, was a chorus girl who longed to sing grand opera. She became a stage star of musicals and operettas instead. Then director Ernst Lubitsch cast her opposite Maurice Chevalier on screen. Mac-Donald was a gifted comedienne, charming and attractive, a star before she appeared with Nelson Eddy and capable of shining without him, as in *San Francisco* (1936), with Clark Gable. Studio quarrels and changing fashions ended her film stardom but she continued on stage and even opera.

Nelson Eddy, born in Providence, Rhode Island, was a newspaper reporter before joining the Philadelphia Civic Opera. Concerts and radio appearances brought him a movie contract. Eddy was stiff in films and detractors nicknamed him 'the singing capon.' Except for his phenomenal success with Jeanette MacDonald, Eddy's screen career lacks luster. Still, he was notable on his own in *The Phantom of the Opera* (1943) and after his movie career was over he was a popular concert performer.

Right: MacDonald and Eddy in *Bitter Sweet* (1940).

Below: I Married an Angel (1942).

FILMOGRAPHY
(Jeanette MacDonald alone)
The Love Parade 1929
The Vagabond King 1930
Annabelle's Affairs 1931
One Hour With You 1932
Love Me Tonight 1932
The Merry Widow 1934
San Francisco 1936
The Firefly 1937
Smilin' Through 1941
Cairo 1942
Three Darling Daughters 1948
The Sun Comes Up 1949
(Nelson Eddy alone)
Student Tour 1934
Rosalie 1937
Let Freedom Ring 1939
Balalaika 1939
The Chocolate Soldier 1941
The Phantom of the Opera 1943
Knickerbocker Holiday 1944
Northwest Outpost 1947
(Jeanette MacDonald and Nelson Eddy together)
Naughty Marietta 1935
Rose Marie 1936
Maytime 1937
The Girl of the Golden West 1938
Sweethearts 1939
New Moon 1940
Bitter Sweet 1940
I Married an Angel 1942

Above: MacDonald and
Eddy in *Maytime* (1937).
*Right: The Girl of the
Golden West* (1938).

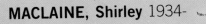

MACLAINE, Shirley 1934-

When Shirley Maclaine was young she was a gamine with a flair for comedy. Over the years she matured as an actress, recouping her film career several times when it headed towards the doldrums, and emerging in the public eye as a celebrity active in left-wing political causes. Like her brother Warren Beatty, she's got a keen head for business, frequently making a lucrative deal for herself when she appears in a film. Secure in her Academy Award for Best Actress for *Terms of Endearment* (1983), Maclaine is right where she belongs again, on top of the heap.

Born Shirley MacLean Beatty in Richmond, Virginia, she began dancing as a child, then took off for New York after graduating from high school. She danced in Broadway chorus lines until she was plucked from the crowd to take an injured Carol Haney's place in *The Pajama Game*. Movie producer Hal Wallis saw the show and signed Maclaine to a contract. She made her debut in the delightful Alfred Hitchcock film, *The Trouble with Harry* (1955). *Some Came Running* (1958), with Frank Sinatra, brought her an Oscar nomination and good reviews. *Ask Any Girl* (1959) and *The Apartment* (1959) won her British Film Academy Awards. Teamed with Jack Lemmon, she played a hooker in *Irma La Douce* (1963), a smash hit.

Though Maclaine fought for and eventually won stronger and more complex roles such as in *The Turning Point* (1977) and *Being There* (1979), she was frequently cast as a soft-headed, soft-hearted female, vaguely bohemian in lifestyle but distinctly unpretentious. While waiting to break out of the mold, Maclaine starred in a television series, *Shirley's World* in 1971, and turned her attention to writing. A successful author, she also wrote, produced and co-directed a documentary, *The Other Half of the Sky: A China Memoir* (1975).

Maclaine, with her background in musicals, has appeared in cabaret and performed in one-woman shows on Broadway and at London's Palladium. When she's not working she travels.

Above left: Maclaine with Kelly – *What a Way to Go* (1964).
Opposite: Shirley Maclaine.
Inset: Maclaine in one of the frenzied moments in *Sweet Charity* (1968).

FILMOGRAPHY

The Trouble with Harry 1955
Around the World in 80 Days 1956
Hot Spell 1957
The Matchmaker 1958
Some Came Running 1958
Ask Any Girl 1959
Can-Can 1959
The Apartment 1959
The Children's Hour 1962
Two for the Seesaw 1962

Irma La Douce 1963
What a Way to Go 1964
Gambit 1966
Sweet Charity 1968
The Bliss of Mrs Blossom 1968
Desperate Characters 1971
The Turning Point 1977
Being There 1979
Loving Couples 1980
Terms of Endearment 1983

MACMURRAY, Fred 1908-

Born in Kankakee, Illinois, Fred MacMurray began as a singer and saxophonist in various bands but he was a lead in Hollywood from the day he signed a contract. He proved a durable performer.

Most of the time MacMurray played decent, likeable leads in comedies. Every once in a while he played a loser and liar as in *Double Indemnity* (1944), one of his best dramatic roles. By the end of MacMurray's career, a television series, *My Three Sons*, and wholesome Walt Disney movies kept him on top. In 1954 he married actress June Haver.

FILMOGRAPHY
The Gilded Lily 1935
Alice Adams 1935
The Trail of the Lonesome Pine 1936
True Confession 1937
Sing You Sinners 1938
Double Indemnity 1944
The Egg and I 1947
Family Honeymoon 1948
The Caine Mutiny 1954
Pushover 1954
The Shaggy Dog 1959
The Apartment 1960
The Absent Minded Professor 1961
The Swarm 1978

Below: MacMurray and Stanwyck – *Double Indemnity* (1944).

MAGNANI, Anna 1907-1973

Anna Magnani was a fiery force, a international star whose unkempt appearance defied convention. Magnani was born in Alexandria, Egypt, an raised in poverty in Rome. She began her career as a nightclub singer, the appeared on stage.

Hers was a minor film career until the 1940s when she appeared in Roberto Rossellini's *Open City* (1945). She was romantically involved with Rossellini until Ingrid Bergman entered his life. Her Hollywood debut came in *The Rose Tattoo* (1955), which won her an Academy Award for Best Actress. Magnani later returned to Italy where she was considered a national treasure.

FILMOGRAPHY
The Blind Woman of Sorrento 1934
Tempo Massimo 1936
Open City 1945
Angelina 1945
The Miracle 1950
Volcano 1953
The Golden Coach 1954
Bellissima 1954
The Rose Tattoo 1955
Wild is the Wind 1957
The Fugitive Kind 1959
Mamma Roma 1962
The Secret of Santa Vittoria 1969

Below right: Anna Magnani in *The Rose Tattoo* (1955).

MALDEN, Karl 1913-

Karl Malden, born Mladen Sekulovich in Gary, Indiana, is a fine actor who made his mark in theater as early as the 1930s. His congenial homely face and husky build made him a natural for working-class character roles in films rather than romantic leads.

Malden can project great innocence and moral strength, infusing his characterizations with complexity. He is consistently good on screen even when the material is unworthy of his talents. He won an Academy Award for Best Supporting Actor for *A Streetcar Named Desire* (1952), re-creating Mitch, the character he played in the Broadway production.

FILMOGRAPHY
Winged Victory 1944
Boomerang 1947
The Gunfighter 1950
A Streetcar Named Desire 1952
Ruby Gentry 1952
On the Waterfront 1954
Baby Doll 1956
The Hanging Tree 1959
One-Eyed Jacks 1961
Gypsy 1962
The Cincinnati Kid 1965
Hotel 1967
Patton 1969
Summertime Killer 1973
Beyond the Poseidon
   Adventure 1979
Billy Galvin 1987

Karl Malden as General Omar Bradley in *Patton* (1969).

MANSFIELD, Jayne 1933-1967

The most flamboyant of the Marilyn Monroe imitators, Jayne Mansfield was always good copy for the gossip columns. She had been a beauty queen and pin-up model before appearing on stage and in films. Her flair for light comedy was rarely shown to good effect; she played in a series of generally dismal films. She was killed in an automobile accident.

FILMOGRAPHY
The Girl Can't Help It 1956
Will Success Spoil Rock Hunter? 1957
The Sheriff of Fractured Jaw 1959
Too Hot to Handle 1960
A Guide for the Married Man 1967

Below: Jayne Mansfield starred with Tom Ewell in *The Girl Can't Help It* (1956).

MARCH, Fredric 1897-1975

Fredric March, born Ernest Frederick McIntyre Bickel in Racine, Wisconsin, started out as a banker. Under the name Fredric March he abandoned himself to his true love, acting, and became a marvelous stage actor and a great screen actor who understood subtlety, nuance and characterization. In 1926 he married Florence Eldridge and they became an important theatrical team.

March could play heroes and romantic leading men. He excelled at light comedy or tragic roles. He won Academy Awards for Best Actor for *Dr Jekyll and Mr Hyde* (1932) and *The Best Years of Our Lives* (1946).

FILMOGRAPHY
Dr Jekyll and Mr Hyde 1932
Death Takes a Holiday 1934
Les Miserables 1935
A Star is Born 1937
I Married a Witch 1942
The Best Years of Our Lives 1946
Death of a Salesman 1952
Inherit the Wind 1960
Seven Days in May 1964

Right: March in *Dr Jekyll and Mr Hyde* (1932).
Below: Martin, Judy Holliday – *Bells Are Ringing* (1960).

FILMOGRAPHY
My Friend Irma 1949
Scared Stiff 1953
Living it Up 1954
Artists and Models 1955
Ten Thousand Bedrooms 1957
The Young Lions 1958
Rio Bravo 1959
Ocean's Eleven 1960
Kiss Me Stupid 1964
The Sons of Katie Elder 1965
Bandolero 1968
Something Big 1971
The Cannonball Run 1982

MARSHALL, Herbert 1890-1966

Herbert Marshall's career spanned four decades. British-born, he was a success on stage and screen, reaching his peak as an urbane romantic lead in Hollywood movies. He made a smooth transition to character roles as he grew older.

FILMOGRAPHY
Blonde Venus 1932
Trouble in Paradise 1932
The Good Fairy 1935
The Dark Angel 1935
Angel 1937
The Little Foxes 1941
The Moon and Sixpence 1942
The Enchanted Cottage 1944
The Razor's Edge 1946
The Third Day 1965

MARTIN, Dean 1917-

Dean Martin, born Dino Crocetti, began as a singer and, teamed with comic Jerry Lewis, made a series of extremely popular comedies in the 1950s. After the pair had a highly publicized break-up in 1956, Martin continued to make films, usually comedies or action films, and was very successful.

MARVIN, Lee 1924-

Lee Marvin has often been compared to Humphrey Bogart and though there is little chance that he will ever achieve Bogey's legendary status (Marvin has never had his *Maltese Falcon*) the comparison is not unjustified. While not conventionally good looking, he projects an aggressive masculinity which can be riveting, and he has many fans.

Marvin started playing mainly heavies – he was as vicious as they come in *The Big Heat* (1953), he challenged Marlon Brando as a rival motorcycle gang leader in *The Wild One* (1954) and he was so mean in *Bad Day at Black Rock* (1955) that when he gets his head bashed in you feel like cheering. Later he played heroes, though often violent ones. Marvin also has a fine comic sense which he displayed to great advantage in a dual role in the Western spoof *Cat Ballou* (1965), which won him an Oscar for Best Actor and the BFA Award. He even did a musical, *Paint Your Wagon* (1969) where he tried – unsuccessfully – to sing with co-star Clint Eastwood. Though he has turned in some excellent performances he has not had a major film success since the early 1970s.

Above: Marvin in *The Big Red One* (1979).
Top: Marvin in *Paint Your Wagon* (1969).

FILMOGRAPHY
You're in the Navy Now 1951
Eight Iron Men 1952
The Big Heat 1953
The Wild One 1954
The Caine Mutiny 1954
Bad Day at Black Rock 1955
Pete Kelly's Blues 1955
Attack 1956
Raintree County 1957
The Man Who Shot Liberty Valance 1962
The Killers 1964
Cat Ballou 1965
Ship of Fools 1965
The Dirty Dozen 1967
Point Blank 1967
Hell in the Pacific 1968
Paint Your Wagon 1969
Emperor of the North Pole 1973
The Big Red One 1979
Death Hunt 1981

Chico (*right*) and Harpo Marx with Louis Calhern in *Duck Soup* (1933).

MARX BROTHERS, The

The Marx Brothers are probably the funniest team that has ever appeared on screen. Their films are as fresh and hilarious today as they were half a century ago. Their props, Groucho's moustache and cigar, Harpo's curly wig and Chico's pseudo-Italian accent are still immediately identifiable.

The brothers were born in New York City and thrown into vaudeville at an early age by their tough, ambitious mother Minna, who appeared on stage with them. Starting primarily as musicians and singers (they were called 'The Six Musical Mascots' and Minna was one of the Mascots) they gradually introduced humor into their act. 'We played in towns I would refuse to be buried in today,' Groucho later

quipped. Their brand of inspired lunacy caught on; they became Broadway successes and then went to Hollywood.

At first there were five Marx Brothers; Gummo (born Milton, 1893-1977), left the act early. Zeppo (born Herbert 1901-1979), who often played straight man or romantic relief, appeared in early films but was unmemorable.

It was Chico (born Leonard 1886-1961), Harpo (born Adolph but called Arthur, 1888-1964) and Groucho (born Julius, 1890-1977), who everyone remembers as *The* Marx Brothers.

They began making films for Paramount in 1929 and their first few films, which grew out of their stage act, were solid but not overwhelming successes. By 1933 their film career was in trouble. Ironically, *Duck Soup*, released that year, is today considered one of their

very best films. The Marxes' contrac was picked up by Irving Thalberg c MGM. Thalberg allowed the Marxes t take key sequences from upcomin, movies on a road tour to test th audience reaction. Thalberg also in sisted the films have a plot with a lov interest and some boring musical pro duction numbers in which the Marxe were barely involved. The result wa: almost like two films inexpertly stitch ed together but the core remained th humor, and films like *A Night at the Opera* (1935) were enormously popular.

After Thalberg's death the quality o the Marx Brothers films declined, and by 1950 they had stopped making film: together, though they occasionally appeared as individuals in other films and Groucho went on to a very suc cessful television career. He won a special Oscar before he died.

Above: The Marx Brothers – *Animal Crackers* (1930) with Margaret Dumont at right. *Right: Go West* (1940).

FILMOGRAPHY

The Coconuts 1929	Duck Soup 1933	Go West 1940
Animal Crackers 1930	A Night at the Opera 1935	The Big Store 1941
Monkey Business 1931	A Day at the Races 1937	A Night in Casablanca 1946
Horse Feathers 1932	Room Service 1938	Love Happy 1950
	At the Circus 1939	

MASON, James 1909-1984

polished performer who added luster every film he was in, the suave and handsome James Mason played villains and gentlemen with equal ease. Though he never won an Academy Award, the highly acclaimed character actor received Britain's highest film honor, the Golden Seal, in 1977. His contribution to movies spanned nearly five decades.

Mason's father was a wool merchant in the Yorkshire town of Huddersfield. Planning on a career in architecture, Mason attended Marlborough College and Cambridge University but during the Depression of the 1930s came to the unusual conclusion that he could better earn a living on stage than by designing buildings. He played in repertory in the provinces, appeared with the Old Vic and with the Gate Company in Dublin, simultaneously beginning a film career as the leading man in a series of 'B' pictures.

Both stage and film roles improved until he hit it big in *The Man in Grey* (1943), a Regency melodrama. For a while he made a successful career out of playing nasty, evil men who browbeat sensitive heroines. From 1944 to 1947 he was the top box-office draw in Britain.

Mason moved to Hollywood in 1946 with his wife of many years, Pamela. The couple had two children. They were divorced shortly afterwards. There was a lot of publicity which irked Mason, who was a very private person, and Hollywood responded by considering him eccentric. He later moved to Switzerland to escape life in a fishbowl, and in 1970 married Clarissa Kay, an Australian actress.

Mason broke away from playing villains and cads but though he hoped to become an internationally recognized leading man it never happened. His range was simply too great and he was, despite his distinctive voice, always more actor than personality. He left his mark on so many important films, including *The Seventh Veil* (1945) and *A Star is Born* (1954), that he achieved the kind of stardom most character actors can only dream of.

Opposite: James Mason as Brutus.
Below: Mason and Judy Garland in *A Star Is Born* (1954).

FILMOGRAPHY
I Met a Murderer 1939
Hatter's Castle 1942
The Night Has Eyes 1942
The Man in Grey 1943
The Seventh Veil 1945
Odd Man Out 1946
The Reckless Moment 1949
Pandora and the Flying Dutchman 1951
The Desert Fox 1951
Five Fingers 1952
The Desert Rats 1953
Julius Caesar 1953
Charade 1953
20,000 Leagues Under the Sea 1954
A Star is Born 1954
North by Northwest 1959
Journey to the Center of the Earth
Lolita 1962
The Pumpkin Eater 1964
The Blue Max 1966
Georgy Girl 1966
The Deadly Affair 1967
Child's Play 1972
The Last of Sheila 1973
The Mackintosh Man 1973
Harrowhouse 1974
Heaven Can Wait 1978
Murder by Decree 1979
The Verdict 1982
The Shooting Party 1985

MASSEY, Raymond 1896-1983

This Canadian-born actor was most identified with the role of Abraham Lincoln on stage and screen and the kindly Dr Gillespie in the long running 'Dr Kildare' TV series. Massey also effectively played a host of other often sinister characters in his long career.

FILMOGRAPHY

The Speckled Band 1931
The Old Dark House 1932
The Scarlet Pimpernel 1934
Things to Come 1936
The Prisoner of Zenda 1937
Abe Lincoln in Illinois 1940
Arsenic and Old Lace 1944
East of Eden 1955
Mackenna's Gold 1968

MASTROIANNI, Marcello 1923-

Marcello Mastroianni – darkly handsome, often cynical, world-weary and jaded on screen, but retaining an air of dignity whatever befalls him, this Italian actor has been an international star since the late 1950s. Mastroianni has appeared opposite some of the most beautiful actresses in Europe, including Sophia Loren, who has co-starred with him in several of his most popular films. He could have become a Hollywood star any time he wished over the past 20 years, a fate he has steadily resisted, and his career hasn't suffered.

Born into a peasant family in Fontana Liri, Italy, he was employed as a draftsman during World War II until the Germans sent him to a labor camp. When the war ended Mastroianni went to Rome, working as a clerk and acting at night. He joined Luchino Visconti's acting company, appearing on stage in plays like *A Streetcar Named Desire* and *Death of a Salesman*. He made his debut in films in an Italian version of *Les Miserables* in 1947. After that he rose steadily both on stage and in pictures until he had a reputation within Italy as a talented, popular leading man.

International success came with *La Dolce Vita* (1959), directed by Federico Fellini. Mastroianni was broodingly brilliant as a man trapped by luxury and decadence. Antonioni's *La Notte* (1961), Germi's clever *Divorce Italian Style* (1962), which won Mastroianni a British Film Academy Award, and Fellini's *8½* (1963), solidified the actor's fame. He won another British Film Academy Award for *Yesterday, Today and Tomorrow* (1963). In the years that followed Mastroianni was such a staple ingredient of films by great directors that at times he seemed to personify the modern European male. There have been few actors before him who have so dominated movies. Off screen Mastroianni's romance with the beautiful actress Catherine Deneuve made gossip columnists happy in the 1970s.

FILMOGRAPHY

I Miserabili 1947
Sunday in August 1949
The Bigamist 1955
White Nights 1957
La Dolce Vita 1959
La Notte 1961
Divorce Italian Style 1962
8½ 1963
Yesterday, Today and Tomorrow 1963
The Organizer 1963
Marriage Italian Style 1964
Casanova 70 1965
The Tenth Victim 1965
Diamonds for Breakfast 1968
Blowout 1973
The Priest's Wife 1974
A Special Day 1977
Traffic Jam 1978
Ginger and Fred 1986

Below: Marcello Mastroianni.

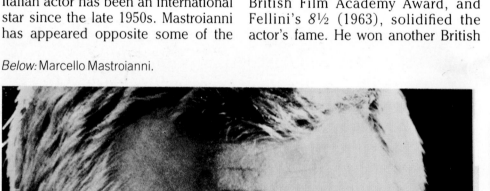

MATTHAU, Walter 1920-

Walter Matthau fills the screen with his expansive talent. An ordinary looking guy with an elastically expressive face and distinctive voice, Matthau, born Walter Matuschanskayasky in New York, was a poor kid who grew up working at menial jobs until returning from service in World War II.

He built a steady career on stage, in movies and on television until hitting stardom with the Broadway hit, *The Odd Couple*. Matthau won an Academy Award for Best Supporting Actor for *The Fortune Cookie* (1966) and became Hollywood's leading comic grouch with the heart of gold.

FILMOGRAPHY
A Face in the Crowd 1957
Charade 1963
Mirage 1965
The Fortune Cookie 1966
A Guide for the Married Man 1967
The Odd Couple 1968
Hello Dolly 1969
Cactus Flower 1969
A New Leaf 1971
Plaza Suite 1971
Pete 'n Tillie 1972
The Front Page 1975
The Sunshine Boys 1975
The Bad News Bears 1976
Casey's Shadow 1977
House Calls 1978
First Monday in October 1981
I Ought to Be in Pictures 1982

Matthau and Jack Lemmon in *Buddy, Buddy* (1981).

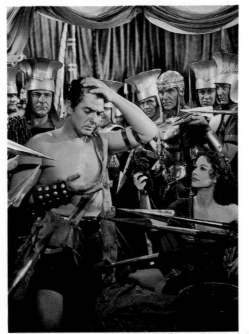

Mature in *Samson and Delilah* (1949).

Left: Matthau and Lemmon in *The Fortune Cookie* (1966).

MATTHEWS, Jessie 1907-

Billed as 'The Dancing Divinity' Jessie Matthews made her first stage appearance at the age of 10, and during her teens was in the chorus line of London musicals. She was a star of musical reviews by the late 1920s and carried her enormous popularity into a string of light screen musicals of the 1930s.

FILMOGRAPHY
The Beloved Vagabond 1923
Straws in the Wind 1924
The Man from Toronto 1932
The Good Companions 1932
Friday the Thirteenth 1933
Evergreen 1934
First a Girl 1935
Climbing High 1939
Candles at Nine 1943
The Hound of the Baskervilles 1977

MATURE, Victor 1915-

Victor Mature was christened 'The Hunk' long before that term became popular. Critics ridiculed his wooden acting, and Mature never took his career very seriously. Yet he was a symbol of male sex-appeal and a major box-office draw during the 1940s and early 1950s. He retired in 1972, though he has made a couple of brief screen appearances since.

FILMOGRAPHY
The Housekeeper's Daughter 1939
One Million BC 1940
I Wake Up Screaming 1941
Fury at Furnace Creek 1948
Samson and Delilah 1949
The Robe 1953
Demetrius and the Gladiators 1954
The Egyptian 1954
After the Fox 1966
Firepower 1979

MCCOY, Tim 1891-1978

Tim McCoy, a former Lieutenant Colonel in the US Army and authority on Indian dialects and customs, first served as a technical advisor for *The Covered Wagon* (1923). He went on to appear in a huge number of Westerns, and during the early 1930s was one of the most popular western stars.

FILMOGRAPHY
The Thundering Herd 1925
War Paint 1926
Beyond the Sierras 1928
The Fighting Fool 1932
Man of Action 1933
The Westerner 1935
Texas Marshal 1941
Around the World in 80 Days 1956
Requiem for a Gunfighter 1965

MCDOWALL, Roddy 1928-

Born in London, Roddy McDowall was a child actor when he came to Hollywood during the London Blitz in 1940. He rose to rapid success in movies like *How Green Was My Valley* (1941), and *Lassie Come Home* (1943). In the 1950s he turned to Broadway and television.

McDowall returned to movies as a polished, engaging supporting actor whose presence in almost any film makes a difference. Besides being a busy professional actor, he's a fine photographer and owns a superb collection of old movies.

FILMOGRAPHY
Murder in the Family 1936
This England 1940
How Green Was My Valley 1941
My Friend Flicka 1943
Lassie Come Home 1943
The White Cliffs of Dover 1944
Macbeth 1950
Cleopatra 1963
The Loved One 1965
The Planet of the Apes 1967
Escape from the Planet of the Apes 1971
The Poseidon Adventure 1972
Evil Under the Sun 1982
Class of 1984 1983
Fright Night 1985
Dead of Winter 1987

Right: McLaglen in *The Informer* (1935).
Below: Roddy McDowall (*left*) with Walter Pidgeon in *How Green Was My Valley* (1941).

MCLAGLEN, Victor 1883-1959

Victor McLaglen had been a miner and a boxer and looked it. The British born McLaglen was one of six brothers, all in films. He usually played a happy-go-lucky tough guy but his finest performance was as the tortured central character in *The Informer* (1935), for which he won an Academy Award for Best Actor.

FILMOGRAPHY
The Call of the Road 1920
Beau Geste 1926
What Price Glory 1926
The Lost Patrol 1934
The Informer 1935
Under Two Flags 1936
She Wore A Yellow Ribbon 1949
Rio Grande 1951
The Quiet Man 1952
Sea Fury 1958

MCQUEEN, Steve 1930-1980

Steve McQueen was one of the hotte stars of the 1960s and 1970s, hitting th box-office top ten year after year. He to Bogart, Cagney and Edward Robinson, he had a cool self-awar ness, ice-blue eyes and a strong sens of independence. McQueen was a anti-hero with heroic traits.

Born Terence McQueen in Slate Missouri, his childhood was anythin but pampered. A messed-up kid abar doned by his father, he wound up i reform school, then became a sailo lumberjack, beachcomber, carniva barker and at last a Marine. The servic didn't cure him. He spent time in th brig for going AWOL and became drifter after he was discharged.

McQueen drifted into acting, study ing at New York's Neighborhoo Theater and with Uta Hagen an Herbert Berghof, debuting in a Yiddis theater in the city's Lower East Side The Actors' Studio followed and th well-schooled McQueen got his firs break when he replaced Ben Gazzar in *Hatful of Rain* on Broadway in 195! Moving to Hollywood McQueen migh have been stuck in bits and in scienc fiction films like *The Blob* (1958) fo ever had he not landed the starring rol in a television series, 'Wanted: Dead o Alive.' This role led to replacin Sammy Davis, Jr in Frank Sinatra' *Never So Few* (1959).

McQueen began an ascent in films In private life a macho type who love car and motorcycle racing, he pe formed his own stunts in *The Grea Escape* (1963) with its spectacula motorcycle-chase scene, and becam a star. He was good in *The Cincinna Kid* (1965), but Edward G Robinso was lots better and not until *Bulli* (1968), with its pace-setting ca chases, did McQueen really carry a filn completely on his own. After that h was a superstar.

McQueen's first wife was actres Neile Adams, his second, movie sta Ali McGraw. They later divorced. I Hollywood McQueen had the reputa tion of being moody, temperamenta and hard to get along with. He wa especially hard on directors. At the ag of 50 McQueen died of cancer. Hi death robbed the world of one of th major rebel heroes of modern movies

Opposite: Steve McQueen in *The Great Escape* (1963).
Inset: McQueen as *Tom Horn* (1980).

FILMOGRAPHY

FILMOGRAPHY
Rashomon 1950
Seven Samurai 1954
The Lower Depths 1957
Throne of Blood 1957
The Hidden Fortress 1958
Yojimbo 1961
Red Beard 1964
Grand Prix 1966
Rebellion 1966
Red Sun 1971
Paper Tiger 1975
Midway 1976
Winter Kills 1979
1941 1979

MIFUNE, Toshiro 1920-

oshiro Mifune, the internationally
spected Japanese actor, first came to
tention in the West with *Rashomon*
950), a movie about the different
erceptions of truth. Set, as so many
panese movies are, in the feudal era,
tells from different points of view the
le of the rape of a nobleman's wife.
ashomon won the Venice Grand Prix
nd the Academy Award for best
reign language film. The movie's
irector, Akira Kurosawa, was recog-
ized as a great artist.

Mifune was Kurosawa's favorite
ading man and their partnership is
gendary. But Mifune, ferocious,
cowling, poignantly sensitive,
ynamic and versatile, was never
erely an interpreter for a director. By
e early 1960s he was the most famous
apanese star since Sessue Hayakawa.

Born in 1920 in Tsingtao, China, into
Japanese family with a long medical
adition, he was in the Japanese Army
uring World War II, then broke into
lms by winning a studio talent con-
est. An actor who has appeared in
novies with meaning and depth, the
Vest knows Mifune chiefly in three
ypes of role. He plays simple ordinary
en, modern executives and officers,
nd samurai. His samurai incarnation
 the most popular. As a medieval
arrior – bold, heroic, but often dis-
usted with cruelty and injustice –
lifune's samurai is more a cross be-
veen Douglas Fairbanks, Gary Cooper
nd Marlon Brando than John Wayne.
lifune brings sanity, sexiness and a
vorld-weary air to historical adventure
novies like *Seven Samurai* (1954),
vhich was the one of the first of its kind
o catch on in the West. *The Lower
Depths* (1957), a Japanese adaptation
f Gorki, and *Throne of Blood* (1957), a
apanese reworking of Macbeth, were
lso well received.

In 1963 Mifune formed his own pro-
luction company, directing *The
Legacy of the Five Hundred Thousand*
1963). *Grand Prix* (1966) was his first
Hollywood film and by 1975 Mifune
rad turned his talents to television,
playing a samurai. More than any other
single actor, Toshiro Mifune has
created an appreciation in the West for
apanese films. He also appeared in
he popular TV mini series *Shogun*.

eft: Toshiro Mifune, the great Japanese
ctor who also appeared in English-
speaking films.

MILES, Sarah 1941-

Sarah Miles, the vivacious and intri-
guing British actress, made her screen
debut in *Term of Trial* (1962) with
Laurence Olivier. In 1967 she married
playwright, screenwriter and director
Robert Bolt. They were divorced in
1976. She is the sister of director
Christopher Miles.

FILMOGRAPHY
Term of Trial 1962
The Servant 1963
Blow Up 1966
Ryan's Daughter 1970
Lady Caroline Lamb 1972
**The Sailor Who Fell from Grace with
  the Sea** 1976
The Big Sleep 1978
Steaming 1985

MILLAND, Ray 1905-1986

Ray Milland made his debut in British
films in 1929 under the name of Spike
Milland. He appeared in literally
hundreds of films and also appeared
on television. Born Reginald Truscott-
Jones in Neath, Wales, he was a Royal
Guardsman in London before becoming an actor.

Charming, attractive and suave, he
was a romantic leading man until *The
Lost Weekend* (1945) earned him an
Academy Award for Best Actor in a
serious film. After that Milland played a
wide range of roles, including villains
and leads in horror films. A real pro, he
also directed.

FILMOGRAPHY
Payment Deferred 1932
The Jungle Princess 1936
Beau Geste 1939
The Doctor Takes a Wife 1940
Skylark 1941
The Uninvited 1944
The Lost Weekend 1945
Kitty 1945
The Big Clock 1948
Alias Nick Beal 1949
Night into Morning 1951
Dial M for Murder 1954
The Man with X-Ray Eyes 1963
Love Story 1970
Oliver's Story 1978

Below: Ray Milland – *The Lost Weekend*
(1945).

MILLER, Ann 1919-

Long legs and plenty of spunk characterize Ann Miller, the great tap dancer who added bright moments even to inferior movies and who was one of the best reasons for going to see some of MGM's banner musicals. Born Lucy Collier in Chireno, Texas, she was a professional dancer from childhood who broke into movies at 17.

Though her acting and her dancing brought her attention early on, it wasn't until the late 1940s that her gifts were fully recognized. After her movie career ended she continued performing in nightclubs and on television. Still stunning and a skillful dancer, she wowed Broadway audiences when she appeared in *Sugar Babies* a few years ago.

FILMOGRAPHY
New Faces of 1937 1937
You Can't Take it With You 1938
The Kissing Bandit 1948
Easter Parade 1948
On the Town 1949
Two Tickets to Broadway 1951
Kiss Me Kate 1953
Deep in My Heart 1954
Hit the Deck 1955

MILLS, Hayley 1946-

Hayley Mills, the talented daughter of actor John Mills and younger sister of actress Juliet Mills, was a child star who received a special Academy Award for *Pollyanna* (1960). Later Mills made the transition to adult roles dramatically via a movie nude scene in the 1960s and a high publicized affair with producer-director Roy Boulting.

FILMOGRAPHY
Tiger Bay 1959
Pollyanna 1960
Whistle Down the Wind 1961
The Chalk Garden 1964
The Family Way 1966
The Kingfisher Caper 1975

Top: Ann Miller in *Small Town Girl* (1953).
Below: Hayley Mills in Walt Disney's *Summer Magic* (1963).

MILLS, Sir John 1908-

nighted in 1976 in honor of his illus-ious acting career, Sir John Mills has resented movie goers with a fine port-olio of screen portraits. Born in North lmham, England, Mills began as a horus boy, then appeared in dramas, ebuting in films in 1932. During World Var II he gained popularity playing toic heroes.

Mills won an Academy Award for est Supporting Actor for *Ryan's* *Daughter* (1971). He is the father of ctresses Hayley Mills and Juliet Mills. Vhether as a lead or character actor, e always excels and though his style s low key, he is extremely versatile.

FILMOGRAPHY
Those Were the Days 1934
Goodbye, Mr Chips 1939
The Young Mr Pitt 1942
In Which We Serve 1942
The Way to the Stars 1945
Great Expectations 1946
Scott of the Antarctic 1948
The History of Mr Polly 1949
Hobson's Choice 1954
Tiger Bay 1959
Tunes of Glory 1960
The Family Way 1966
Ryan's Daughter 1971
The Human Factor 1976
Gandhi 1982

John Mills (*right*) and Trevor Howard in *Ryan's Daughter* (1971).

MINNELLI, Liza 1946-

Singer and actress Liza Minnelli is the daughter of the legendary Judy Garland and director Vincente Minnelli. A vibrant talent, she won a Academy Award for Best Actress for her portrayal of Sally Bowles in *Cabaret* (1972). Her dynamic style has made her a smash success in live productions.

FILMOGRAPHY
Charlie Bubbles 1967
The Sterile Cuckoo 1969
Cabaret 1972
Lucky Lady 1976
New York, New York 1976
Arthur 1981

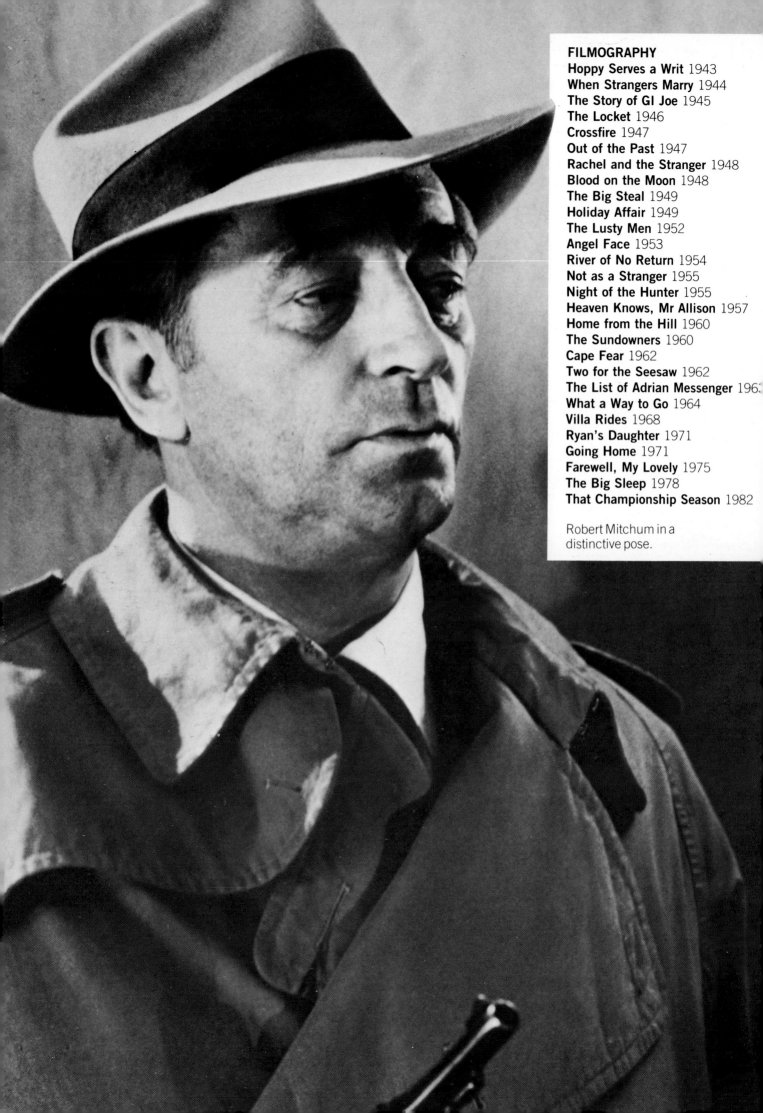

FILMOGRAPHY
Hoppy Serves a Writ 1943
When Strangers Marry 1944
The Story of GI Joe 1945
The Locket 1946
Crossfire 1947
Out of the Past 1947
Rachel and the Stranger 1948
Blood on the Moon 1948
The Big Steal 1949
Holiday Affair 1949
The Lusty Men 1952
Angel Face 1953
River of No Return 1954
Not as a Stranger 1955
Night of the Hunter 1955
Heaven Knows, Mr Allison 1957
Home from the Hill 1960
The Sundowners 1960
Cape Fear 1962
Two for the Seesaw 1962
The List of Adrian Messenger 196:
What a Way to Go 1964
Villa Rides 1968
Ryan's Daughter 1971
Going Home 1971
Farewell, My Lovely 1975
The Big Sleep 1978
That Championship Season 1982

Robert Mitchum in a
distinctive pose.

MITCHUM, Robert 1917-

Sleepy eyes and a lethargic manner are Robert Mitchum's distinctive features. A strong, durable actor he was always a forceful on-screen personality, even though in the beginning critics carped that he was no actor at all. Because he was husky and sexy they tended to dismiss him as pure beefcake. Yet he was good even in bad films and he played brutal villains better than practically anyone else.

Born in Bridgeport, Connecticut, he had a knock-about childhood and a footloose youth, working as a nightclub bouncer, a promoter for an astrologer and an engine wiper on a freighter. He tried boxing, then married his childhood sweetheart and went to work for Lockheed Aircraft. In 1942 he joined the Long Beach Theater Guild in California and then broke into films as a bit player in a series of Hopalong Cassidy westerns. After that he played supporting roles in comedies, westerns and war films.

It was *The Story of GI Joe* (1945) which made him a star and won him an Oscar nomination. Then it was off to the army; when he returned he was appealingly rugged and casual in lead roles. In 1948 Mitchum was convicted for smoking marijuana. In those days it was the stuff of scandal and Mitchum assumed his career was ruined but audiences did not desert him. Though it would be a while before he made movies equal to *Crossfire* (1947) and *Out of the Past* (1947), *River of No Return* (1954) with Marilyn Monroe made big money and *Not as a Stranger* (1955) was a smash hit.

Mitchum was superb as a psychotic killer in *Night of the Hunter* (1955) and as the vicious relentless pursuer in *Cape Fear* (1962). He was also well cast as a detective in Raymond Chandler remakes in the 1970s. Katharine Hepburn once told Mitchum, 'You know you can't act.' Over the years he's proven that he most assuredly can.

Below: Mitchum in *The Enemy Below* (1957).

171

Tom Mix and his horse, Tony.

MIX, Tom 1880-1940

Though he was born in the eastern state of Pennsylvania, Tom Mix's early career made him a natural for westerns. He had been a Texas Ranger and a US Marshal; he fought in the Spanish-American war and the Mexican Revolution and when he ran out of wars he toured with the circus as a trick rider.

Mix turned to films in 1910, appearing in one- and two-reel silents which he often wrote and directed. His real co-star in most of the films was his horse Tony. The films were straight-forward conflicts of good – Tom Mix – against evil, with good inevitably winning. Just to keep the moviegoer from getting confused, the good guys wore white hats while the bad guys wore black ones. Film historians have complained that the pictures were based on such a simple formula that it was difficult to tell one from the other, yet for years Tom Mix was extremely popular, second only to William S Hart as the world's favorite western hero. His career waned after the coming of sound and at the time of his death in an automobile accident his large fortune had been dissipated.

FILMOGRAPHY
The Escape of Jim Dolan 1913
The Way of the Redman 1914
Western Blood 1918
North of Hudson Bay 1923
The Trouble Shooter 1924
Riders of the Purple Sage 1925
Dick Turpin 1925
The Last Trail 1927
Painted Post 1928
The Drifter 1929
Destry Rides Again 1932
The Rustlers' Roundup 1933

MONROE, Marilyn 1926-1962

Marilyn Monroe was the 1950s favorite blonde, cuddly and vulnerable. But the vulnerability was real and her Cinderella story ended at midnight with the coach vanished and the glass slipper shattered. Born Norma Jean Baker in Los Angeles she was an illegitimate child who was abused and neglected in a series of foster homes. A teenage marriage ended in failure but she had the beauty and drive to break into modeling and from there into movies.

She was merely another blonde doing bit parts until *The Asphalt Jungle* (1950) made audiences sit up and take notice. A born scene-stealer who knew how to flirt with a camera and a genius at self-promotion she made it to the top with little help from her studio, 20th Century Fox. The news that Marilyn had posed nude for a calendar in 1948 only enhanced her sex symbol status.

A musical, *Gentlemen Prefer Blondes* (1953), and *How To Marry a Millionaire* (1953), in cinemascope, made her one of the top-ten box-office draws. In 1954 Marilyn married famed baseball player Joe DiMaggio and as far as the public knew had found her way to happiness. Though *The Seven Year Itch* (1955) was a big success, Marilyn's marriage to DiMaggio didn't last and despite her hefty salary she had debts. Marilyn fled to New York and the Actors' Studio but she returned to Hollywood to make *Bus Stop* (1956), possibly her best movie.

Her 1956 marriage to playwright Arthur Miller was a surprise, though it shouldn't have been. Marilyn Monroe

The magnificent Marilyn Monroe.

173

Opposite: Marilyn Monroe.
Above: Monroe, *River of No Return* (1954).
Left: Monroe, Russell – *Gentlemen Prefer Blondes* (1953).

was never the dumb blonde she played on screen and she fought hard for better roles. She failed in her quest to be taken seriously, never receiving an Academy Award nomination, not even for her clever performance in *Some Like It Hot* (1959).

Marilyn's last film, *The Misfits* (1961), written by Miller and co-starring Clark Gable, was excellent, but by then things had gone drastically wrong for America's golden girl. Divorced from Miller, in and out of psychiatric hospitals, Marilyn Monroe died in 1962 of an overdose of barbiturates. It was probably suicide. After her death the legend of Marilyn as doomed victim grew. The subject of books, articles and plays, she is the image of a beautiful loser, the poor kid who tried but never really succeeded.

FILMOGRAPHY
The Asphalt Jungle 1950
All About Eve 1950
Niagara 1952
Gentlemen Prefer Blondes 1953
How to Marry a Millionaire 1953
There's No Business Like Show Business 1954
The Seven Year Itch 1955
Bus Stop 1956
The Prince and the Showgirl 1957
Some Like It Hot 1959
The Misfits 1961

MONTAND, Yves 1921-

Yves Montand, born Ivo Levi in Italy, became a popular French singer and married actress Simone Signoret. Edith Piaf got him started in films and the sexy, handsome Montand starred in French, European and Hollywood films, giving especially fine performances in the political suspense dramas of director Costa-Gavras.

FILMOGRAPHY
Star Without Light 1946
The Wages of Fear 1953
The Crucible 1957
Let's Make Love 1960
The Sleeping Car Murders 1965
Z 1968
The Son 1972
Clair de Femme 1979

MONTGOMERY, Robert 1904-1981

Most of the time Robert Montgomery was a charming polished light comedian and romantic leading man. Occasionally he played against type with fine results; witness his chilling performance as the villain in *Night Must Fall* (1937). Montgomery, who only entered acting after failing as a writer, became an innovative director in films and television.

FILMOGRAPHY
Private Lives 1931
Night Must Fall 1937
Busman's Honeymoon 1940
Here Comes Mr Jordan 1941
The Lady in the Lake 1946
Eye Witness 1950

Dudley Moore as *Arthur* (1982).

MOORE, Dudley 1935-

A highly talented versatile performer, London-born Dudley Moore is an actor, composer, writer, musician and comedian. A serious student of piano, he has worked closely with Peter Cook and was a member of the hilarious *Beyond the Fringe* group.

Having sparkled on stage, television and in cabaret, it remained for Moore to conquer film which he did with *10* (1980), getting a boost from beautiful Bo Derek. *Arthur* (1982) made Moore a bigger star yet. Subsequent films have proved a disaster, in part because Moore, short and not at all the usual leading man, chooses to play romantic roles. A good solid comedy could cement his career once again.

FILMOGRAPHY
The Wrong Box 1966
Thirty is a Dangerous Age, Cynthia 1967
Foul Play 1978
The Hound of the Baskervilles 1978
10 1980
Wholly Moses 1981
Arthur 1982
Lovesick 1983
Micki and Maude 1984
Santa Claus – The Movie 1985

Left: Montand – *Goodbye Again* (1961).

MOORE, Roger 1928-

Handsome and charming with a debonair style and a twinkling sense of humor, London-born actor Roger Moore hit stardom on television, most notably as 'The Saint.' His film career boomed when he replaced Sean Connery in the James Bond series.

FILMOGRAPHY
The Sins of Rachel Cade 1961
Crossplot 1969
The Man Who Haunted Himself 1970
Live and Let Die 1973
The Spy Who Loved Me 1977
Moonraker 1979
For Your Eyes Only 1981
Octopussy 1983
A View to A Kill 1985

MOOREHEAD, Agnes 1906-1974

One of the best character actresses Hollywood ever produced, Agnes

Roger Moore in *Moonraker* (1979).

Moorehead received five Academy Award nominations. A singer, ballet dancer and drama coach as well, her career really took off once she worked with Orson Welles. She was popular as Endora in the television series *Bewitched*.

FILMOGRAPHY
Citizen Kane 1941
The Magnificent Ambersons 1942
The Lost Moment 1947
Johnny Belinda 1948
Jeanne Eagels 1957
The Bat 1959
Hush...Hush, Sweet Charlotte 1964
Dear Dead Delilah 1975

MORE, Kenneth 1914-1984

An amiable image made Kenneth More one of Britain's most popular stars. He was born in Gerrard's Cross, England, and made his debut in films in the mid-1930s. But it wasn't until he returned from naval service in World War II that his career really took hold.

More received a British Film Academy Award for his appearance in *Doctor in the House* (1954). As a leading man he played both comic and dramatic roles, as well as devoting his efforts to stage and television. The BBC television series *The Forsyte Saga* won him new admirers.

FILMOGRAPHY
Scott of the Antartic 1948
Now Barabbas 1949
The Franchise Affair 1950
Appointment With Venus 1951
Genevieve 1953
Doctor in the House 1954
The Deep Blue Sea 1955
Reach for the Sky 1956
Sink the Bismarck 1960
The Comedy Man 1963
Leopard in the Snow 1978
King Arthur 1979

Kenneth More – *The Sheriff of Fractured Jaw* (1959).

MOREAU, Jeanne 1928-

An international star, Jeanne Moreau was born in Paris where she studied acting, making her stage and film debuts in 1948. It was a decade before her film career exploded, thanks to director Louis Malle. She became extremely popular, a serious actress who was sophisticated and sensual, capable of playing a wide variety of roles.

She's worked with several great directors including Antonioni and Truffaut, whose *Jules et Jim* (1961) highlighted Moreau's on-screen charisma. Moreau made her debut as a director with *La Lumière* (1976), writing the movie's script and starring in it as well.

FILMOGRAPHY
Lift to the Scaffold 1957
The Lovers 1959
La Notte 1961
Jules et Jim 1961
Diary of a Chambermaid 1964
Viva Maria 1965
Chimes at Midnight 1966
The Bride Wore Black 1967
Monte Walsh 1970
La Lumière 1976

Michele Morgan (*right*), with Pier Angeli in *The Vintage* (1957).

MORGAN, Michele 1920-

Blessed with a delicate classic beauty, Michele Morgan was a leading lady while still in her teens. Born Simone Roussel in Neuilly-sur-Seine, France, she is both a French and international star noted for her fascinating on-screen aloofness, sophistication and wonderfully expressive eyes.

It didn't take Morgan long to become France's most popular film actress and she received the Best Actress Award at the Cannes festival for her appearance in *La Symphonie Pastorale* (1946). Though she has appeared in Hollywood films she is at her best in European productions.

FILMOGRAPHY
Orage 1936
Quai des Brumes 1938
Joan of Paris 1941
Passage to Marseilles 1944
La Symphonie Pastorale 1946
The Fallen Idol 1948
The Seven Deadly Sins 1951
Les Grandes Maneouvres 1955
Marguerite de la Nuit 1956
The Mirror Has Two Faces 1960
Landru 1963
Lost Command 1966
Benjamin 1968
Seven Steps to Murder 1977
Cat and Mouse 1978

MORLEY, Robert 1908-

Rotund, irresistibly charming, a master of jolly or pompous comedy roles, Robert Morley is popular on both sides of the Atlantic. Actor and playwright Morley was born in Semley, England. He prepared for a diplomatic career but opted for the stage instead, debuting in 1929. He later played the title role in *Oscar Wilde*.

In 1938 he made his film debut as Louis XVI opposite Norma Shearer in *Marie Antoinette* (1938), winning an Oscar nomination. Since then he has had supporting roles in numerous films and is a familiar figure on television.

FILMOGRAPHY
Marie Antoinette 1938
Major Barbara 1940
The Young Mr Pitt 1942
I Live in Grosvenor Square 1945
An Outcast of the Islands 1951
Gilbert and Sullivan 1953
Beat the Devil 1953
The Doctor's Dilemma 1959
Oscar Wilde 1960
Murder at the Gallop 1963
Topkapi 1964
Theatre of Blood 1973
Who is Killing the Great Chefs of Europe 1978
The Human Factor 1980

MURPHY, Audie 1924-1971

Audie Murphy was America's most decorated soldier during World War II, and it was this fame that got him a movie career. Murphy appeared primarily in B Westerns but in a few films, notably *To Hell and Back* (1955), based on his autobiography, he displayed real talent. His personal life was marred by violence and financial troubles and he was killed in the crash of a private plane.

FILMOGRAPHY
Beyond Glory 1948
The Red Badge of Courage 1951
Destry 1955
To Hell and Back 1955
The Quiet American 1958
Cast a Long Shadow 1959
The Quick Gun 1964
Arizona Raiders 1965
Guns of Apache Pass 1967
A Time for Dying 1971

Right: Audi Murphy (*right*), *Apache Rifles* (1964).
Above: Muni (*Right*) – *The Life of Emile Zola* (1937).

MUNI, Paul 1896-1967

Few American actors were as highly respected as Paul Muni (born Muni Weisenfreund), an Austrian immigrant from a theatrical family who got his start with New York's Yiddish Art Theater Company. Conscientious, with a meticulous eye for details of costume, make-up, walk, gestures and other externals, Muni approached his craft in a rigidly controlled way and had a thriving stage and film career.

Social dramas and costume epics which celebrated famous people were his mainstay. His movie debut in *The Valiant* (1928) brought him as Oscar nomination. Muni won an Academy Award for Best Actor for *The Story of Louis Pasteur* (1936).

FILMOGRAPHY
The Valiant 1928
Scarface 1932
I Am a Fugitive from a Chain Gang 1932
The Story of Louis Pasteur 1936
The Good Earth 1937
The Life of Emile Zola 1937
Juarez 1939
We Are Not Alone 1939
A Song to Remember 1944
The Last Angry Man 1959

Paul Muni in *The Good Earth* (1937).

MURPHY, Eddie 1961-

Eddie Murphy, the young black comedian, began writing comic routines for himself at 15 and before he was 20 he was a cast member of television's popular *Saturday Night Live*. A superb mimic and impressionist as well as a talented actor, he radiates star quality.

FILMOGRAPHY
48 Hours 1981
Trading Places 1982
Beverly Hills Cop 1984
The Golden Child 1987

NALDI, Nita 1899-1961

Nita Naldi, born Donna Dooley in New York City, began in the Ziegfeld Follies and became famous as a silent movie star in the 1920s. She tempted Valentino in *Blood and Sand* (1922) and, after her film career faded when sound movies replaced silent pictures, she appeared occasionally on the stage and later on television.

FILMOGRAPHY
Dr Jekyll and Mr Hyde 1920
Blood and Sand 1922
Cobra 1925
The Marriage Whirl 1926
The Lady Who Lied 1927
What Price Beauty 1928

NEGRI, Pola 1897-

A successful stage actress who led a colorful life, Pola Negri, born Appolonia Chalupek in Janowa, Poland, became a German film star, at her best when directed by Ernst Lubitsch. Then she came to Hollywood, where she was an exotic attraction on the silent screen. Talkies killed her American career but she never wholly abandoned pictures.

FILMOGRAPHY
Die Bestie 1915
Madame du Barry 1918
Bella Donna 1923
Forbidden Paradise 1926
Madame Bovary 1935
Hi Diddle Diddle 1943
The Moonspinners 1964

Below: Pola Negri.

NEWMAN, Paul 1925-

A lucky man, Paul Newman has looks, talent, a successful marriage, a reputation for being a nice guy who gives time and money to worthy liberal causes and a man whose acting career merits acclaim. As if this wasn't enough, Newman possesses the bluest pair of eyes ever to look out from a movie screen.

Born into a wealthy family in Cleveland, Ohio, Newman entered Kenyon College after serving in World War II. His family expected him to go into business and, as the film deals he would later negotiate proved, he was more than competent when it came to making money. But Newman preferred acting to economics. He attended the Yale Drama School and New York's prestigious Actors Studio.

His appearance on Broadway in *Picnic* led to a movie contract, but his first film, *The Silver Chalice* (1954), a costume epic, only served to embarrass him. Eager to continue his stage career and skeptical of Hollywood, Newman decided to make his home near New York. He developed a knack for choosing good scripts and many of his movies have been box-office blockbusters.

Newman won the Cannes Film Festival Award for Best Actor for *The Long Hot Summer* (1958). He has been showered with Oscar nominations; for *Cat on a Hot Tin Roof* (1958); *The Hustler* (1961), which brought him a British Film Academy Award; *Hud* (1963); *Cool Hand Luke* (1967); *Absence of Malice* (1981) and *The Verdict* (1982). He won a British Film Academy Award for the smash hit, *Butch Cassidy and the Sundance Kid* (1969), which matched him brilliantly with Robert Redford and allowed Newman's unsuspected gift for comic frivolity to shine.

In 1968 Newman made his directing debut with the film *Rachel, Rachel* (1968), starring his second wife, the talented actress Joanne Woodward. He went on to further directing and producing under the aegis of First Productions, a company formed by Newman, Sidney Poitier, Barbra Streisand and other stars during the 1970s. The one blight on the seemingly charmed life of Paul Newman was the death of his son by his first wife, Jacqueline Witte, from a drug overdose in 1978.

Right: Paul Newman in *Hombre* (1967).

NEWTON, Robert 1905-1956

[R]obert Newton had thunder in his [v]oice and fire in his rolling eyes. This [B]ritish actor was a gripping scene [st]ealer, a top box-office star who [p]layed villains with panache. His Bill [S]ikes in *Oliver Twist* (1948) and Long [J]ohn Silver in *Treasure Island* (1950) [a]re bravura performances.

FILMOGRAPHY
[F]arewell Again 1937
[M]ajor Barbara 1940
[H]atter's Castle 1941
[T]his Happy Breed 1944
[H]enry V 1945
[O]liver Twist 1948
[T]reasure Island 1950
[T]om Brown's Schooldays 1951
[T]he Beachcomber 1954

NICHOLSON, Jack 1937-

[O]ne of the most charismatic and indi[v]idualistic of Hollywood stars, Jack [N]icholson generally plays rebels, [d]rifters, outsiders and free spirits. [N]icholson's sarcastic grin and wry [b]itterness have illuminated some of [t]he finest movies of the 1970s and [1]980s. With his talent and idiosyncratic [s]tyle, he looks like a safe bet for lead roles and stardom yet he spent over a decade making cheap horror films.

Born in Neptune, New Jersey, Nicholson visited California at age 17 and became hooked on motion pictures, finding work as an office boy in MGM's cartoon department. He joined the Players Ring Theater and appeared on stage and in television before producer-director Roger Corman cast him in horror and action cheapies. Soon Nicholson began producing and writing low-budget films with Corman's protégé, Monte Hellman. Nicholson wrote *Head* (1968) for the rock group The Monkees.

He must have felt he would be stranded forever in the netherworld of 'B' movies, but on a stroke of luck he wound up in *Easy Rider* (1969), a box-office smash and a pace setter in films geared to the young. Nicholson was great as a man who abandoned respectability to join his hippie friends. In many ways a hippie himself, the irreverent Nicholson was in tune with the mood of the 1960s and early 1970s. Audiences sensed this, and *Five Easy Pieces* (1970) made him a superstar.

Nicholson began collecting Oscar nominations with some regularity. Though *Chinatown* (1974) earned him a New York Film Critics Award, it wasn't until *One Flew Over the Cuckoo's Nest* (1976), that he won an Academy Award for Best Actor. He gave an eccentric but fascinating performance in Stanley Kubrick's *The Shining* (1979), a horror film again, but this time grade 'A.' Like other superb movie actors, Nicholson rebounds resiliently from commercial failures, and he's had his share, coming up with the critical part at the critical moment to save his career. Movies don't get much bigger than *Terms of Endearment* (1983), which won him an Academy Award for Best Supporting Actor.

FILMOGRAPHY
The Cry Baby Killer 1958
Studs Lonigan 1961
The Little Shop of Horrors 1962
The Raven 1963
Hell's Angels on Wheels 1967
Easy Rider 1969
Five Easy Pieces 1970
Carnal Knowledge 1971
The Last Detail 1974
Chinatown 1974
One Flew Over the Cuckoo's Nest 1976
The Shining 1979
The Postman Always Rings Twice 1982
Reds 1982
Terms of Endearment 1983
Prizzi's Honor 1985
Heartburn 1986

Opposite: Jack Nicholson as the crazed writer in *The Shining* (1979).
Below: Nicholson won an Academy Award for *One Flew Over the Cuckoo's Nest* (1976).

Sophia Loren and Niven – *Lady L* (1966).

NIVEN, David 1909-1983

Debonair and urbane, David Niven was a dashing light comedian and an attractive romantic lead. Born James David Graham Niven in Scotland, he came from a long line of professional soldiers and attended the Royal Military Academy, Sandhurst, then served with the Highland Light Infantry in Malta.

But the military life was not for Niven and he began drifting around the world aimlessly, working as a lumberman, a reporter, a promotor and even becoming a small-time crook. When he hit Los Angeles he decided to try his luck as a movie extra.

His looks, charm and gentlemanly diction helped him move quickly into leading and strong supporting roles and he learned his craft as he went along. *Dodsworth* (1936) set him on the road to stardom. He was noteworthy in *Bluebeard's Eighth Wife* (1938) and *Bachelor Mother* (1939).

By the start of World War II Niven was a seasoned pro – competent and reliable – adding a touch of class to many films. He left Hollywood to join the British Army as a lieutenant and rose to the rank of colonel. After the war Niven regularly appeared in both British and American movies, moving comfortably between Hollywood and London, continuing in well-bred roles. He was often far superior to the vehi-cles he appeared in.

In the 1950s Niven branched out into television and he also had the biggest box-office smash of his career, *Around the World in Eighty Days* (1956). He played Phileas Fogg in this sweeping costume epic. Niven was long overdue for an Oscar and at last he won an Academy Award for Best Actor and the New York Critics Best Actor Award for his touching performance in *Separate Tables* (1958). A gifted author, he wrote a novel and two exceedingly popular autobiographies. Then he just went on being polished, intelligent, elegant and dapper in movies until he died.

FILMOGRAPHY

Thank You Jeeves 1936
The Charge of the Light Brigade 1936
Dodsworth 1936
The Prisoner of Zenda 1937
Bluebeard's Eighth Wife 1938
Wuthering Heights 1939
Bachelor Mother 1939
Raffles 1940
The First of the Few 1941
The Way Ahead 1944
A Stairway to Heaven 1946
The Other Love 1947
The Bishop's Wife 1947
Enchantment 1948
A Kiss in the Dark 1949
The Toast of New Orleans 1950
The Moon is Blue 1953
Carrington VC 1955
Around the World in Eighty Days 1956
Bonjour Tristesse 1958
Separate Tables 1958
Ask Any Girl 1959
Please Don't Eat the Daisies 1960
The Guns of Navarone 1961

The Pink Panther 1964
Casino Royale 1967
The Brain 1969
Paper Tiger 1975
Murder By Death 1976
Death on the Nile 1978
A Nightingale Sang in Berkeley Square 1980
Curse of the Pink Panther 1983

NORMAND, Mabel 1894-1930

Mabel Normand, a great comedienne, actress and director, was a radiant star in silent films. The daughter of a poor vaudeville pianist, she was a model at 13 and in films at 16. By 1912 she was Mack Sennett's prize female performer.

Normand appeared with and directed Charlie Chaplin. *Tillie's Punctured Romance* (1914), starring both of them, was a smash hit and Sennett established the Mabel Normand Feature Film Company. Later Normand signed with Goldwyn and began living the movie star's life at fever pitch. Scandals over drugs swirled about her and her name was dragged into two sordid murder cases. Normand broke under the strain, making her last major film in 1923, and dying seven years later of pneumonia and tuberculosis.

FILMOGRAPHY

Barney Oldfield's Race for Life 1912
Tillie's Punctured Romance 1914
Fatty and Mabel Adrift 1915
Mickey 1917
Sis Hopkins 1918
Molly O 1921
Suzanna 1922
The Extra Girl 1924
Raggedy Rose 1926

Niven and Capuchine – *The Pink Panther* (1964).

OBERON, Merle 1911-1979

Born in Tasmania and educated in India Merle Oberon, born Merle O'Brien Thompson, was an exquisite brunette beauty who generally played rich and glamorous women in British and American films. She was discovered by Alexander Korda playing bit roles in movies under the name Estelle Thompson. She was married to Korda from 1939 to 1945.

Oberon is best remembered for costume dramas like *The Scarlet Pimpernel* (1934) and *Wuthering Heights* (1939). Oberon's private life was almost as glamorous as her on-screen image. Married four times, she was a glittering international socialite.

FILMOGRAPHY
The Private Life of Henry VIII 1933
The Scarlet Pimpernel 1934
The Dark Angel 1935
These Three 1936
The Divorce of Lady X 1938
The Cowboy and the Lady 1938
Wuthering Heights 1939
Lydia 1941
The Lodger 1944
Dark Waters 1944
A Song to Remember 1945
Desiree 1954
Hotel 1967
Interval 1973

O'CONNOR, Donald 1925-

Donald O'Connor is an amusing singe and a very good light comedian, but h was at his best when he danced. Th Chicago-born son of circus performer turned vaudevillians, the engagin O'Connor was a pro by age 11 when h made his film debut.

He graduated from kids' roles t playing juvenile leads in a string of 'E movies opposite young starlets. H had a talking mule for a companion i the 'Francis' movie series. But hi shining hour came in *Singin' in th Rain* (1952). Several other goo musicals followed, plus televisio roles and composing music.

FILMOGRAPHY
Sing You Sinners 1938
Tom Sawyer, Detective 1938
Beau Geste 1939
Mister Big 1943
Patrick the Great 1945
Francis 1949
Singin' in the Rain 1952
Call Me Madam 1953
There's No Business Like Show Business 1954
The Buster Keaton Story 1957
That Funny Feeling 1965

Left: Oberon in *Wuthering Heights* (1939).
Below: O'Connor, Gene Kelly and Debbie Reynolds in *Singin' in the Rain* (1952).

O'HARA, Maureen 1920-

Born Maureen Fitzsimmons in Mill-wall, near Dublin, Ireland, Maureen O'Hara was a gloriously beautiful red-head with an engaging personality and a Hollywood star of the 1940s and 1950s. An ingénue at the Abbey Theatre, she made her British film debut in 1938.

She was beautiful in Technicolor costume pictures but was at her best in two perky contemporary films, *Miracle on 34th Street* (1947) and *Sitting Pretty* (1948). *The Quiet Man* (1952) won director John Ford an Oscar but O'Hara's acting performance was one of the reasons he won it.

FILMOGRAPHY
Jamaica Inn 1939
The Hunchback of Notre Dame 1939
A Bill of Divorcement 1940
How Green Was My Valley 1941
The Black Swan 1942
Miracle on 34th Street 1947
Sitting Pretty 1948
The Quiet Man 1952
The Magnificent Matador 1955
The Parent Trap 1961
The Deadly Companions 1961
The Rare Breed 1966
Big Jake 1971

The glamorous red-haired
Maureen O'Hara.

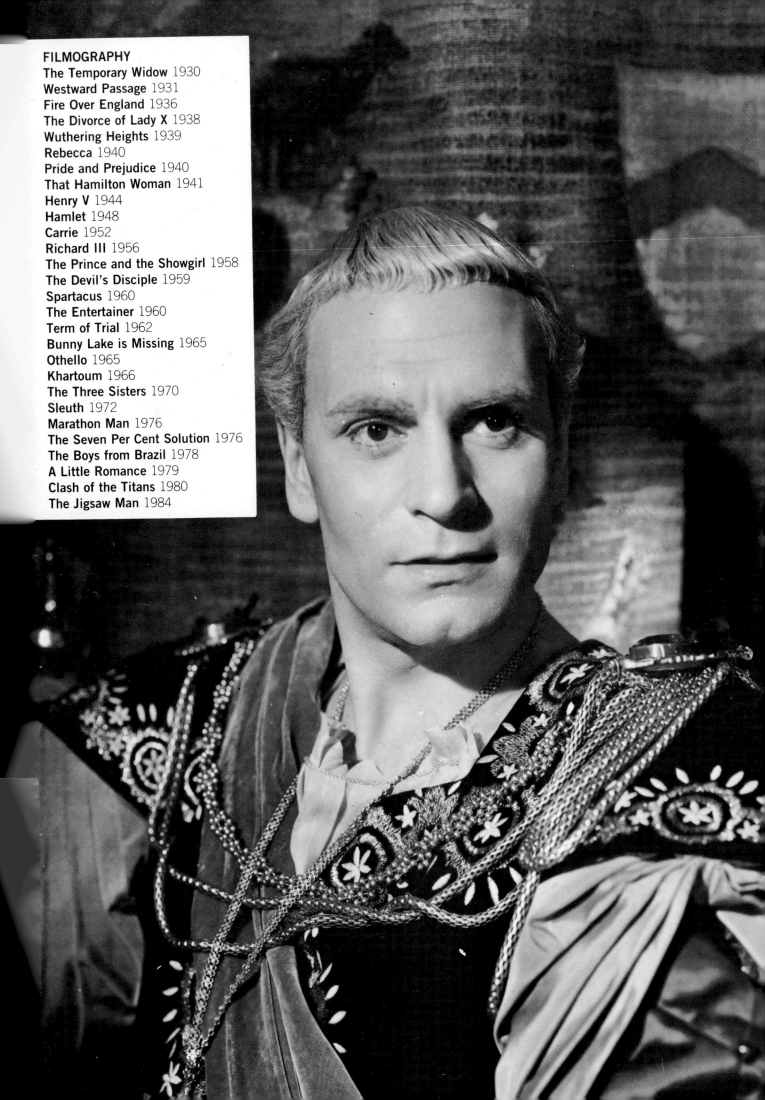

FILMOGRAPHY
The Temporary Widow 1930
Westward Passage 1931
Fire Over England 1936
The Divorce of Lady X 1938
Wuthering Heights 1939
Rebecca 1940
Pride and Prejudice 1940
That Hamilton Woman 1941
Henry V 1944
Hamlet 1948
Carrie 1952
Richard III 1956
The Prince and the Showgirl 1958
The Devil's Disciple 1959
Spartacus 1960
The Entertainer 1960
Term of Trial 1962
Bunny Lake is Missing 1965
Othello 1965
Khartoum 1966
The Three Sisters 1970
Sleuth 1972
Marathon Man 1976
The Seven Per Cent Solution 1976
The Boys from Brazil 1978
A Little Romance 1979
Clash of the Titans 1980
The Jigsaw Man 1984

O'NEAL, Ryan 1941-

Boyishly handsome O'Neal, father of movie actress Tatum O'Neal, was a lifeguard and amateur boxer who began his career as a television stuntman. He was the star of several hit films, including *Love Story* (1970), and his playboy lifestyle keeps his name in the news.

FILMOGRAPHY
Love Story 1970
What's Up Doc? 1972
Paper Moon 1973
Barry Lyndon 1975
Nickelodeon 1976
Oliver's Story 1979
The Main Event 1979
Partners 1982
Irreconcilable Differences 1984
Fever Pitch 1985

O'TOOLE, Peter 1932-

When it comes to flamboyance, range, and sex appeal there are few actors as winning as Peter O'Toole, who burst into stardom with *Lawrence of Arabia* (1962). O'Toole's career sometimes hits snags because of his bouts with alcohol but he was wonderful in *My Favorite Year* (1982), taking a Best Actor Academy Award Nomination.

FILMOGRAPHY
Lawrence of Arabia 1962
Becket 1964
What's New, Pussycat 1965
The Lion in Winter 1968
The Stuntman 1978
My Favorite Year 1982
Supergirl 1984
Club Paradise 1986

Peter O'Toole – *How to Steal a Million* (1966).

Above: O'Neal, Milland – *Oliver's Story* (1979).
Opposite: Laurence Olivier.

OLIVIER, Lord (Laurence) 1907-

aurence Olivier just may be the reatest actor of the century. Born in orking, England, into a clergyman's amily he made a rather peculiar stage ebut playing Katharine in a school roduction of *The Taming of the hrew*. In 1926 he joined the Birmingam Rep, then did a number of plays in ondon's West End and made his roadway debut in 1929. His looks and alent did not go unnoticed but the vorld did not fall at his feet and he had o struggle like many other young ctors. He made his debut on screen in 930, appeared in a few innocuous lms. Hired to play opposite Garbo in *ueen Christina* (1933), he was re- laced by John Gilbert.

Yet just a few years later he would merge as an actor whose gifts were nparalleled. Joining the Old Vic, he layed one great Shakespearian role fter another and *Wuthering Heights* 1939) and *Rebecca* (1940) established im as a superb romantic lead in films.

In 1944 Olivier was appointed co- irector of the Old Vic. He produced,

directed and starred in the movie *Henry V* (1944), a magnificent achievement which won him a special Academy Award. *Hamlet* (1948) brought him a step closer to being recognized as a genius. The film took an Academy Award for Best Picture and Olivier won the Oscar for Best Actor. He received a special Academy Award again at the 1978 ceremonies for his contribution to films.

Olivier married actress Jill Esmond in 1930. The couple divorced in 1940 and Olivier married stage and film star Vivien Leigh. They appeared together on stage frequently. In 1961 Olivier married actress Joan Plowright.

Resourceful and entrepreneurial, there are few aspects of theater, films and television that Olivier has overlooked. In 1963 he became director of England's National Theatre Company. Olivier was knighted in 1947. In 1970 he was made a peer of the realm. In 1971 he took his seat in the House of Lords, the only actor ever to be given this honor.

PACINO, Al 1939-

Al Pacino – intensity and depth are the hallmarks of this serious actor. Born into a working-class Sicilian-American family in New York City, Pacino attended the High School of Performing Arts, dropping out and doing odd jobs to earn the money to study at Herbert Berghof's acting school and the Actors' Studio.

Pacino appeared in off-Broadway and Broadway productions, earning critical praise and receiving awards. With little film work behind him he was chosen to play Michael Corleone, a difficult and complex character, in *The Godfather* (1972). The movie was a blockbuster and Pacino became a star. He often plays tough but intelligent and sensitive anti-heroes on screen, frequently accepting challenging and controversial roles. However the theater has remained his first love.

FILMOGRAPHY
Panic in Needle Park 1971
The Godfather 1972
Serpico 1973
The Godfather, Part II 1974
Dog Day Afternoon 1975
And Justice for All 1979
Author! Author! 1982
Scarface 1983
Revolution 1985

PALANCE, Jack 1920-

Jack Palance, born Walter Palahnui was burned severely in a bomber cras during World War II. Plastic surge gave his face a taut, almost skull-li appearance. With a sinister voice match, Palance has frequently appea ed as a villain in Hollywood, and mo recently in international films.

FILMOGRAPHY
Panic in the Streets 1950
Shane 1953
Sign of the Pagan 1954
The Big Knife 1955
I Died a Thousand Times 1955
Che! 1969
Oklahoma Crude 1973
Ladyfingers 1980

Left: Al Pacino in *Serpico* (1973).
Below: Pacino in *The Godfather, Part II* (1974).

PALMER, Lilli 1914-

lli Palmer, an elegant Austrian ctress who fled the Nazis, made her m debut in London in 1935, appearg regularly in British movies until oming to America in 1945 with her rst husband, actor Rex Harrison. ollywood movies and Broadway ays followed. Then she continued er career in Europe.

ILMOGRAPHY
hunder Rock 1942
he Rake's Progress 1945
ly Girl Tisa 1947
he Fourposter 1952
he Pleasure of His Company 1961
ebastian 1967
ight Hair Child 1971
he Boys from Brazil 1978

PARKER, Eleanor 1922-

leanor Parker was a stunning redhead vho kept getting better and better roles ntil she became a leading lady in the 950s. Never typecast, she played a vide variety of characters and was iominated for an Academy Award hree times. Later she shifted to supiorting roles.

FILMOGRAPHY
Of Human Bondage 1946
The Voice of the Turtle 1947
Caged 1950
Detective Story 1951
Scaramouche 1952
nterrupted Melody 1955
The Sound of Music 1965
Eye of the Cat 1969
Sunburn 1979

PECK, Gregory 1916-

Gregory Peck is a leading man who projects strength, sincerity, moral fiber, intelligence, kindness and conviction rather than flashy heroics. What's more he conveys all this virtue in a likeable way, a rare achievement. Dark and broodingly handsome, Peck is also a sex symbol but the kind who'd make a good son-in-law. He was one of the first of the post World War II actors to take advantage of the crumbling Hollywood studio system, working out financially rewarding deals for himself and working only in pictures he chose.

His steady stoic style was sometimes called wooden by critics but when he had good material he was an easy to love blockbuster star.

Born Eldred Gregory Peck in La Jolla, California, he attended San Diego State College, then enrolled in New York's Neighborhood Playhouse, making his debut on Broadway in *The Morning Star* by Emlyn Williams in 1942. A spinal injury prevented him seeing any military service and in the war years, when leading men were at a premium in Hollywood, he was snatched up. Peck proved strong on classy sex appeal and a hit in many kinds of movies.

Peck – *The Man in the Gray Flannel Suit* (1956).

Peck starred in *Spellbound* (1945), Hitchcock's famous psychological thriller; *Gentlemen's Agreement* (1947), an Oscar winning movie about anti-semitism and *The Gunfighter* (1950), an innovative and mature western. He fell in love with Audrey Hepburn in *Roman Holiday* (1953), was Captain Ahab in *Moby Dick* (1956) and won an Academy Award for Best Actor playing a liberal Southern lawyer in *To Kill a Mockingbird* (1963).

Peck's career went on the downswing as he grew older and there were rumors he was through, especially

when he took the lead in *The Om*[...]
(1976). It made more money than a[...]
thing he had ever done and he ca[...]
bouncing back, this time as a N[...]
doctor in *The Boys From Brazil* (197[...]
Active in many charities, Peck w[...]
the recipient of the Medal of Freed[...]
Award and the Academy of Motion P[...]
ture Arts and Sciences Jean Hersh[...]
Humanitarian Award.

FILMOGRAPHY

Days of Glory 1943
The Keys of the Kingdom 1944
The Valley of Decision 1944
Spellbound 1945
The Yearling 1946
Duel in the Sun 1946
The Macomber Affair 1947
Gentlemen's Agreement 1947
The Paradine Case 1947
Twelve O'Clock High 1949
The Gunfighter 1950
Captain Horatio Hornblower 1951
The Snows of Kilimanjaro 1952
Roman Holiday 1953
The Man in the Gray Flannel Suit 1956
Moby Dick 1956
The Big Country 1958
On the Beach 1959
The Guns of Navarone 1961
Cape Fear 1962
To Kill a Mockingbird 1963
Captain Newman, MD 1963
Mirage 1965
Arabesque 1966
The Stalking Moon 1968
The Omen 1976
The Boys from Brazil 1978
Sea Wolves 1980

Left: Peck, Bergman – *Spellbound* (1945).
Below left: Peck, Anthony Quinn in *The Guns of Navarone* (1961).
Below: Peck – *Duel in the Sun* (1946).

PEPPARD, George 1928-

A good-looking leading man who tends towards playing tough heroes, George Peppard has had a few golden moments in films but often the vehicles he appears in are not up to his talents. Peppard has achieved some of his greatest success on television in 'Banacek' and 'The A Team.'

FILMOGRAPHY
The Strange One 1957
Home from the Hill 1960
Breakfast at Tiffany's 1961
How the West was Won 1962
The Victors 1963
The Carpetbaggers 1964
The Blue Max 1966
Newman's Law 1974
Battle Beyond the Stars 1980

Above: Peppard – *The Blue Max* (1966).
Below: Anthony Perkins in *Psycho* (1960).

PERKINS, Anthony 1932-

Son of actor Osgood Perkins, Anthony Perkins has been both a leading and fine supporting actor. Tall, slightly-built and boyishly charming, Perkins made a splash in *Friendly Persuasion* (1956), but is most famous for his role as Norman Bates in *Psycho* (1960).

FILMOGRAPHY
Friendly Persuasion 1956
Desire Under the Elms 1957
Fear Strikes Out 1957
The Matchmaker 1958
Psycho 1960
Catch 22 1970
Murder on the Orient Express 1974
Psycho II 1983
Crimes of Passion 1984
Psycho III 1986

PICKFORD, Mary 1893-1979

Mary Pickford was 'America's Sweetheart' and 'The World's Sweetheart,' a bigger box-office draw than any of her peers, including Charles Chaplin. Though she tried a wide variety of roles, audiences preferred her as the plucky, innocent young girl, rich only in spirit, for whom a happy ending waits. For almost 25 years Pickford may have been the most famous female on earth, a star known even in remote rural villages where movies were shown but plays were not seen.

.Born Gladys Smith in Toronto, Canada, she became a child actress at age five after her father's death. Touring as 'Baby Gladys' she was the chief source of income for her family, though eventually her sister Lottie and her brother Jack also went into acting.

Left: Mary Pickford at a World War I bond drive.
Below: Mary — America's Sweetheart.

At age 14 she was on Broadway and at 16 she became a Biograph player, working for DW Griffith. Like the other players, her name wasn't listed in the movie credits, but her blonde ringlets won her the nickname 'the girl with the golden curls,' and as such she became very popular.

Pickford moved from film company to film company, negotiating the best deal she could get. Her salary was soon astronomical and she remained fabulously wealthy all her life. Accused of having 'a mind like a cash register' she actually fought hard for artistic control. In 1919 she joined Chaplin, Griffith and husband-to-be Douglas Fairbanks in forming United Artists so that the stars could produce, release, and distribute their own films and the films of others.

Fairbanks and Pickford were Hollywood's royal couple living in a 'palace' called Pickfair. It was the second marriage for each and considerably less rosy than the fan magazines painted it. Besides, a career crisis loomed for Pickford. She had played Pollyanna on screen as late as 1919 and continued doing Cinderella roles into her thirties. By 1928 she was sick of ringlets and appeared in her first talkie, *Coquette* (1929), all grown up with her hair cut short. She won an Academy Award for her performance but the movie didn't catch on with the public.

Pickford retired from films in the 1930s, though she appeared frequently on radio. In 1936 she divorced Fairbanks and married Charles 'Buddy' Rogers. In 1975 Mary Pickford received a special Academy Award for her contribution to films.

FILMOGRAPHY
Her First Biscuits 1909
The Violin Maker of Cremona 1910
The Paris Hat 1913
Madame Butterfly 1915
Less Than the Dust 1916
The Little Princess 1917
Rebecca of Sunnybrook Farm 1917
Stella Maris 1918
Pollyanna 1919
Suds 1920
Little Lord Fauntleroy 1921
The Love Light 1921
Tess of the Storm Country 1922
Rosita 1923
Dorothy Vernon of Haddon Hall 1924
Little Annie Rooney 1925
My Best Girl 1927
The Taming of the Shrew 1929
Coquette 1929
Kiki 1931
Secrets 1933

PIDGEON, Walter 1897-1984

Walter Pidgeon was strong without being threatening, reassuring without being insipid, a comfortable benign leading man, especially appealing during World War II when audiences dreamed of peaceful domesticity. Pidgeon was born in St John, New Brunswick, Canada, and went to the New England Conservatory of Music.

Entering films in the silent era, he began as a supporting actor, then sang in early musicals after sound came in. During the 1940s he appeared in a number of important movies and was especially effective opposite Greer Garson. He switched to character roles in the 1950s.

FILMOGRAPHY
The Thirteenth Juror 1927
Society Lawyer 1939
Man Hunt 1941
Blossoms in the Dust 1941
How Green was My Valley 1941
Mrs Miniver 1942
Madame Curie 1943
That Forsyte Woman 1949
The Bad and the Beautiful 1952
Executive Suite 1954
Forbidden Planet 1956
Advise and Consent 1962
Funny Girl 1968
Sextette 1978

Below: Plummer, Julie Andrews — *The Sound of Music* (1965).

Above: Walter Pigeon in *Dark Command* (1940) with Roy Rogers (*left*) and John Wayne.

PLUMMER, Christopher 1927-

Christopher Plummer had a formidable stage reputation in his native Canada before going to Broadway and then to Hollywood. Plummer was the Baron in the extremely popular *The Sound of Music* (1965) and was effective as Sherlock Holmes in *Murder by Decree* (1978). Plummer has also appeared frequently on TV, often in Shakespeare.

FILMOGRAPHY
Stage Struck 1958
The Fall of the Roman Empire 1964
The Sound of Music 1965
Inside Daisy Clover 1966
Oedipus the King 1968
The Return of the Pink Panther 1975
The Man Who Would be King 1975
The Disappearance 1977
Murder by Decree 1978
International Velvet 1978
Somewhere in Time 1981
The Amateur 1982

POWELL, Dick 1904-1963

Born in Mountain View, Arkansas, Dick Powell began his career as a singer and instrumentalist and had several hit records. He was a good juvenile lead in movie musicals, frequently opposite Ruby Keeler. In an amazing role reversal, Powell became one of the tough-guy types of the 1940s playing characters like detective Marlowe.

A versatile survivor, Powell pulled off another coup when he began producing and directing films in the 1950s and headed a successful television production company. Powell was married twice, first to actress Joan Blondell, then to actress June Allyson.

FILMOGRAPHY
Forty-Second Street 1933
Gold Diggers of 1933 1933
Footlight Parade 1933
Dames 1934
Christmas in July 1940
Model Wife 1941
It Happened Tomorrow 1944
Murder My Sweet 1944
Cornered 1945
Johnny O'Clock 1947
Pitfall 1948
The Reformer and the Redhead 1950
Cry Danger 1951
The Bad and the Beautiful 1952
Susan Slept Here 1954

Above: Dick Powell, Gloria Stuart in *Gold Diggers of 1935* (1935).
Below: Poitier and Dorothy Dandridge in *Porgy and Bess* (1959).

POITIER, Sidney 1924-

A handsome black actor who broke many racial barriers making it easier for blacks to achieve commercial success in films, Sidney Poitier was born in Miami, Florida, and raised in the Bahamas. Though sometimes cast as a symbol rather than a character, he was still able to turn out magnetic performances in movies like *The Blackboard Jungle* (1955).

Lilies of the Field (1963), made Poitier the first black actor to receive an Academy Award for Best Actor and *Guess Who's Coming to Dinner* (1967) was a blockbuster hit dealing with the then touchy subject of black/white romance. Poitier also directs movies.

FILMOGRAPHY
No Way Out 1950
The Blackboard Jungle 1955
Edge of the City 1957
The Defiant Ones 1958
Lilies of the Field 1963
In the Heat of the Night 1967
To Sir with Love 1967
Guess Who's Coming to Dinner 1967
Brother John 1971
A Piece of the Action 1977

POWELL, William 1892-1984

Most famous for *The Thin Man* (1934), William Powell was one of the most sophisticated of leading men, and certainly one of the best dressed. Born in Pittsburgh, Pennsylvania, Powell began his stage career in 1912 and a decade later was in silent films, often playing the villain.

With the coming of sound he became a good guy, though a highly cynical one, starting with a series of light mysteries in which he was detective Philo Vance. From 1931 to 1933 Powell was married to actress Carole Lombard. He was engaged to Jean Harlow when she died. His best on-screen sweetheart was Myrna Loy. They made a great team.

FILMOGRAPHY
Sherlock Holmes 1922
Romola 1924
Beau Geste 1926
The Canary Murder Case 1929
Street of Chance 1930
One Way Passage 1932
Manhattan Melodrama 1934
The Thin Man 1934
The Great Ziegfeld 1936
My Man Godfrey 1936
Another Thin Man 1939
Life With Father 1947
Mister Roberts 1955

Above: William Powell (*center*) – *The Thin Man* (1934).
Below: Tyrone Power and Alice Faye in *Alexander's Ragtime Band* (1938).

POWER, Tyrone 1913-1958

A member of a famous Irish acting family, Tyrone Power was born in Cincinnati, Ohio. His stage and silent-movie actor father, also named Tyrone Power, encouraged him to seek a theatrical career. Power was extraordinarily good looking, with soft velvety eyes and he quickly developed into one of Hollywood's leading romantic stars.

Power was sometimes taken to be nothing more than a pretty boy but he was a fine actor when given the right material, as in *Nightmare Alley* (1947) and *Witness for the Prosecution* (1957). Power died in his forties of a heart attack.

FILMOGRAPHY
Lloyds of London 1937
In Old Chicago 1938
Alexander's Ragtime Band 1938
Rose of Washington Square 1939
Jesse James 1939
Johnny Apollo 1940
The Mark of Zorro 1940
Blood and Sand 1941
The Razor's Edge 1946
Nightmare Alley 1947
The Eddie Duchin Story 1956
The Sun Also Rises 1957
Witness for the Prosecution 1957

PRESLEY, Elvis 1935-1977

Elvis Presley's fans still call him th
King of Rock and Roll and his career i
different from that of practically an
other movie star. All of his films wer
predictable, tailor-made vehicle
which gave him a chance to sing
Though he sometimes had good co
stars, the scripts were mediocre o
worse. Critics hated Presley films an
most ordinary moviegoers avoide
them, but the films were not made fo
the ordinary moviegoer, they wer
made for Elvis Presley fans, and ther
were millions of them, enough to mak
Presley one of the top box-office draw
from the mid-1950s through the mid
1960s. After 1967 both the quality and
popularity of Presley films declined
and he appeared only in document
aries after 1969. However, his sudde
death spawned a large and loya
Presley cult, and his movies are now
popular on TV and in video cassettes

PRESTON, Robert 1917-1987

Changing his image to meet the chang
ing times did a lot for Rober
Preston, the vigorous actor who begar
in films in 1938. He brought vitality to
the wholesome *The Music Man* (1961)
and to the impudent *Victor, Victoria*
(1982). In early films he was often a
coward or villain.

FILMOGRAPHY
Beau Geste 1939
This Gun for Hire 1942
The Dark at the Top of the Stairs 1960
The Music Man 1961
All the Way Home 1963
SOB 1981
Victor, Victoria 1982

PRICE, Vincent 1911-

He progressed from playing a fop, a
cad and a villain to playing a full-scale
monster and becoming the king of
horror films in the 1950s and 1960s.
Price was born in St Louis, Missouri
and educated as an art history major at
Yale, but he got his start in acting on
the London stage. His stage appear
ances led to a Hollywood contract. He
first appeared in costume dramas and
some notable films like *Laura* (1944),
but he hit his stride in the enormously

FILMOGRAPHY

Love Me Tender 1956	**Kid Galahad** 1962
Loving You 1956	**Roustabout** 1964
Jailhouse Rock 1957	**Girl Happy** 1965
King Creole 1958	**Frankie and Johnny** 1966
GI Blues 1960	**Double Trouble** 1967
Blue Hawaii 1961	**Stay Away, Joe** 1968
Wild in the Country 1961	**Change of Habit** 1969
	Elvis on Tour 1970

opular horror film *House of Wax* (1953) and in a series of films based on Edgar Allen Poe stories made by director Roger Corman. Price generally adds a hammy and humorous touch to even his most horrific roles.

FILMOGRAPHY
The Tower of London 1939
The Invisible Man Returns 1940
The House of the Seven Gables 1940
The Song of Bernadette 1943
Laura 1944
Dragonwyck 1946
The Three Musketeers 1948
House of Wax 1953
The Fly 1958
The Fall of the House of Usher 1960
The Pit and the Pendulum 1961
The Raven 1963
The Masque of the Red Death 1964
The Tomb of Ligeia 1964
Witchfinder General 1968
The Abominable Dr Phibes 1971
Theatre of Blood 1973
Romance in the Jugular Vein 1980

Opposite: Elvis Presley in *Charro!* (1969).
Below: Vincent Price as Prince Prospero in *The Masque of the Red Death* (1964).

PRYOR, Richard 1940-

Richard Pryor, an undeniable comic genius and potentially a fine actor, has appeared on the screen mostly in minor roles or weak vehicles. Only in films of his stage performances such as *Richard Pryor – Live in Concert* (1979) has he been able to display the full force of his extraordinary talent. A deal which gives him control of his own films may herald a better future.

FILMOGRAPHY
Wild in the Streets 1968
The Phynx 1970
Lady Sings the Blues 1971
Some Call It Loving 1973
Uptown Saturday Night 1974
The Bingo Long Traveling All-Stars and Motor Kings 1976
Silver Streak 1976
Richard Pryor – Live in Concert 1979
Stir Crazy 1980
Bustin' Loose 1981
Richard Pryor Live on the Sunset Strip 1982
Superman III 1983
Critical Condition 1987

Above: Anthony Quinn in *Flap* (1970).

QUINN, Anthony 1915-

The forceful but engaging Anthony Quinn, born in Chihuahua, Mexico to Irish and Mexican parents, is an international superstar who grew up in America and began appearing in films during the 1930s. Despite his marriage to Kathrine DeMille, the daughter of director-producer Cecil B de Mille, he made it big on his own after years of playing bit and supporting roles as tough guys or American Indians.

Success on Broadway gave his career a boost, as did winning Academy Awards for Best Supporting Actor for *Viva Zapata* (1952) and *Lust for Life* (1956). After that he played virile leads and is especially famous for *Zorba the Greek* (1964).

FILMOGRAPHY
Blood and Sand 1941
The Ox-Bow Incident 1943
The Brave Bulls 1951
Viva Zapata 1952
La Strada 1954
Lust for Life 1956
Requiem for a Heavyweight 1963
Zorba the Greek 1964
The Shoes of the Fisherman 1968
The Destructors 1974
Valentina 1983

RAFT, George 1895-1980

George Raft had been a prizefighter and a gigolo and he was reputed to be the world's fastest Charleston dancer. Raft never denied his close associations with mobsters and that was the part he always played best. He came to Hollywood in the 1920s and was briefly heralded as a second Valentino, but it was his role as the coin-flipping gangster Guido Rinaldo in *Scarface* (1932) that made him a major star and he remained one for over a decade.

Fights with the studios, a remarkably poor choice of scripts and his own limited acting talents threw his career into permanent decline. Raft was, however, instrumental in creating two screen legends. In 1932 he invited an old girlfriend from vaudeville days, Mae West, to appear with him in *Night After Night*. He later turned down *Casablanca* (1942), *The Maltese Falcon* (1941), *Dead End* (1937) and *High Sierra* (1941), all of which were eagerly snapped up by Bogart.

Below left: George Raft, Dietrich in *Manpower* (1941).
Below: Claude Rains in *Here Comes Mr Jordan* (1941).

RAINS, Claude 1889-1967

Though his face appeared only briefly Claude Rains had the title role in his first film, *The Invisible Man* (1933) and Rains' stage-trained voice dominated the production. He had been in the British theater from age 11. Often appearing in villainous or cynical parts he became one of Hollywood's best character actors.

FILMOGRAPHY
Queen of the Night Clubs 1929
Scarface 1932
Night After Night 1932
The Eagle and the Hawk 1933
Bolero 1934
The Glass Key 1935
Souls at Sea 1937
Spawn of the North 1938
The Lady from Kentucky 1939
Background to Danger 1943
Rogue Cop 1954
Black Widow 1954
Some Like it Hot 1959
Hammersmith is Out 1972
The Man With Bogart's Face 1980

FILMOGRAPHY
The Invisible Man 1933
The Mystery of Edwin Drood 1935
Anthony Adverse 1936
The Adventures of Robin Hood 1938
Mr Smith Goes to Washington 1939
Casablanca 1942
Caesar and Cleopatra 1945
Lawrence of Arabia 1962

Aldo Ray – a voice like a fog horn characterized this beefy leading man who specialized in playing brawny but lovable tough guys. Casting agents spotted him when he ran for sheriff in a California town. He was at his best in *The Naked and the Dead* (1958).

FILMOGRAPHY
The Marrying Kind 1951
Pat and Mike 1952
We're No Angels 1955
The Naked and the Dead 1958
Johnny Nobody 1961
The Bad Bunch 1976
Human Experiments 1980

Above: Basil Rathbone as Sherlock Holmes.
Above right: Ronald Reagan played a soldier in *This Is the Army* (1943).

RATHBONE, Basil 1892-1967

Basil Rathbone will probably be best remembered as Sherlock Holmes in a series of films made during the 1940s based on the Conan Doyle stories and frequently reshown on television. But in most of his films he played a villain, everything from Pontius Pilate to Nazis, and he was usually superb.

Rathbone was born in South Africa and educated in England. He began appearing on the stage in Shakespearian roles in 1913, often taking such parts as Iago and Cassius – the sharp featured actor did indeed have a lean and hungry look. After service in World War I he began making films in England, and in the mid-1920s went to Hollywood where his career did not prosper at first. It was an American film, *David Copperfield* (1935), where he played an absolutely loathsome Mr Murdstone, that set him up for a long series of wonderful roles as the heavy, though he wasn't quite a villain in one of his most famous films, *Son of Frankenstein* (1939). He played the overcurious, but basically decent son of the original monster maker. Rathbone frequently returned to the stage, but by the end of his career the quality of his films had deteriorated badly.

FILMOGRAPHY
The Last of Mrs Cheyney 1929
Captain Blood 1935
David Copperfield 1935
Anna Karenina 1935
The Garden of Allah 1936
The Adventures of Robin Hood 1938
The Adventures of Marco Polo 1938
Son of Frankenstein 1939
Tower of London 1939
The Hound of the Baskervilles 1939
The Adventures of Sherlock Holmes 1940
The Mark of Zorro 1940
Sherlock Holmes and the Spider Woman 1944
The Scarlet Claw 1945
We're No Angels 1955
The Last Hurrah 1958
The Comedy of Terrors 1963
Hillbillies in a Haunted House 1968

REAGAN, Ronald 1911-

Starting as a sportscaster, Ronald Reagan went to Hollywood in the mid-1930s. He appeared, often as a romantic lead, in some 50 films, most of them unmemorable. Reagan's declining film career was revived by television. He served as president of the Screen Actors Guild and became increasingly involved in politics. In 1966 he was elected Governor of California and in 1980 President of the United States; he was re-elected in 1984.

FILMOGRAPHY
Love is on the Air 1937
Brother Rat 1938
Dark Victory 1939
Knute Rockne – All American 1940
King's Row 1941
Desperate Journey 1942
The Girl from Jones Beach 1949
The Hasty Heart 1950
Bedtime for Bonzo 1951
Law and Order 1953
Hellcats of the Navy 1957
The Killers 1964

REDFORD, Robert 1936-

Assuredly his striking blond good looks helped make Robert Redford a star but he has turned out to be far more than just another Hollywood sex object or conventional leading man. Redford is an actor of sensitivity and integrity.

Born Charles Redford in Santa Monica, California, he was a high-school athlete who attended the University of Colorado on a baseball scholarship. Along the way he decided he wanted to be an artist, so he dropped out of college and traveled through Europe. He returned to study art at Brooklyn, New York's Pratt Institute. When he continued to get nowhere as a painter he studied acting at the American Academy of Dramatic Arts.

Television followed as well as stage acting. It was in *Barefoot in the Park* on Broadway in 1963 that he scored his biggest success up to that time. Redford began appearing in movies as early as 1961. Oddly enough his looks were something of a handicap at first. He was in danger of being typecast as an attractive but bland executive type but he fought for a wide range of roles and won.

The film *Butch Cassidy and the Sundance Kid* (1969) made Redford a blockbuster superstar. He and Paul Newman were fantastic together and they never looked better. They were great again in the charming movie *The Sting* (1973). Women fell in love with Redford in droves and by 1974 he was the number-one box-office star in America. He more than held his own against Barbra Streisand in *The Way We Were* (1973), a fine romantic film. Redford, a strong athlete off screen, and an agile performer of stunts on, proved popular with men, too, especially in adventure films.

In private life Redford is a serious conservationist who owns a huge tract of land in Utah. An active supporter of liberal causes, he produced and starred in *All the President's Men* (1976), about the Watergate Investigation. Redford is not a compulsive performer and after staying away from the screen since *Brubaker* (1979), pundits wondered whether he still had the golden touch. *The Natural* (1984), was a major success, proving that Redford still has that special charisma.

Opposite: Robert Redford in *The Candidate* (1972).
Bottom: Redford as *The Natural* (1984).
Below: Redford, Paul Newman, Katharine Ross in *Butch Cassidy and the Sundance Kid* (1969).

FILMOGRAPHY
Inside Daisy Clover 1965
The Chase 1966
Barefoot in the Park 1967
Tell Them Willie Boy is Here 1969
Butch Cassidy and the Sundance Kid 1969
Downhill Racer 1969
Little Fauss and Big Halsy 1970
Jeremiah Johnson 1972
The Candidate 1972
The Way We Were 1973
The Sting 1973
The Great Waldo Pepper 1975
Three Days of the Condor 1975
All the President's Men 1976
The Electric Horseman 1979
Brubaker 1979
The Natural 1984
Out of Africa 1985

abc

Mc Kay
the better way

REDGRAVE, Lynn 1943-

The London-born daughter of actor Sir Michael Redgrave and sister of actress Vanessa Redgrave, Lynn Redgrave is especially good at comedy. She was plump and touching in *Georgy Girl* (1966), her most famous film. She has continued on stage and in movies and has appeared often on television.

FILMOGRAPHY
Tom Jones 1963
Georgy Girl 1966
The Deadly Affair 1967
Blood Kin 1969
Every Little Crook and Nanny 1972
The National Health 1973
The Happy Hooker 1975
The Big Bus 1976

REDGRAVE, Sir Michael 1908-1985

Sir Michael Redgrave was an eminent British actor, director, producer and playwright who was knighted for services to the theater in 1959. Born in Bristol, England, and educated at Cambridge, he was a journalist and teacher before becoming an actor.

Versatility and intelligence marked Redgrave as a consummate performer early on – witness his performance in *The Lady Vanishes* (1938). He was a man who preferred challenging roles. Redgrave had a distinguished stage and screen career and was the father of actresses Vanessa and Lynn Redgrave.

FILMOGRAPHY
The Lady Vanishes 1938
The Stars Look Down 1939
Kipps 1941
Thunder Rock 1942
The Way to the Stars 1945
Dead of Night 1945
Fame is the Spur 1947
Mourning Becomes Electra 1947
The Browning Version 1950
The Importance of Being Ernest 1952
The Quiet American 1958
The Loneliness of the Long Distance Runner 1963
The Go-Between 1971

REDGRAVE, Vanessa 1937-

A powerful and celebrated British actress, Vanessa Redgrave is the daughter of actor Sir Michael Redgrave. She is also a colorful and controversi presence off-screen, known for h support of left-wing causes.

Redgrave attended London's Centr School of Music and Drama. A sti with the Royal Shakespeare Compar enhanced her budding reputation the theater and with movies lik *Morgan* (1966) and *Blow Up* (1966) her credit, she became an importa film actress. *Julia* (1977) won her a Academy Award for Best Supportir Actress.

FILMOGRAPHY
Morgan 1966
Blow Up 1966
Camelot 1967
The Charge of the Light Brigade 1968
Isadora 1968
The Seagull 1969
The Trojan Women 1971
Mary Queen of Scots 1972
Murder on the Orient Express 1974
The Seven Per Cent Solution 1976
Julia 1977
Agatha 1979
Yanks 1979
The Bostonians 1984
Wetherby 1985

Vanessa Redgrave with Sean Connery in *Murder on the Orient Express* (1974).

Christopher Reeve as *Superman* (1978).

REED, Oliver 1938-

Burly and scowling, Oliver Reed makes a super villain but he is a good actor in general. The nephew of director Sir Carol Reed, he was born in England, dropped out of school in his teens and worked as a bouncer, a boxer and cab driver.

In 1961 Reed began playing bit roles in British films and landed a lead in a Hammer Studios horror movie, *The Curse of the Werewolf* (1962). Stardom came when he played the vicious Bill Sikes in the movie musical *Oliver!* (1968). Reed comes across as forcefully masculine on screen.

FILMOGRAPHY
The Curse of the Werewolf 1962
The Damned 1962
Paranoic 1963
The System 1964
The Trap 1966
The Shuttered Room 1966
The Jokers 1966
Oliver! 1968
Women in Love 1969
The Devils 1971
Sitting Target 1972
The Three Musketeers 1973
The Four Musketeers 1974
Burnt Offerings 1976
The Brood 1979
The Sting II 1983

Oliver Reed – *The Three Musketeers* (1973).

REEVE, Christopher, 1952-

Superman (1978) made a star of Christopher Reeve the handsome, charming, and gifted actor. Born in New York City, he studied acting under John Houseman, struggling to survive until his screen success. Despite a promising career as a movie star, Reeve's basic love is the stage and, though good in light comedy and romance, he has been anxious to try a wide variety of parts.

FILMOGRAPHY
Superman 1978
Somewhere in Time 1980
Superman II 1980
Deathtrap 1982
Superman III 1983
The Bostonians 1984
The Aviator 1984

REMICK, Lee 1935-

Lee Remick acted and danced on stage and television before making her film debut in *A Face in the Crowd* (1957). Flirtatious and pretty in her early movies, she matured into an actress of depth and skill. She played Jennie Jerome, the mother of Winston Churchill, in the 1975 television production *Jennie.*

FILMOGRAPHY
A Face in the Crowd 1957
The Long Hot Summer 1958
Anatomy of a Murder 1959
Days of Wine and Roses 1963
The Europeans 1979
The Competition 1980

RENNIE, Michael 1909-1971

Tall, thin, almost gaunt, Michael Rennie began as an extra in British films and moved on to substantial roles in Hollywood films particularly during the 1950s. He also gained popularity as the hero of the TV series 'The Third Man.'

FILMOGRAPHY
Secret Agent 1936
Dangerous Moonlight 1940
The Wicked Lady 1945
The Black Rose 1950
Five Fingers 1952
Les Misérables 1952
The Day the Earth Stood Still 1952
The Robe 1953
Desiree 1954
The Rains of Ranchipur 1955
The Lost World 1960
The Devil's Brigade 1968
The Battle of El Alamein 1968

Opposite: Burt Reynolds in *Hustle* (1975).
Below: Reynolds in trouble in *Paternity* (1981).

REYNOLDS, Burt 1936-

Burt Reynolds – a good sense of humor and easy-going charm are two reasons why this handsome star is so popular. Reynolds made it to the top the modern way via television and mass-media publicity. Alas, critics rarely take him seriously, which is a shame because he is talented. He has shown wit and sparkle in several light comedies.

Reynolds was born in Waycross, Georgia. His paternal grandmother was a Cherokee Indian and later Reynolds was frequently cast as an Indian on television. He grew up in Palm Beach, Florida, the son of the town's police chief and was a wild kid who ran away from home at 14, but returned and won a football scholarship to Florida State University. A knee injury and an auto accident put an end to his promising athletic career and he shifted to acting, moving to New York. Despite the move, Reynolds remained deeply attached to the South.

Things did not go easily for Reynolds at first but eventually he appeared in television's *Riverboat* and *Gunsmoke*.

He broke into films as a stuntman. Appearances on television talk shows where he proved an amusing guest, a much publicized romance with singer Dinah Shore and the fuss raised over his becoming the first nude male centerfold in the April 1972 issue of *Cosmopolitan* magazine brought the fans in to see his movies. *Deliverance* (1972), a terrifying but excellent film gave him superstar status.

One of Hollywood's foremost male sex symbols, Reynolds fascinated gossip columnists. In 1963, before he became famous, he married television's *Laugh-In* 'sock-it-to-me' comedienne British actress Judy Carne. Later his name was linked with tennis champion Chris Evert and actress Sally Field.

Though *Smokey and the Bandit* (1977) and *The Cannonball Run* (1981) made huge sums of money, Reynolds was at his best in the exciting *The Longest Yard* (1974), the off-beat *The End* (1978) and opposite Goldie Hawn in *Best Friends* (1982). It would be interesting to see what Reynolds could do with a demanding dramatic role which called upon him to be more versatile.

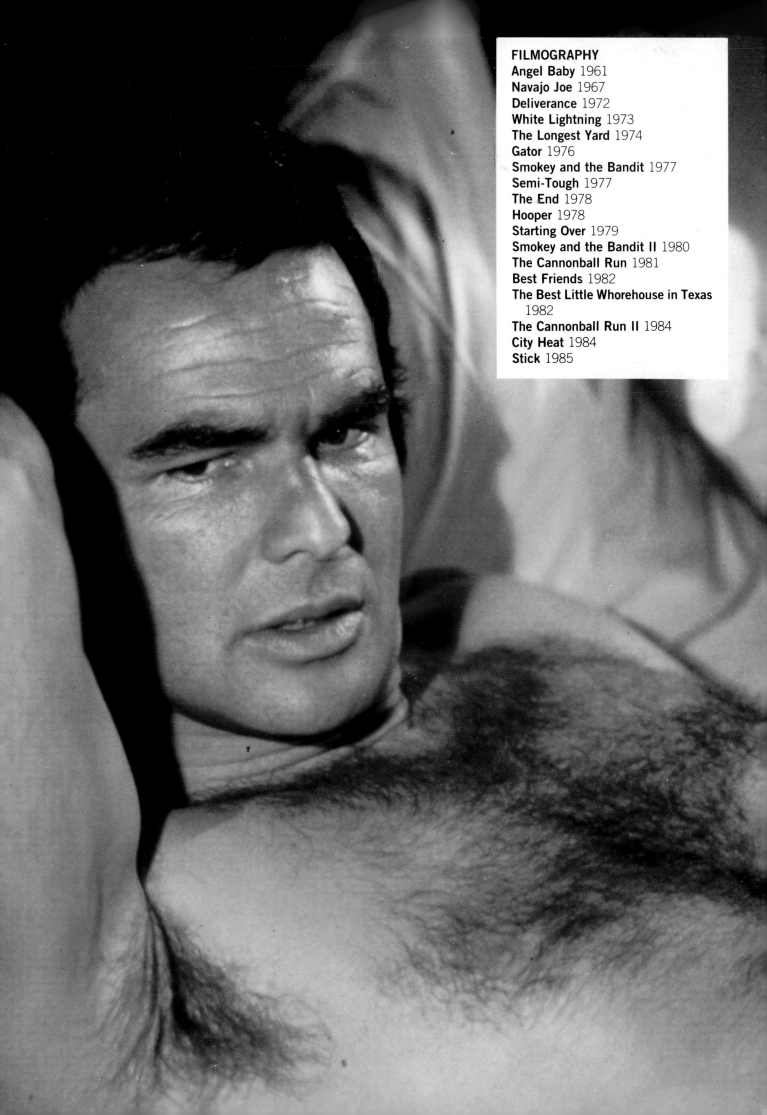

FILMOGRAPHY
Angel Baby 1961
Navajo Joe 1967
Deliverance 1972
White Lightning 1973
The Longest Yard 1974
Gator 1976
Smokey and the Bandit 1977
Semi-Tough 1977
The End 1978
Hooper 1978
Starting Over 1979
Smokey and the Bandit II 1980
The Cannonball Run 1981
Best Friends 1982
The Best Little Whorehouse in Texas
   1982
The Cannonball Run II 1984
City Heat 1984
Stick 1985

REYNOLDS, Debbie 1932-

Debbie Reynolds was a cute perky little teenager when she entered films and she became a popular star of musicals and light comedies, the image of the wholesome girl-next-door. Fans sided with her when husband, singer Eddie Fisher, left her for Elizabeth Taylor in 1959.

FILMOGRAPHY
Singin' In the Rain 1952
Susan Slept Here 1954
Hit the Deck 1955
The Tender Trap 1955
Tammy and the Bachelor 1957
The Unsinkable Molly Brown 1964
What's the Matter with Helen? 1971

Above: Donald O'Connor, Debbie Reynolds, Gene Kelly in *Singin' in the Rain* (1952).
Below: Sir Ralph Richardson as a barrister in *Witness for the Prosecution*.

RICHARDSON, Sir Ralph 1902-1984

Sir Ralph Richardson was one of Britain's great actors, admired around the world. He appeared in movies chiefly in character roles partly because he lacked his colleague Laurence Olivier's good looks, a prime requisite for a romantic lead. Especially good on screen playing basically ordinary well-bred types or intellectuals, he projected integrity, blunt intelligence and an underlying vulnerability. His characterizations were always unique, often eccentric and usually memorable. Theater was his true love, not film, and it was on stage that he was most brilliant.

Born in Cheltenham, Gloucester, Richardson began working as an office boy in an insurance company. A small legacy freed him to study acting. He toured for a while, then joined the Birmingham Rep and went to the Old Vic in 1930. He was to return to it several times, becoming one of its mainstays, playing many important Shakespearean roles, including Petruchio, Henry V, Iago, Brutus and Sir Toby Belch. He also appeared frequently on Broadway.

Richardson made his debut in films in 1933. He was a villain in *Bulldog Jack* (1934) and delightful in *The Man Who Could Work Miracles* (1936). Some think his finest screen role was the squire in *South Riding* (1938). He had smaller parts than Laurence Olivier in *The Divorce of Lady X* (1938) or than Robert Donat in *The Citadel* (1938), but he was a match for them.

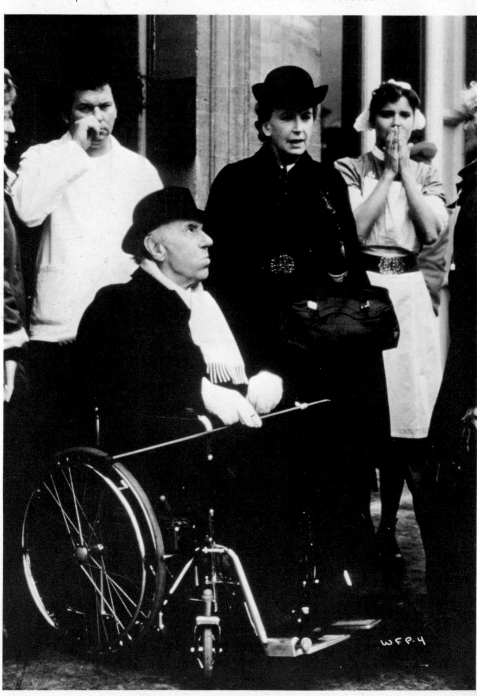

Richardson (*center*) in *Our Man in Havana* (1959). Noel Coward is at right.

FILMOGRAPHY

The Ghoul 1933
The Return of Bulldog Drummond 1934
Bulldog Jack 1934
The Man Who Could Work Miracles 1936
South Riding 1938
The Divorce of Lady X 1938
The Citadel 1938
Q Planes 1939
The Four Feathers 1939
The Silver Fleet 1943
Anna Karenina 1948
The Fallen Idol 1948
The Heiress 1949
Outcast of the Islands 1951
Breaking the Sound Barrier 1952
Richard III 1956
Our Man in Havana 1959
Oscar Wilde 1960
Long Day's Journey into Night 1962
Woman of Straw 1964
Doctor Zhivago 1965
The Wrong Box 1966
Khartoum 1967
Lady Caroline Lamb 1972
A Doll's House 1973
O Lucky Man 1973
Charlie Muffin 1979
Dragonslayer 1981
Time Bandits 1981

During the 1940s he married actress Meriel Forbes and was knighted in 1947. His dedication to the stage at this point made it difficult for him to accept film roles, but he made *Anna Karenina* (1948) with Vivien Leigh and was so good in Graham Greene's *The Fallen Idol* (1948) that Greene considered his performance the finest interpretation of any of his characters ever.

The Heiress (1949) brought Richardson an Academy Award nomination and *Breaking the Sound Barrier* (1952) won him the British Film Academy's Best British Actor Award. He was outstanding in many later films, but along with the gems were mediocre movies, always enriched by his presence. Meanwhile he was busy giving his all to the theater.

RITTER, Tex 1905-1974

Born Woodward Maurice Ritter, Tex Ritter was popular both as a Western singer and recording artist and star of innumerable Western features. He was often labeled 'America's Most Beloved Cowboy' and may be best remembered for singing the title song in the Gary Cooper classic *High Noon*.

FILMOGRAPHY

Song of the Gringo 1936
Sing Cowboy Sing 1937
Rainbow Over the Range 1940
Deep in the Heart of Texas 1942
The Old Chisholm Trail 1942
Marshal of Gunsmoke 1944
The Girl From Tobacco Row 1966

ROBARDS, Jason Jr 1920-

Jason Robards, Jr, the son of acto Jason Robards, first gained attention for his performances in the plays o Eugene O'Neill. Television and movi stardom followed. He won Academy Awards for Best Supporting Actor fo *All the President's Men* (1976) and *Julia* (1977). His third wife was the legendary Lauren Bacall.

FILMOGRAPHY
Tender is the Night 1961
Long Day's Journey into Night 1962
The Hour of the gun 1967
Isadora 1968
All the President's Men 1976
Julia 1977
Comes A Horseman 1978
Melvin and Howard 1979
Max Dugan Returns 1983

ROBINSON, Edward G 1893-1973

Edward G Robinson was the quintes sential tough guy actor. To this day there is a bit of Robinson in many gangster characterizations in films and on television. But he was skillful in other roles as well.

Born Emmanuel Goldenberg in Bucharest, Rumania, he came to America at age 10. After years on Broadway he went to Hollywood making it big with *Little Caesar* (1930).

Attacks by the House Un-American Activities Committee during the 1950s led to career problems and financia difficulties. Family and personal prob lems plagued him as well but he con tinued to act and received a special Academy Award posthumously.

FILMOGRAPHY
Little Caesar 1930
Five Star Final 1931
The Whole Town's Talking 1934
Kid Galahad 1937
Dr Ehrlich's Magic Bullet 1940
Double Indemnity 1944
The Woman in the Window 1944
Scarlet Street 1945
Key Largo 1948
House of Strangers 1949
A Bullet for Joey 1955
Two Weeks in Another Town 1962
The Cincinnati Kid 1965
Soylent Green 1973

Left: Edward G Robinson as Enrico Bandello – *Little Caesar* (1930).

Dame Flora Robson, a great British character actress of stage and screen, graduated from the Royal Academy of Dramatic Art as a Bronze Medallist. She debuted on stage in the 1920s and on screen in the 1930s. Many of her performances are memorable and she was created Dame of the British Empire in 1960.

FILMOGRAPHY
Fire Over England 1936
Wuthering Heights 1939
Saratoga Trunk 1943
Caesar and Cleopatra 1945
Black Narcissus 1946
Innocent Sinners 1957
Murder at the Gallop 1963
Seven Women 1965
Dominique 1978

ROGERS, Ginger 1911-

Ginger Rogers, sassy and sexy with a tart tongue, was a clever wisecracking comedienne who longed for dramatic roles but who was swept into movie immortality in the arms of Fred Astaire instead. The movies they danced in during the 1930s are the best musicals Hollywood ever made.

She was born Virginia McRath in Independence, Missouri. Her divorced mother, for a time a Hollywood script writer, was ambitious and she groomed her daughter early for a show business career. It began in Fort Worth, Texas, when Rogers, aged 14, debuted professionally with Eddie Foy's vaudeville troop. A year later she won a Charleston contest and sang and danced on the vaudeville circuit. In 1928 with first husband Jack Pepper she was half of the team, 'Ginger and Pepper.' Later she sang with a band, appeared in film shorts and found some success in Broadway musicals.

She was a bright addition to movie musicals like *Gold Diggers of 1933* (1933) and *Forty-Second Street* (1933). Even in such early films Rogers projected toughness, calculating shrewdness and self-sufficiency with engaging charm. There was no top billing for her or Fred Astaire in *Flying Down to Rio* (1933), but she provided the common touch to his elegance and they stole the picture dancing 'The Carioca.' From

Right: Ginger Rogers as a young chorus girl in *Gold Diggers of 1933* (1933).

then on they were top box-office stars. Rogers made other films on her own during her years with Astaire and afterwards tackled a variety of roles, winning an Academy Award for Best Actress for *Kitty Foyle* (1940). She was delicious posing as a child in *The Major and the Minor* (1943).

Though Rogers continued in films through the 1950s and even into the 1960s, she devoted more and more of her time to the stage, pulling in crowds after taking over the lead in *Hello Dolly* on Broadway and *Mame* in London. She was married several times, and her second husband was actor Lew Ayres. When Rogers is not acting she's hard at work in Republican Party politics.

Left: Rogers in *Lady in the Dark* (1943).
Below: Ginger and Fred – *Top Hat* (1935).

ROGERS, Roy 1912-

Roy Rogers succeeded Gene Autry as 'King of the Cowboys,' particularly the singing cowboys. Born Leonard Slye, he formed a singing group 'Sons of the Pioneers' under the name Dick Weston. Often teamed with sidekick George 'Gabby' Hayes and his wife Dale Evans and riding his horse Trigger, he made a series of mild but popular Westerns during the 1940s and early 1950s. A shrewd businessman, he is estimated to be a millionaire many times over.

FILMOGRAPHY
Tumbling Tumbleweeds 1935
Under Western Skies 1938
Red River Valley 1941
Robin Hood of the Pecos 1942
The Man From Music Mountain 1944
Roll on, Texas Moon 1947
Son of Paleface 1952
Pals of the Golden West 1953
Mackintosh and TJ 1975

ROGERS, Will 1879-1935

Beginning as a trick rider and rope twirler in wild west shows, Will Rogers gradually introduced bits of humor and homespun philosophy into his act. Rogers moved on to vaudeville and films and the talkies were a great boost to his career. By the time of his death in an air crash he was regarded a spokesman for the common man and virtually a national hero.

FILMOGRAPHY
Laughing Bill Hyde 1918
Jubilo 1919
The Ropin' Fool 1922
Don't Park There 1924
The Cowboy Sheik 1924
They Had to See Paris 1929
Young as You Feel 1931
State Fair 1933
David Harum 1934
Handy Andy 1934
Judge Priest 1934
Life Begins at Forty 1935
Steamboat Round the Bend 1935

ROLAND, Gilbert 1905-

Gilbert Roland, born Luis Antonio Damaso de Alonso in Mexico, first trained as a bullfighter (his father's pro-

Roy Rogers, the 'King of the Cowboys,' with his horse Trigger.

fession). He often starred as a dashing 'Latin lover' in silent films and matured into a durable character actor in a huge number of Hollywood and international films.

FILMOGRAPHY
The Plastic Age 1925
Camille 1927
Men of the North 1929
She Done Him Wrong 1933
Last Train from Madrid 1937
Juarez 1939
The Sea Hawk 1940
Captain Kidd 1945
We Were Strangers 1949
The Bullfighter and the Lady 1951
Beyond the Twelve Mile Reef 1953
The Big Circus 1959
Islands in the Stream 1977
The Black Pearl 1977

ROMERO, Cesar 1907-

Cesar Romero was one of Hollywood's chief 'Latin lovers' of the 1930s, 1940s and 1950s, later moving to character parts. Romero played the Cisco Kid in early instalments of that film series and on TV he was The Joker in the popular 'Batman' series.

FILMOGRAPHY
The Shadow Laughs 1933
The Thin Man 1934
The Devil Is a Woman 1935
Wee Willie Winkie 1937
Ride on, Vaquero 1942
Springtime in the Rockies 1942
Captain from Castile 1948
Vera Cruz 1954
Marriage on the Rocks 1965
Batman 1966
Madigan's Millions 1968
The Spectre of Edgar Allen Poe 1973

ROONEY, Mickey 1920-

Known for his small size, his energy and versatility, his numerous marriages to tall women, and his ability to bounce back from adversity, Mickey Rooney (born Joe Yule, Jr into a vaudeville family) made his film debut at age six.

A year later he appeared in the 'Mickey McGuire' film series, legally adopting the name of the series character, and later becoming Mickey Rooney in 1932. Popular in the 'Andy Hardy' movie series and the musicals he made with Judy Garland, he shared a special juvenile Academy Award with Deanna Durbin in 1938. His adult credits include a stint on Broadway in *Sugar Babies*. In 1983 Rooney was given another special Academy Award.

FILMOGRAPHY
A Midsummer Night's Dream 1935
Ah Wilderness 1935
A Family Affair 1937
Boys' Town 1938
Babes in Arms 1939
Strike Up the Band 1940
Babes on Broadway 1941
The Human Comedy 1943
National Velvet 1944
The Bold and the Brave 1956
Requiem for a Heavyweight 1962
The Black Stallion 1979

RUGGLES, Charles 1886-1970

Charles Ruggles, a character actor and brother of actor and director Wesley Ruggles, was frequently cast as a henpecked husband opposite Mary Boland. Audiences loved Ruggles's wistful timidity and he was in numerous stage productions and nearly 100 films.

FILMOGRAPHY
Charley's Aunt 1930
Trouble in Paradise 1932
Ruggles of Red Gap 1935
Bringing Up Baby 1938
A Stolen Life 1946
The Pleasure of His Company 1961
The Ugly Dachshund 1966

Below: Mickey Rooney and Judy Garland – *Strike Up the Band* (1940).

Left: Rooney and June Preisser in *Judge Hardy & Son* (1939) – one of the films in the seemingly endless Andy Hardy series.

Left: The glamorous Jane Russell – *Gentlemen Prefer Blondes* (1953).

RUSSELL, Rosalind 1908-1976

Rosalind Russell – wit, elegance, and class were her strong points. She was terrific playing bold independent working women who tossed quips at the men in their lives. But she was never too tough to be a lady and there was no hard edge to the romance in her films.

Born into a wealthy family in Waterbury, Connecticut (her father a lawyer, her mother a fashion editor), Russell made her stage debut in the 1920s, her film debut in 1934. She received the Jean Hersholt Award for her charitable works but, despite four nominations, she never won the Oscar her strong performances deserved.

FILMOGRAPHY
Evelyn Prentice 1934
China Seas 1935
Craig's Wife 1936
Night Must Fall 1937
The Citadel 1938
The Women 1939
His Girl Friday 1940
Design for Scandal 1941
My Sister Eileen 1942
Sister Kenny 1946
Mourning Becomes Electra 1948
Picnic 1956
Auntie Mame 1958
Gypsy 1962
The Unexpected Mrs Pollifax 1970
Below: Rosalind Russell (*center*), with Natalie Wood and Karl Malden in *Gypsy* (1962).

RUSSELL, Jane 1921-

A striking brunette, Jane Russell set the trend for bosomy sex symbols when Howard Hughes cast her in the then notorious *The Outlaw* (1940). But she proved she was more than a passing fad when she co-starred in comedies with Bob Hope and went on to Broadway and commercials.

FILMOGRAPHY
The Outlaw 1940
The Paleface 1948
Son of Paleface 1952
Gentlemen Prefer Blondes 1953
The Tall Men 1956
Waco 1966
Darker than Amber 1970

RUTHERFORD, Dame Margaret 1892-1972

Dame Margaret Rutherford was wonderful playing eccentric characters. A British actress of stage and film she specialized in dotty spinsters like the medium in *Blithe Spirit* (1945). Rutherford won an Academy Award for Best Supporting Actress for *The VIPs* (1963). She was married to actor Stringer Davis.

FILMOGRAPHY
The Demi Paradise 1943
Blithe Spirit 1945
Miranda 1947
The Happiest Days Of Your Life 1950
The Importance of Being Earnest 1952
Murder She Said 1962
Murder at the Gallop 1963
The VIPs 1963
Arabella 1968

RYAN, Robert 1909-1973

A fine versatile leading man and character actor, Robert Ryan was a college athlete who tried boxing and modeling before becoming an actor. Consistently good in films of all kinds and a success on stage, the modest and low-key Ryan never became as famous as less talented but flashier stars.

FILMOGRAPHY
Gangway for Tomorrow 1943
Crossfire 1947
The Set-Up 1949
The Racket 1951
Clash By Night 1952
Bad Day at Black Rock 1955
God's Little Acre 1958
Odds Against Tomorrow 1959
Billy Budd 1962
The Outfit 1974

215

SANDERS, George 1906-1972

Before ending his life with an overdose of sleeping pills, George Sanders wrote a note mentioning boredom as the main reason for his suicide. It seemed perfectly in keeping with the cynical, world-weary character he had played so often on the screen.

Sanders was born of British parents in St Petersburg, Russia. The family returned to England during the Russian Revolution. He first tried business, but became an actor in the early 1930s. Sanders went to Hollywood in 1936, and made most of his films in America. Though he usually played a villain or cad, he also starred as the hero of 'The Saint' and 'The Falcon' series. When given a meaty part, such as that of the cynical critic in *All About Eve* (1950), Sanders could excel. That role won him an Academy Award for Best Supporting Actor.

FILMOGRAPHY
Dishonor Bright 1936
Lloyds of London 1937
The Saint Strikes Back 1939
Rebecca 1940
Foreign Correspondent 1940
The Gay Falcon 1941
The Moon and Sixpence 1942
The Black Swan 1942
The Ghost and Mrs Muir 1947
All About Eve 1950
Ivanhoe 1952
Call Me Madame 1953
That Certain Feeling 1956
Village of the Damned 1950
Psychomania 1972

SAVALAS, Telly 1924-

Telly Savalas was born Aristotle Savalis on Long Island, New York. He had a modest film career primarily playing heavies from Genghis Khan to Al Capone. It was as the shaven-headed detective Kojak in the popular TV series of that name that he became a real star. Savalas has been unable to turn his TV fame into major big-screen success.

FILMOGRAPHY
The Young Savages 1961
Cape Fear 1962
Birdman of Alcatraz 1962
The Man From the Diners Club 1963
Battle of the Bulge 1965
The Greatest Story Ever Told 1965
Beau Geste 1966
The Dirty Dozen 1967
On Her Majesty's Secret Service 1969
Kelly's Heroes 1970
Killer Force 1975

Below right: George C Scott in *The Hustler* (1961).
Below: George Sanders, Gene Tierney in *The Ghost and Mrs Muir* (1947).

SCHEIDER, Roy 1934-

Some actors always give solid performances but don't project star quality even when they're leading men, and this is the case with Roy Scheider. Thin and ordinary-looking, his large nose the result of being broken when he was a Golden Gloves boxer in high school, he has been an important addition to several Oscar nominated films and has a lot more to offer than many better looking and more colorful actors.

Born in Orange, New Jersey, he made his professional stage debut in 1961 as Mercutio in the New York Shakespeare Festival production of *Romeo and Juliet*. He continued to appear in classic roles on stage, debuted in films in the mid-1960s and during the 1970s became a major movie lead and character actor.

Right: Roy Scheider in *All That Jazz* (1979).

FILMOGRAPHY
Klute 1971
The French Connection 1972
Jaws 1975
Marathon Man 1976
Jaws 2 1979
All That Jazz 1979
Still of the Night 1982
Blue Thunder 1983
2010 1984

SCOTT, George C 1926-

Impressive and magnetic, George C Scott is a shrewd, aggressive actor and a cranky individualist off-screen. Born in Wise, Virginia, he was a Marine and an aspiring writer and teacher before he became an actor.

Off-Broadway, Broadway and television brought him acclaim. Despite great success in movies he is openly contemptuous of Hollywood and returns to the stage periodically. He refused to accept an Academy Award for Best Actor for *Patton* (1970), referring to the Academy Awards as 'a meaningless self-serving meat parade.' Formerly married to actress Colleen Dewhurst, his present wife is actress Trish Van Devere. He has also tried his hand at directing.

FILMOGRAPHY
Anatomy of a Murder 1959
The Hustler 1961
The List of Adrian Messenger 1963
Dr Strangelove 1963
The Bible 1966
Patton 1970
They Might be Giants 1971
The Hospital 1972
The New Centurions 1972
The Prince and the Pauper 1977
Islands in the Stream 1977
Movie Movie 1978
Hardcore 1979
The Changeling 1979
Taps 1982

Randolph Scott (*left*) as Hawkeye in *The Last of the Mohicans* (1936).

Selected for the title role in Otto Preminger's *Saint Joan* (1957), novice Jean Seberg did not become a Hollywood star despite massive publicity French films gave her career a boost. She was a tragic figure, and personal difficulties coupled with harassment by the FBI because of her left-wing activism are the reasons given for her suicide.

FILMOGRAPHY
Saint Joan 1957
The Mouse That Roared 1959
Breathless 1960
In the French Style 1963
Lilith 1964
Pendulum 1969
Airport 1970
The Wild Duck 1979

SEGAL, George 1934-

George Segal, a leading man and former jazz musician, received acclaim for his stage performances before appearing in films. Nominated for an Oscar for *Who's Afraid of Virginia Woolf?* (1966), he is a light comedian as well as a dramatic actor.

FILMOGRAPHY
King Rat 1965
Who's Afraid of Virginia Woolf? 1966
The Owl and the Pussycat 1970
Where's Poppa? 1973
Blume in Love 1973
A Touch of Class 1973
Fun with Dick and Jane 1977
Rollercoaster 1977
Who is Killing the Great Chefs of Europe? 1978
The Last Married Couple in America 1979
Carbon Copy 1981

Segal in *The St Valentine's Day Massacre* (1967).

SCOTT, Randolph 1898-1987

Tall and ruggedly handsome, Randolph Scott appeared in a huge number of 'B' Westerns, yet near the end of his career he made a surprising series of excellent low-budget westerns that indicated his potential as an actor was far greater than most people had realized.

Scott was born Randolph Crane in Virginia, and managed to lie his way into the army at the age of 14. He got into films accidentally after meeting eccentric producer and billionaire Howard Hughes on the golf course. Scott began his career in romantic comedies but soon switched almost exclusively to Westerns. He invested his money wisely and when he retired in the early 1960s he was reputedly one of the wealthiest men in Hollywood.

FILMOGRAPHY
The Far Call 1929
Hot Saturday 1932
The Lone Cowboy 1933
Murders in the Zoo 1933
Wagon Wheels 1934
She 1935
Roberta 1935
The Last of the Mohicans 1936
Rebecca of Sunnybrook Farm 1938
Western Union 1941
The Shores of Tripoli 1942
Home, Sweet Homicide 1946
Return of the Badman 1948
Sugarfoot 1951
Man in the Saddle 1951
Man Behind the Gun 1953
The Bounty Hunter 1954
Seven Men from Now 1956
The Tall T 1957
Ride Lonesome 1959
Comanche Station 1960
Ride the High Country 1962

eter Sellers, a masterful mimic, was a rilliantly original comic with an intinct for satire who often combined athos with humor, the mark of a great lown. He described himself as a man rithout personality, a vacuum waiting b be filled by a character. Whether true r not, the characters he created were xtraordinarily real and complete.

Born in Southsea, England, into a amily of music-hall performers, ellers began his acting career as a hild and at 17 joined the RAF where he vas a camp entertainer. Beginning in 1949 Sellers appeared on BBC radio on *The Goon Show*. He also did television and made short films. His first feature film, *Penny Points to Paradise* (1951), included fellow Goons Harry Secombe and Spike Milligan.

The Ladykillers (1955), starring Sellers's idol, Alec Guinness, gave Sellers's career a big boost. He played three characters in *The Mouse That Roared* (1959), which was especially popular in America. *I'm All Right, Jack* (1959) was a massive hit in Britain, winning Sellers the British Film Academy Best British Actor Award.

Sellers's wonderful interpretation of the bumbling but dignified detective, Inspector Clouseau, was first seen in *The Pink Panther* (1963), which launched a blockbuster series. When director Stanley Kubrick cast Sellers as the ex-Nazi scientist in *Dr Strangelove* (1963), Sellers made screen history. Sellers also played the president of the United States and an RAF officer in the movie. Kubrick wanted Sellers to play even more roles because nobody else could match his talent and versatility. Sellers had arrived as an international star.

His private life was different. Besides marrying four times, he was a compul-

Sellers (*left*) – *The Wrong Arm of the Law* (1963) with Bernard Cribbins.

sive worker who was barely slowed even by heart attacks, driven at fever pitch right to the moment of his untimely death.

Sellers's final film, *Being There* (1979), features one of his best performances, and the one of which he was most proud. It is comforting to remember this when one contemplates the patched-together butchered version of the Pink Panther series released after his death.

FILMOGRAPHY

Penny Points to Paradise 1951
The Ladykillers 1955
The Naked Truth 1958
The Mouse that Roared 1959
I'm All Right, Jack 1959
The Battle of the Sexes 1960
Two-Way Stretch 1960
Only Two Can Play 1962
Lolita 1962
The Wrong Arm of the Law 1963
The Pink Panther 1963
Dr Strangelove 1963
The World of Henry Orient 1964
What's New, Pussycat? 1966
I Love You Alice B Toklas 1968
The Return of the Pink Panther 1975
Murder by Death 1976
Being There 1979

Right: Peter Sellers in *Being There* (1979).
Below: Sellers, Niven – *The Pink Panther* (1963).

Sharif, Julie Christie – *Dr Zhivago* (1965).

SHARIF, Omar 1932-

orn Michael Shalhoub in Alexandria, gypt, Omar Sharif entered acting over e objections of his wealthy family. lis good looks and the influence of ome of his friends got him a lead pposite the popular Egyptian actress aten Hamama, whom he later married. The couple has since divorced.

Sharif made a large number of gyptian films, few of which were seen utside of the Arab world. He became n international star when he was hosen to play Sherif Ali Ibn El Kharish n the epic *Lawrence of Arabia* (1962).

US and European producers decided at Sharif looked 'foreign' but it didn't atter what nationality. He has played verything from a Spanish priest to the longol conqueror Genghis Khan. He as been a Nazi and a Jew; Prince udolph of Austria and Che Guevara.

His greatest success came in the title ole of *Doctor Zhivago* (1965), where he played a Russian and traded the sands of Arabia for the snows of the steppe.

Sharif has often expressed his boredom with acting, and insists that he far prefers bridge, at which he is an international champion.

FILMOGRAPHY
The Struggle for the Valley 1953
Goha 1957
The Agony of Love 1960
Lawrence of Arabia 1962
The Fall of the Roman Empire 1964
Behold a Pale Horse 1964
The Yellow Rolls Royce 1964
Genghis Khan 1965
Doctor Zhivago 1965
The Night of the Generals 1967
Funny Girl 1967
Mayerling 1968
Mackenna's Gold 1969
Che! 1969
The Tamarind Seed 1974
Bloodline 1979
Top Secret 1984

SHAW, Robert 1927-79

Robert Shaw, an actor, novelist, and playwright born in Westhoughton, England, appeared in movies from the 1950s. A character actor who was often a villain, Shaw, a vigorous expansive talent, suddenly blossomed into stardom in the 1970s. He was felled by a heart attack just as he was reaching his full stride.

FILMOGRAPHY
From Russia with Love 1963
The Luck of Ginger Coffey 1964
A Man For All Seasons 1966
The Sting 1973
The Taking of Pelham One-Two-Three 1974
Jaws 1975
Robin and Marian 1976
Black Sunday 1977
Force 10 From Navarone 1978

221

Norma Shearer.

SHEARER, Norma 1900-1983

MGM billed Norma Shearer as 'The First Lady of the Screen.' Her elegance and style won her a wide public following and critical praise. Born in Montreal, Canada, she trained for the theater from childhood.

Shearer got no farther than bit parts in films until she met and later married Irving Thalberg, vice-president and supervisor of production at MGM. From then on she had her pick of co-stars, directors and roles. Frequently nominated, Shearer won an Academy Award for *The Divorcee* (1930). When Thalberg died in 1936 her career declined in part because of poor script choices. She retired from movies in 1942 and married a young ski instructor.

SHERIDAN, Ann 1915-1967

Ann Sheridan – expressive eyes, warmth, sexiness, a sense of humor and down-to-earth charm made her a winner. Born in Denton, Texas, Sheridan planned to be a teacher and headed for Hollywood only because she won a beauty contest which offered a bit part in a movie as a prize.

She made her way up with the help of a publicity campaign billing her as the 'Oomph Girl.' Despite the sex-object image, she had real talent and was good in comedy, drama and even musicals, thanks to her contralto voice. Later she turned to television.

FILMOGRAPHY
Angels with Dirty Faces 1938
They Made Me a Criminal 1939
They Drive by Night 1940
King's Row 1941
The Man Who Came to Dinner 1941
Shine on Harvest Moon 1944
The Unfaithful 1947
I Was a Male War Bride 1949
Woman on the Run 1950
Come Next Spring 1956
Woman and the Hunter 1957

Right: Shields, Christopher Atkins – *The Blue Lagoon* (1980).
Below: Sheridan, Reagan, *King's Row* (1941).

SHIELDS, Brooke 1965-

Brooke Shields was a professional model before she was one year old, becoming the 'Ivory Snow Baby' and was featured in advertisements for many other popular products. She made her first film when she was 11 and two years later had a major role in the controversial film *Pretty Baby* (1978). At times her face seems to be everywhere, but as to whether Shields is an actress or just a very beautiful celebrity, the jury is still out.

FILMOGRAPHY
Alice Sweet Alice 1978
Pretty Baby 1978
King of the Gypsies 1978
Tilt 1979
Wanda Nevada 1979
Just You and Me, Kid 1979
The Blue Lagoon 1980
Endless Love 1981

SIGNORET, Simone 1921-1985

When she was young, Simone Signoret was the most gorgeous and sensual movie actress of her era. The combination of strength and vulnerability she projected was unique. She retained her star quality till the end of her life.

Born Simone Kaminker to French parents living in Wiesbaden, Germany, she was raised in Paris. During the German Occupation of France in World War II, Signoret's Jewish father escaped to London to join Charles De Gaulle's Free French. Signoret and her mother and brothers remained in France where Signoret was forced to quit school to support her family. She began working as a typist but became a film extra instead. She also joined a theater group.

Signoret married movie director Yves Allegret who cast her in her first leading role in *Les Démons de l'Aube* (1945). She played a prostitute in *Dédée d'Anvers* (1948), the movie which first brought her significant attention. She would often play prostitutes and lovesick women, ultimately

Simone Signoret with the British Film Academy's award for *Room at the Top* (1958).

FILMOGRAPHY
Les Démons de l'Aube 1945
Macadam 1945
Against the Wind 1947
Dédée d'Anvers 1948
Manèges 1949
La Ronde 1950
Casque d'Or 1952
Thérèse Racquin 1953
Les Diaboliques 1954
Les Sorcières de Salem 1957
Room at the Top 1958
Term of Trial 1962
The Day and the Hour 1963
Ship of Fools 1965
The Sleeping Car Murders 1965
The Deadly Affair 1967
The Seagull 1968
Le Chat 1972
Madame Rosa 1978

naturing into more complex and in-
eresting roles.

In 1951 Signoret, now divorced,
married singer and actor Yves
Montand. *La Ronde* (1950) made her
an international star and she won a
British Film Academy Best Foreign
Actress Award for *Casque d'Or* (1952).
She would win one again for *Les
Sorcières de Salem* (1957), the French
version of Arthur Miller's play *The
Crucible*, and a third for *Room at the
Top* (1958), which would bring her a
Cannes Film Festival Award and an
Academy Award for Best Actress as
well.

Les Diaboliques (1954), was not
only one of the best horror/suspense
films ever made, but it was one of the
first foreign language films to get wide
distribution in Britain and America.
Signoret was wonderful in it.

Signoret refused all offers to go to
Hollywood until *Ship of Fools* (1965),
which brought her an Oscar nomination. Unlike many actresses, she
allowed herself to gain weight and
grow older without a battle, switching
comfortably to character roles. Sometimes working for little or no fee to
promote worthwhile movies, she won
fresh acclaim again for *Le Chat* (1972),
with Jean Gabin, and *Madame Rosa*
(1978), which gained her a Cesar, the
French equivalent of an Oscar. Not that
she needed any more acclaim; Signoret had won all the laurels.

Below: Jean Simmons in *Desiree* (1954).

SIM, Alastair 1900-1976

Alastair Sim's face and voice were
utterly unique and he created an un-
matched gallery of eccentric and
usually hilarious characters. Sim was
born in Edinburgh and was a professor
of elocution before making his stage
debut at age 30. He is best remembered
for his role as Scrooge in the 1951
version of *A Christmas Carol*, revived
on television every Christmas, and in
the dual role of the dotty headmistress
and her bookie brother in *The Belles of
St Trinian's* (1954). He also appeared
frequently on the London stage in plays
which he produced or directed.

Below: Sim in *A Christmas Carol* (1951).

FILMOGRAPHY
Riverside Murder 1935
The Terror 1938
Alf's Button Afloat 1938
This Man is News 1938
Inspector Hornleigh 1939
Cottage to Let 1941
Let the People Sing 1942
Green For Danger 1946
London Belongs to Me 1948
The Happiest Days of Your Life 1949
Laughter In Paradise 1951
A Christmas Carol 1951
An Inspector Calls 1954
The Belles of St Trinian's 1954
Wee Georgie 1955
The Green Man 1956
Blue Murder at St Trinian's 1957
School for Scoundrels 1960
Royal Flash 1975

SIMMONS, Jean 1929-

Delicately beautiful, Jean Simmons
became a professional actress in her
early teens, blossoming into a leading
lady. British-born Simmons came to
Hollywood with her husband of the
time, Stewart Granger, appearing in a
number of films. She was always good
regardless of her material. Recently
she has appeared on television.

FILMOGRAPHY
Great Expectations 1946
Black Narcissus 1946
Hamlet 1948
The Robe 1953
Desiree 1954
Guys and Dolls 1955
The Big Country 1958
Home Before Dark 1958
Elmer Gantry 1960
The Happy Ending 1969
Dominique 1979

SINATRA, Frank 1915-

Frank Sinatra was the singing idol of the bobby soxers of the 1940s; then just when his career seemed finished he rescued it with his surprisingly fine acting. Sinatra was born in Hoboken, New Jersey and began his career as a band singer. His popularity soared during the post-World War II era and he appeared in a number of musicals, often in secondary roles.

In 1952 his vocal cords haemorrhaged and he was dropped by his record company. Sinatra begged Columbia to give him a dramatic role in *From Here to Eternity* (1953) for which he was paid a paltry $8000. His performance as the tragic Maggio was superb and won him an Oscar for Best Supporting Actor. His voice recovered and he has risen to legendary status as the 'Chairman of the Board of Show Business.'

Though Sinatra performances in films like *The Man With the Golden Arm* (1955) and *The Detective* (1968) have been excellent, he has often relied on his image, not his acting. Since 1970 he has rarely appeared in films.

FILMOGRAPHY
Higher and Higher 1943
Anchors Aweigh 1945
It Happened in Brooklyn 1947
Take Me Out to the Ball Game 1949
From Here to Eternity 1953
Guys and Dolls 1955
The Tender Trap 1955
The Man With the Golden Arm 1955
High Society 1956
The Joker is Wild 1957
Pal Joey 1957
Some Came Running 1959
Ocean's Eleven 1960
The Manchurian Candidate 1962
Von Ryan's Express 1965
The Detective 1968
The First Deadly Sin 1980

Left: Sinatra and Kelly in *Anchors Aweigh* (1945)

Below: Sinatra as Tony Rome (1967)

226

Smith in *Dr Jekyll and Mr Hyde* (1941).

SMITH, Sir C Aubrey 1863-1948

To a generation of American movie-goers Sir C Aubrey Smith, the bushy-eyebrowed character actor, was the image of the crusty English gentleman. Smith had been a member of England's national cricket team before making his stage debut at age 30. He appeared in a huge number of silent and sound films in both Britain and America.

FILMOGRAPHY
Builder of Bridges 1915
The Witching Hour 1916
Trader Horn 1931
Bachelor Father 1931
Tarzan the Ape Man 1932
Love Me Tonight 1932
Trouble in Paradise 1932
Morning Glory 1933
Queen Christiana 1933
Cleopatra 1934
Lives of a Bengal Lancer 1935
The Prisoner of Zenda 1937
The Four Feathers 1939
Another Thin Man 1939
Rebecca 1940
Dr Jekyll and Mr Hyde 1941
The White Cliffs of Dover 1944
And Then There Were None 1945
An Ideal Husband 1947
Little Women 1949

SMITH, Maggie 1934-

Maggie Smith is a British light comedienne and dramatic actress and rave reviews have followed her throughout her career. Chiefly a stage actress, her screen appearances have also been notable. She won an Academy Award for Best Actress for *The Prime of Miss Jean Brodie* (1969), and an Academy Award for a Best Supporting Actress for *California Suite* (1978).

FILMOGRAPHY
The VIPs 1963
Othello 1966
The Prime of Miss Jean Brodie 1969
Travels with My Aunt 1973
California Suite 1978
Death on the Nile 1978
Evil Under the Sun 1982
A Room With a View 1986

SPACEK, Sissy 1949-

Sissy Spacek, once considered an oddity who specialized in creepy teen-age parts, has shown herself to be one of the most accomplished of the modern screen actresses with a potential for true greatness. Born Mary Elizabeth Spacek in Quitman, Texas, she had originally wanted to be a country-rock singer. Even though her first film was a disaster, critics noticed the uniqueness of the tiny, freckle-faced girl with the froggy voice.

Though in her mid-twenties, she could convincingly play teenagers, as she did when she played a tormented high-school girl with murderous powers in *Carrie* (1976). She received her first Oscar nomination for the film. She took the best actress Oscar in 1979 for her portrayal of country and western singer Loretta Lynn in *Coal Miner's Daughter* (1979), and she did her own vocals. She was brilliant again in *Missing* (1982) opposite Jack Lemmon.

FILMOGRAPHY
Prime Cut 1972
Bandlands 1973
Carrie 1976
Coal Miner's Daughter 1979
Raggedy Man 1981
Missing 1982
The River 1984
'night Mother 1986
Crimes of the Heart 1986

Sissy Spacek as Carrie (1976).

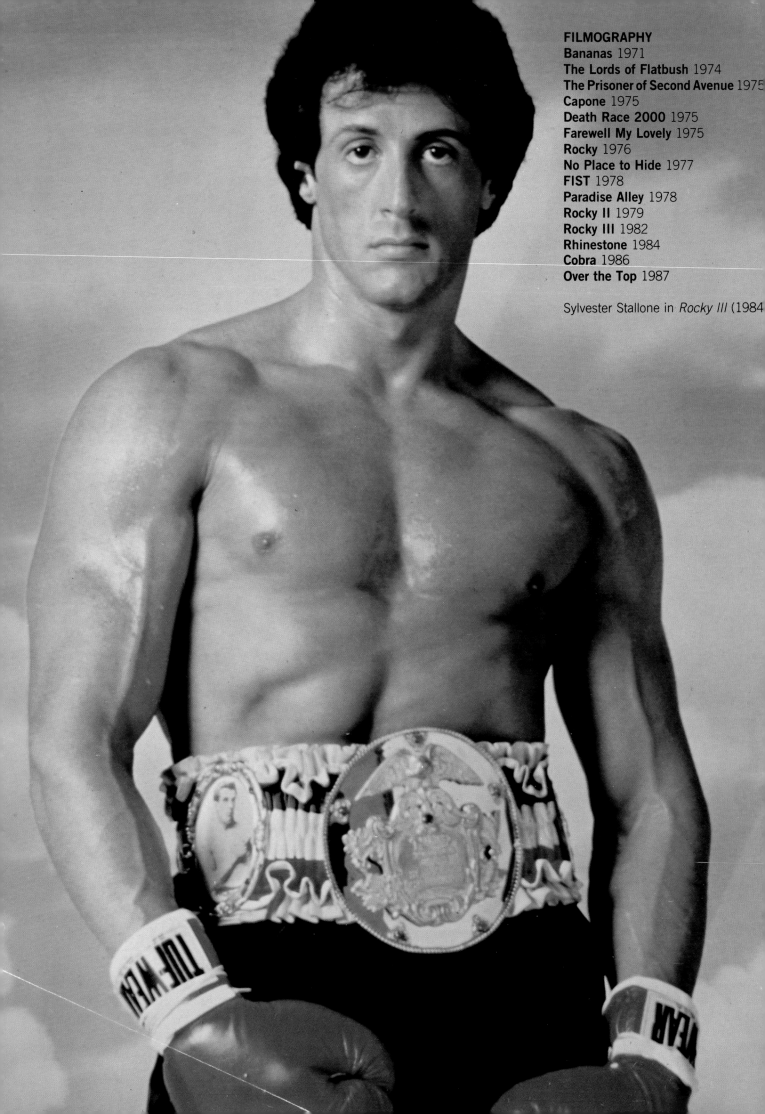

Sylvester Stallone in *Rocky III* (1984

STALLONE, Sylvester 1946-

Sylvester Stallone was a down and nearly out actor when he wrote a screenplay about a down and nearly out boxer who triumphs over the odds. Stallone sold the script on the provision that he play the lead character, Rocky Balboa. The film *Rocky* (1976) was a huge hit, and it propelled Stallone from obscurity to stardom.

Stallone's road to success had not been easy. He was born into poverty in New York City, but grew up primarily in Philadelphia (the scene of *Rocky*) after his parents' divorce. Stallone was in and out of foster homes and in and out of schools for years.

His well-muscled physique got him some off-Broadway parts and a few film roles, but his career was going nowhere until *Rocky*. Two *Rocky* sequels

have also been smash hits. Aside from the Rocky films, Stallone's *Rambo* has made him one of Hollywood's most popular actors.

STANWYCK, Barbara 1907-

Barbara Stanwyck – directors admired her professionalism, lack of temperament and her enthusiastic love of her craft. Born Ruby Stevens in Brooklyn, New York, she was orphaned early and quit school at 13.

By 15 she was a Ziegfeld chorus girl. Stage roles followed, as did minor parts in silent films. In 1928 Stanwyck married vaudeville star Frank Fay. When Fay went to Hollywood, so did Stanwyck. By the late 1930s she was a durable leading lady. In the 1940s,

Stanwyck with Robert Preston – *Union Pacific* (1939).

playing aggressive women, she was a joy to watch. She later appeared on television. Her second husband was actor Robert Taylor.

FILMOGRAPHY
Baby Face 1933
Annie Oakley 1935
Stella Dallas 1937
Golden Boy 1939
The Lady Eve 1941
Meet John Doe 1941
Ball of Fire 1941
Double Indemnity 1944
The Strange Love of Martha Ivers 1946
The Lady Gambles 1949
Clash by Night 1952
Executive Suite 1954
Roustabout 1964
The Night Walker 1965

STEIGER, Rod 1925-

Born in Westhampton, New York, Rod Steiger quit school at 16 to join the Navy, staying on as a civilian clerk and acting in amateur productions. Next, it was on to New York City and serious theater studies, including a stint with the prestigious Actors Studio.

Steiger, burly and imposing, emerged as a foremost 'Method' actor in the 1950s, receiving kudos for his stage performances and for his appearance on television in *Marty*. He has since been impressive in films. He won a British Film Academy Award and an Oscar for *In the Heat of the Night* (1967). His second wife was actress Claire Bloom.

FILMOGRAPHY
On the Waterfront 1954
The Big Knife 1954
The Harder They Fall 1956
Al Capone 1958
Cry Terror 1958
The Mark 1961
The Pawnbroker 1964
Doctor Zhivago 1965
In the Heat of the Night 1967
No Way to Treat a Lady 1968
The Amityville Horror 1979
The Chosen 1982

Top: Steiger and Sidney Poitier – *In the Heat of the Night* (1967).
Right: Stewart and Jeff Chandler – *Broken Arrow* (1950).

STEWART, James 1908-

James Stewart was appealingly shy, the gawky nice fellow with the drawling nasal voice who epitomized the best of American small-town values, the on-screen embodiment of good sense, modesty and decency. Yet the unassuming characters Stewart created were never maudlin, dull or foolishly sentimental, and they never struck a false note.

Born in Indiana, Pennsylvania, a small town which loves him and which he loves, Stewart first acted in a Boy Scout play and he became an amateur magician and accordionist. He attended Princeton University, appearing in college productions but taking a degree in architecture. He was persuaded to follow his true love, theater, and joined an acting group which included Henry Fonda and Margaret Sullavan. He and Fonda became close friends though political differences later came

Stewart in *The Glenn Miller Story* (1953).

FILMOGRAPHY
Next Time We Love 1936
The Gorgeous Hussy 1936
Seventh Heaven 1937
Of Human Hearts 1938
Vivacious Lady 1938
You Can't Take it With You 1938
Mr Smith goes to Washington 1939
Destry Rides Again 1939
The Shop Around the Corner 1940
The Mortal Storm 1940
The Philadelphia Story 1940
It's a Wonderful Life 1946
Call Northside 777 1949
The Stratton Story 1949
Winchester 73 1950
Broken Arrow 1950
Harvey 1950
No Highway 1951
The Glenn Miller Story 1953
Rear Window 1954
The Man from Laramie 1955
Vertigo 1958
Bell, Book and Candle 1958
Anatomy of a Murder 1959
The Man Who Shot Liberty Valence 1962
Shenandoah 1965
The Flight of the Phoenix 1965
Firecreek 1968
The Cheyenne Social Club 1970
The Magic of Lassie 1978

between them, as Fonda was a supporter of liberal causes and Stewart became a strong conservative. Sullavan had Stewart cast in many of her films once she reached Hollywood.

Though at first an unusual leading man and hero, Stewart's sincerity and his air of being slightly embarrassed at all times caught on with the public. He was simply grand in *You Can't Take It with You* (1938), *Mr Smith Goes to Washington* (1939) and *The Philadelphia Story* (1940), which brought him an Academy Award. During World War II Stewart became a bomber pilot, flying 20 missions over Germany and achieving the rank of full colonel. He was a brigadier general in the Air Force Reserve until retiring in 1968, the highest-ranking Hollywood entertainer in the United States military.

Stewart moved smoothly into a wider variety of roles after the war, dazzling critics and fans alike with his wonderful performance in the gentle *Harvey* (1950), but also playing detectives, western heroes and leads in Alfred Hitchcock blockbusters. Despite his position as one of Holywood's top personalities, Stewart has kept his private life private, marrying in 1941.

Left: James Stewart was a physician in *The Shootist* (1976).

Meryl Streep in *The French Lieutenant's Woman* (1981).

STREEP, Meryl 1953-

Blonde and delicately beautiful, Meryl Streep is one of the brightest stars to appear in years, a winner of numerous awards and much critical acclaim. Born in Basking Ridge, New Jersey, Streep began taking voice lessons at age 12, aiming for a career as an opera singer, but appearing in school plays made her decide to become an actress.

Streep majored in Drama at Vassar and attended the Yale School of Drama. She made a splash on Broadway in *27 Wagons Full of Cotton*, joined the New York Shakespeare Festival, and rose to the top in films almost instantly. Streep won an Academy Award for Best Supporting Actress for *Kramer vs Kramer* (1979), and an Academy Award for Best Actress for *Sophie's Choice* (1982).

FILMOGRAPHY
Julia 1977
The Deer Hunter 1978
Manhattan 1979
Kramer vs Kramer 1979
The French Lieutenant's Woman 1981
Sophie's Choice 1982
Silkwood 1983
Falling in Love 1984
Out of Africa 1985
Heartburn 1986

STREISAND, Barbra 1942-

A force of nature, that's what Barbra Streisand is, the kind of monumental combination of talent and drive that comes along once in a generation. Without looks or money, influence or connections, she broke into show business and built a legendary career. Accused of being an egomaniac who controls every aspect of her films, she's actually a self-confident artist, a charismatic presence with a voice of glorious brass.

Above: Streisand – *On a Clear Day You Can See Forever* (1970).
Top left: Streisand in *Funny Girl* (1968).
Left: Streisand, Sharif – *Funny Girl.*

Born in Brooklyn, New York, after she graduated from high school she worked as a switchboard operator and theater usher while trying to become an actress. After winning a Greenwich Village nightclub contest, Streisand had some modest success in night-clubs and appeared in an off-Broadway revue. She debuted on Broadway in *I Can Get It for You Wholesale* in 1962 opposite Elliot Gould, whom she married but later divorced. He was good, too, but she got the raves. Critics loved her gift for comedy and she won the New York Critics Award.

Superstardom came practically over-night with television performances, live supper club shows and a dazzling Broadway success in the musical *Funny Girl* based on the life of enter-

Barbra Streisand played a boy in *Yentl* (1983).

tainer Fanny Brice. Hit records also made Streisand a winner.

Streisand made her debut on screen in *Funny Girl* (1968), and won an Academy Award. In 1970 she won a special Broadway Tony Award· for being the actress of the decade. She soon established herself as a major Hollywood star, a smashing box-office draw. As she gobbled up fame and fortune, critics began to attack her, accusing her of overreaching her talents. When she made the popular *A Star is Born* (1976), invidious comparisons were made between her and Judy Garland, who starred in the definitive version of the film. But Streisand still received an Oscar for composing the song 'Evergreen.'

Streisand's movies are not always good, but *The Way We Were* (1973) with Robert Redford is one of the great classic romantic films of all time. Streisand is primarily a singer and personality rather than an actress, and her movies are often merely vehicles to display her gifts. But she's what her vast audiences want to see and isn' that what being an old-fashioned super-star is all about?

SUTHERLAND, Donald 1934-

Donald Sutherland is a tall, talented Canadian-born actor who went to England and studied at the London Academy of Music and Dramatic Art. Basically a versatile character actor, he is also a popular leading man, at his best in off-beat movies.

FILMOGRAPHY
The Dirty Dozen 1967
M*A*S*H 1970
Klute 1971
Don't Look Now 1973
The Day of the Locust 1975
1900 1976
Casanova 1976
Invasion of the Body Snatchers 1978
Murder by Decree 1979
Ordinary People 1980
Eye of the Needle 1981
Heaven Help Us 1985

Sutherland – *The Invasion of the Body Snatchers* (1978).

SWANSON, Gloria 1897-1983

Silent film star Gloria Swanson had glamor. A genius at self-promotion, she caused fans to go mad over her high-fashion clothes, her marriage to a genuine marquis and her exceptional beauty. She was born Josephine Swenson in Chicago, Illinois. Swanson married Wallace Beery in 1916 and did romantic comedies for Mack Sennett.

Dramas and suggestive comedies were her forté and it was director Cecil B DeMille who made her a star. She lost most of her money producing *Queen Kelly* (1928), never released in America, eventually retiring from the screen only to return in triumph as the aging silent film star and recluse in *Sunset Boulevard* (1950).

Right: The glorious Gloria Swanson.

FILMOGRAPHY
The Meal Ticket 1915
Shifting Sands 1918
Male and Female 1919
The Affairs of Anatol 1921
Madame Sans Gene 1925
Sadie Thompson 1928
Queen Kelly 1928
Indiscreet 1931
Father Takes a Wife 1941
Sunset Boulevard 1950
Airport 1975 1974

TAYLOR, Elizabeth 1932-

Elizabeth Taylor typifies what most people mean when they say movie star. Born in London to American parents, she arrived in Los Angeles with her family in 1939. Liz, as she is popularly called, was already a beauty. Her ambitious mother worked tirelessly to make her a child star.

National Velvet (1944) showcased a lovely and sensitive Liz and it may still rank as her finest film. Early on she matured into a radiant woman, capable of playing romantic roles well beyond her years, famous for her dark hair, violet eyes and ripe figure. She was courted by industrialist Howard Hughes before she married the heir to the Hilton Hotel chain, Nicky Hilton, while still in her teens. The marriage lasted only long enough to make *Father of the Bride* (1950) a hit film.

Liz began taking acting seriously with *A Place in the Sun* (1951). By then she was secure in her position as top box-office superstar, one of the most well-publicized women in the world. Her exciting private life and many

Below: The young Elizabeth Taylor in a glamorous pose.

Above: Elizabeth Taylor and Mickey Rooney in *National Velvet* (1944).

marriages continued fueling public interest. In 1952 Liz married British actor Michael Wilding. In the late 1950s she married colorful show business impresario Michael Todd. After he died in a plane crash she married singer Eddie Fisher. Fans painted her as the wicked temptress who lured Fisher away from wholesome wife Debbie Reynolds. Liz won back the sympathy of fans when she almost died of pneumonia, also winning an Academy Award for Best Actress for *Butterfield 8* (1960), ostensibly also because of her long illness.

Next began the Richard Burton phase of Liz's life. Her romance with the British actor on the set of *Cleopatra* (1962) fed gossip columns. Taylor and Burton married, divorced, remarried, redivorced. One of the films they made together, *Who's Afraid of Virginia Woolf?* (1966), brought Taylor an Oscar for Best Actress which she certainly deserved.

When their movie appeal faltered, the Burtons appeared on stage together quite successfully. Taylor also fared well on Broadway on her own. Over the years she has emerged as a magnificent character; fat, vulgar, a survivor of the Hollywood studio system at its most vicious – yet glamorous.

Above: Taylor — *Who's Afraid of Virginia Woolf?* (1966).

Above: Taylor in *Raintree County* (1957).

Right: Taylor as *Cleopatra* (1962).

FILMOGRAPHY

Lassie Come Home 1943
Jane Eyre 1943
The White Cliffs of Dover 1944
National Velvet 1944
Cynthia 1947
Little Women 1949
Father of the Bride 1950
A Place in the Sun 1951
Ivanhoe 1952
Elephant Walk 1954
Giant 1956
Raintree County 1957
Cat on a Hot Tin Roof 1958
Suddenly Last Summer 1959
Butterfield 8 1960
Cleopatra 1962
The VIPs 1963
Who's Afraid of Virginia Woolf? 1966
The Taming of the Shrew 1967
Reflections in a Golden Eye 1967
Secret Ceremony 1968
Zee and Company 1971
Ash Wednesday 1973
The Mirror Crack'd 1980

Robert Taylor and Garbo in *Camille* (1937).

Broadway Melody of 1936 1935
Magnificent Obsession 1936
His Brother's Wife 1936
The Gorgeous Hussy 1936
Camille 1937
A Yank at Oxford 1938
Waterloo Bridge 1940
Billy the Kid 1941
Johnny Eager 1942
Bataan 1943
Undercurrent 1946
Conspirator 1950
Quo Vadis 1951
Ivanhoe 1952
Knights of the Round Table 1953
Saddle the Wind 1958
Party Girl 1958
The Glass Sphinx 1968

Shirley Temple – *Poor Little Rich Girl* (1936).

TEMPLE, Shirley 1928-

Golden ringlets, bright eyes and dimples galore made Shirley Temple a child star like no other child star before or since. She was a good little dancer and singer with terrific on-screen personality, as indelibly a phenomenon of Hollywood movies of the 1930s as Astaire and Rogers's flashing feet. The style of her era seems coy and cutsy to modern audiences and she lacked the staying power of child actors like Elizabeth Taylor or Mickey Rooney, but she had great star quality. Reruns of Shirley's films – some of them 50 years old – still go over big on television.

She was born in Santa Monica, California, where her father worked as a bank teller. It was her mother who

TAYLOR, Robert 1911-1969

Robert Taylor was a hard-working professional who, if he rarely soared, rarely crashed and he was blessed with very good looks. Born Spangler Arlington Brugh in Filley, Nebraska, he dreamed of becoming a cellist and went to California to study music.

Instead he wound up 'The Man with the Perfect Profile' at MGM, a romantic lead who played opposite some of the screen's most beautiful female stars. Later in his career he took on less glamorous roles, performing solidly. His first wife was actress Barbara Stanwyck.

spotted baby Shirley's potential and the child started dancing lessons at the age of three. Before she was four she beat the competition and appeared in a series of one-reel films called *Baby Burlesks*, parodying famous stars like Marlene Dietrich. A song and dance rendition of 'Baby Take a Bow' in *Stand Up and Cheer* (1934) was highly precocious and took the minds of the masses off the Depression.

Within a year Shirley was wildly popular, even winning a special Academy Award. Old ladies wept over her, mothers would have traded their offspring for her and little girls wanted to be her. Her famous rendering of 'On the Good Ship Lollipop' in *Bright Eyes* (1934) gave the song immortality.

By 1938 she was a national treasure – the number-one box-office Hollywood star, with fans snapping up Shirley Temple dolls, mugs, dresses and coloring books. A massive publicity campaign portrayed her as sweet, unspoiled and naively charming.

As Shirley grew older, her hair grew darker and audiences cooled. Though she showed charm in *The Bachelor and the Bobbysoxer* (1947), her public seemed never to forgive her for leaving childhood behind. She had been a storybook princess, a plucky little angel, and that was the only way audiences wanted to see her. At 17 Shirley Temple married actor John Agar, later divorcing him and marrying business executive Charles Black. She is active in Republican Party politics, and has retired from films.

FILMOGRAPHY
The Red-Haired Alibi 1932
To the Last Man 1933
Stand Up and Cheer 1934
Little Miss Marker 1934
Now and Forever 1934
Bright Eyes 1934
The Little Colonel 1935
Curly Top 1935
The Littlest Rebel 1935
Captain January 1936
Poor Little Rich Girl 1936
Dimples 1936
Wee Willie Winkle 1937
Heidi 1937
Rebecca of Sunnybrook Farm 1938
Little Miss Broadway 1938
The Little Princess 1939
Susannah of the Mounties 1939
Miss Annie Rooney 1942
Since You Went Away 1944
I'll Be Seeing You 1944
Kiss and Tell 1945
The Bachelor and the Bobbysoxer 1947
Fort Apache 1948
Mr Belvedere Goes to College 1949
A Kiss for Corliss 1949

Above: Temple, Menjou – *Little Miss Marker* (1934).

Left: Shirley in trouble in *Poor Little Rich Girl* (1936).

TOMLIN, Lily 1939-

Lily Tomlin, born Mary Jean Tomlin, was already a successful television and cabaret performer when she made an impressive film debut in *Nashville* (1975). Yet despite her obvious talents as a comedienne and dramatic actress her film career has not really taken off as it might.

FILMOGRAPHY
Nashville 1975
The Late Show 1977
Moment by Moment 1978
9 to 5 1980
All of Me 1984
Pete 'N Tillie 1984

TRACY, Spencer 1900-1967

Actors from Humphrey Bogart to Laurence Olivier admired Spencer Tracy. Unlike most performers who, if they're around long enough, generally need at least one or two strong comeback films, Tracy's popularity rose steadily. In his extraordinary film career he rarely received so much as a bad review. His low-key style and his ability to react to other actors in a completely natural way have never been bettered. It is sad and a bit ironic that today he is less famous than many other leading men of his era. If Bogie deserves to be a cult figure so does Tracy.

Born in Milwaukee, Wisconsin, he was educated at a Jesuit Prep School and originally planned to become a priest. In 1917 he joined the navy, then went to Ripon College where he discovered acting. Though he had altered his life goals, Tracy remained a devout Catholic. In 1923 he married actress Louise Treadwell. They never divorced even though Tracy's name was later linked romantically with screen star Loretta Young and his long-standing intimate relationship with Katharine Hepburn is a Hollywood legend.

Tracy studied acting in New York, eventually appearing on Broadway. On stage he had the reputation of being solidly dependable and disciplined during performances. But off stage he was moody, quarrelsome, short-tempered and had a drinking problem. These characteristics carried over to his film career. Tracy's craggy, rugged appearance led to his being typecast as a tough guy at first. Yet he soon became a star, playing a wide range of roles, though never a typical leading man.

He received many Oscar nominations, winning two in succession for *Captains Courageous* (1937) and *Boys Town* (1938). He and Katharine Hepburn were terrific together in a series of films such as *Adam's Rib* (1949) and *Father of the Bride* (1950). They teamed for *Guess Who's Coming to Dinner* (1967), and Tracy won a British Film Academy Award. He died shortly after the film was made. Audiences went to see the movie in droves to honor the man whose humor, masculinity, sincerity and dignified unpretentiousness on screen had brought so much pleasure to so many of them.

Above right: Tracy in *Bad Day at Black Rock* (1955).

FILMOGRAPHY
Quick Millions 1931
Twenty Thousand Years in Sing Sing 1932
The Power and the Glory 1933
A Man's Castle 1933
Fury 1936
San Francisco 1936
Captains Courageous 1937
Boys' Town 1938
Stanley and Livingstone 1939
Northwest Passage 1940
Edison, the Man 1940
Boom Town 1940
Dr Jekyll and Mr Hyde 1941
Woman of the Year 1942
The Seventh Cross 1944
State of the Union 1948
Adam's Rib 1949
Father of the Bride 1950
Pat and Mike 1952
Bad Day at Black Rock 1955
The Last Hurrah 1958
Inherit the Wind 1960
Judgment at Nuremberg 1961
Guess Who's Coming to Dinner 1967

That wonderful team – Tracy and Hepburn in *Woman of The Year* (1942).

Right: Spencer Tracy as Dr Jekyll in *Dr Jekyll and Mr Hyde* (1941).

TRAVOLTA, John 1954-

The TV series 'Welcome Back Kotter' brought John Travolta to the public's attention and *Saturday Night Fever* (1977) made him a superstar. Though some of his later films have also been huge financial successes, they have been critical failures, and his superstar status is threatened.

FILMOGRAPHY
Carrie 1975
Saturday Night Fever 1977
Grease 1978
Moment by Moment 1978
Urban Cowboy 1980
Blow Out 1982
Staying Alive 1983

Left: Travolta in *Staying Alive* (1983).

TREVOR, Claire 1909-

Born Claire Wemlinger in New York city, Claire Trevor was a highly gifted actress who projected vulnerability so well she wound up typecast as the tramp with the heart of gold or the gangster's moll in 'B' movies. Yet Trevor was superb when given the rare chance to act in a good film.

Dead End (1937), *Stagecoach* (1939) and *The High and the Mighty* (1954) brought her the recognition she deserved. *Key Largo* (1948) did even more for her. The movie won Trevor an Academy Award for Best Supporting Actress.

FILMOGRAPHY
The Mad Game 1933
Dead End 1937
The Amazing Dr Clitterhouse 1938
Stagecoach 1939
Honky Tonk 1941
Murder My Sweet 1944
Crack Up 1946
Key Largo 1948
Hard, Fast and Beautiful 1951
The High and the Mighty 1954
Marjorie Morningstar 1958
Two Weeks in Another Town 1962
The Stripper 1963
How to Murder Your Wife 1965
The Cape Town Affair 1967

Above right: The beautiful Lana Turner.
Below: The gifted Claire Trevor.

FILMOGRAPHY

They Won't Forget 1937	**Homecoming** 1948
Love Finds Andy Hardy 1939	**The Three Musketeers** 1948
Ziegfeld Girl 1941	**The Merry Widow** 1952
Honky Tonk 1941	**The Bad and the Beautiful** 1952
Somewhere I'll Find You 1942	**Peyton Place** 1957
The Postman Always Rings Twice 1945	**Imitation of Life** 1959
Green Dolphin Street 1946	**Portrait in Black** 1960
Cass Timberlane 1947	**Bittersweet Love** 1976

TURNER, Lana 1920-

Lana Turner – as a teen-aged blonde starlet she became Hollywood's 'Sweater Girl,' then matured into a glamorous star. Born Julia Turner in Wallace, Idaho, she went to California at age nine with her mother after her father was robbed and murdered.

Her private life kept her in the news. Married numerous times, including to band leader Artie Shaw and ex-Tarzan Lex Barker, she was the center of a well-publicized scandal when in 1958 her daughter stabbed her gangster lover Johnny Stompanato to death. Turner has remained a glittering celebrity and appears on television.

TURPIN, Ben 1874-1940

Ben Turpin's long film career was built primarily around his severely and hilariously crossed eyes. After years in vaudeville Turpin began making films in 1907 and appeared in some early Chaplin shorts, but worked mainly for Mack Sennett. He made his final film in 1939, the year before his death.

FILMOGRAPHY
Uncle Tom's Cabin 1919
Small Town Idol 1921
The Prodigal Bridegroom 1926
Show of Shows 1929
The Love Parade 1930
Million Dollar Legs 1939

ULLMANN, Liv 1939-

Liv Ullmann, a great dramatic actress and earthy natural beauty, has appeared in numerous Swedish and international films. Born in Tokyo, Japan, to Norwegian parents, she went with her family to Canada at the beginning of World War II, and later to New York. After her father's death she moved to Norway, achieving prominence on stage in Oslo and in Norwegian films.

She has worked closely with Swedish film director Ingmar Bergman, starring in some of his greatest films. They also lived together for several years and are the parents of a daughter.

FILMOGRAPHY
The Wayward Girl 1959
Persona 1966
Hours of the Wolf 1967
Shame 1968
A Passion 1970
The Emigrants 1971
Pope Joan 1971
Cries and Whispers 1972
Scenes From a Marriage 1973
Lost Horizon 1973
The New Land 1973
Face to Face 1976
A Bridge Too Far 1977
The Serpent's Egg 1977
Autumn Sonata 1978
The Wild Duck 1985

Right: Liv Ullmann – *The Abdication* (1974).
Below: Ustinov (*center*) with David Niven and Bette Davis – *Death on the Nile* (1978).

USTINOV, Peter 1921-

Peter Ustinov, the talented actor, screenwriter, director, playwright and novelist, was born in London to a Russian father and French mother. Ustinov debuted on stage at 17, turned to films early, impressing critics with his gifts. He won Academy Awards for *Spartacus* (1960) and *Topkapi* (1964). His wit and charm make him a popular television talk-show guest.

FILMOGRAPHY
Private Angelo 1949
Hotel Sahara 1951
Quo Vadis 1951
Beau Brummel 1954
The Egyptian 1954
We're No Angels 1955
The Sundowners 1960
Spartacus 1960
Romanoff and Juliet 1961
Topkapi 1964
Death on the Nile 1978

VALENTINO, Rudolph 1895-1926

Talk about star quality – nobody ever had more of it than Rodolfo Alfonzo Raffaele Pierre Philibert Guglielmi of Castellaneta, Italy, otherwise known to the world as Rudolph Valentino. His animal magnetism, flashing dark eyes, elegant taste in clothes and aura of mystery and wickedness made him the great idol and male sex symbol of the silent-movie era.

His early life is a record of failure. In 1912 he was begging on the streets of Paris. In 1943 he was in New York, where he was booked several times by the police on suspicion of petty theft and blackmail. He found work as a taxi dancer, moved into the nightclub class, toured with a show and wound up in Hollywood.

He began in films playing gigolos, villains and seductive dancers. While still a bit player he married actress Jean Acker who later divorced him, claiming the marriage was never consummated. Contacts and luck brought him the lead in *The Four Horsemen of the Apocalypse* (1921), a record-breaking smash hit. *The Sheik* (1921) made women swoon and started an Arabic fad in interior decorating.

Valentino's second wife was Natasha Rambova (born Winifred Shaunessy) and until they separated she managed his career. Valentino was arrested for bigamy after marrying her because their wedding took place before his divorce from Acker was finalized. Rambova and Valentino went on an extensive dance tour and he published a popular book of poetry called *Day Dreams*.

If women loved Valentino, men despised him. In 1926 the Chicago *Tribune* attacked him for being a 'Pink Powder Puff,' a 'painted pansy.' Valentino did appear in some of his films in elaborate and highly decorative costumes, but he often appeared in very little, which seemed to be the way his fans liked him best.

In 1926 Valentino was rushed to a New York hospital suffering from a perforated ulcer. When newspapers reported he had died, many American women became hysterical. His funeral was an enormous event. Valentino's fan clubs developed into cults and there were reports of women committing suicide over his death. The reaction did not go unnoticed on Wall Street. Thanks to Valentino, movies

were taken seriously as a business. He did a lot to create the movie industry, though perhaps not very much for the art form of film.

FILMOGRAPHY
Alimony 1918
The Delicious Little Devil 1919
The Cheater 1920
Once to Every Woman 1920
The Four Horsemen of the Apocalypse 1921
Unchained Seas 1921
Camille 1921
The Sheik 1921
The Young Rajah 1922
Blood and Sand 1922
Monsieur Beaucaire 1924
A Sainted Devil 1924
Cobra 1924
The Eagle 1925
Son of the Sheik 1926

Above: Valentino delighted his fans in *Son of the Sheik* (1926).
Right: Veidt (in the cabinet) in *The Cabinet of Dr Caligari* (1919).

VAN CLEEF, Lee 1925-

Originally a villain in Hollywood westerns, this durable character actor achieved his greatest success in the so called 'Spaghetti Westerns' that made an international star of Clint Eastwood.

FILMOGRAPHY
High Noon 1952
The Man Who Shot Liberty Valance 1962
For a Few Dollars More 1965
The Good the Bad and the Ugly 1967
Kid Vengeance 1977

VEIDT, Conrad 1893-1943

Conrad Veidt appeared on stage first in Max Reinhardt's celebrated theater in Berlin, and started making German films in 1917. His tall gaunt figure and expressive face led him to be cast in tormented or demonic roles, notably as the murderous sleepwalker in *The Cabinet of Dr Caligari* (1919). He was also in *The Student of Prague* (1926) and *The Hands of Orlac* (1926).

Veidt was unpopular with the Nazis and when they rose to power he chose to live in Britain. When he returned to Germany briefly to make a film, the Nazi Government created an international incident by refusing to let him leave. The Nazis finally relented, and when Veidt went to Hollywood he ironically specialized in playing Nazis, most memorably in *Casablanca* (1942).

FILMOGRAPHY
The Cabinet of Dr Caligari 1919
Waxworks 1924
Lucrezia Borgia 1925
The Student of Prague 1926
The Hands of Orlac 1926
The Man Who Laughs 1927
Congress Dances 1931
Rome Express 1932
The Wandering Jew 1933
The Passing of the Third Floor Back 1935
Under the Red Robe 1936
Dark Journey 1937
The Spy in Black 1939
The Thief of Baghdad 1949
Nazi Agent 1942
Casablanca 1942

VOIGHT, Jon 1938-

Jon Voight might have become a conventional good-looking leading man but he is far too gifted, serious, and adventurous for that. After appearing on stage in musicals, Voight rose to stardom quickly in films as the naive hustler in *Midnight Cowboy* (1969). His career has had its share of peaks and valleys but he won an Academy Award for Best Actor for *Coming Home* (1978).

FILMOGRAPHY
Midnight Cowboy 1969
Catch 22 1970
Deliverance 1972
The Odessa File 1974
Coming Home 1978
Table for Five 1983
The Runaway Train 1985

VON STROHEIM, Erich 1885-1957

Contrary to popular myth, often spread by Erich von Stroheim himself, he was not the descendent of Prussian aristocracy, but Erich Oswald Stroheim, son of a Jewish hatter in Vienna. Though he served briefly in the Austro-Hungarian Army, most of his youth was spent managing his father's hat factory.

Stroheim came to America around 1906 and wound up in Hollywood in 1914 as part of D W Griffith's company. During World War I he was billed as 'The Man You Love to hate,' often playing a cruel Prussian officer with a sarcastic monocled gaze.

After the war he began directing films and established a reputation as a perfectionist, a genius and a profligate spender. His epic *Greed* (1923) ran seven hours and was released only in a severely cut form. The original is said to be a masterpiece but it lost a fortune and he was given few additional opportunities to direct. Stroheim went back to acting, usually in his 'Man You Love to Hate' character.

FILMOGRAPHY
Blind Husbands 1919
Foolish Wives 1921
Three Faces East 1930
La Grande Illusion 1937
Five Graves to Cairo 1943
32 Rue de Montmartre 1947
Sunset Boulevard 1950
Napoleon 1954

Max Von Sydow in *The Emigrants* (1972).

VON SYDOW, Max 1929-

Strikingly gaunt, tall, blond and impressive, Max von Sydow is a great international film star who was frequently cast in the movies of Swedish director Ingmar Bergman. Born in Lund, Sweden, von Sydow's family was middle-class. His father was a university professor.

Von Sydow attended Stockholm's Royal Dramatic Theater School, debuting in films in 1949, frequently playing modern man at his most tortured. His brooding intensity, rich voice and imposing screen presence impressed audiences worldwide, and led to his portraying Christ in *The Greatest Story Ever Told* (1965).

FILMOGRAPHY
Miss Julie 1951
The Seventh Seal 1956
Wild Strawberries 1957
The Face 1959
The Virgin Spring 1960
Through a Glass Darkly 1961
Winter Light 1962
The Greatest Story Ever Told 1965
Hawaii 1966
The Emigrants 1972
The Exorcist 1973
The New Land 1975
Three Days of the Condor 1976
Hurricane 1979
Hannah and Her Sisters 1986
Duet for One 1987

WAGNER, Robert 1930-

Born into a wealthy family in Detroit, Michigan, Robert Wagner expected to go into business but changed his mind. His good looks and pleasant personality made him a teenage movie idol early. Later he matured into a solid leading man and popular television star. He was married to movie actress Natalie Wood.

FILMOGRAPHY
The Happy Years 1950
With a Song in My Heart 1952
A Kiss Before Dying 1956
The War Lover 1962
The Pink Panther 1964
Harper 1966
Winning 1969
The Towering Inferno 1976
Airport 79 1979

Below right: John Wayne (*center*) with Glen Campbell in *True Grit* (1969).

WALLACH, Eli 1915-

Eli Wallach is a distinguished American 'Method' actor, noted for his range and versatility, whose career spans stage, films and television. Wallach was born in Brooklyn, New York, and attended the University of Texas and the City College of New York, planning to become a teacher. But since his first appearance on stage in amateur theater at the age of 15, he had really dreamed of becoming an actor.

He made his Broadway debut in 1945 and his screen debut in *Baby Doll* (1956), an enormous hit. He often plays villains and tough guys in movies. His favorite co-star is his wife, actress Anne Jackson.

FILMOGRAPHY
Baby Doll 1956
The Magnificent Seven 1960
The Misfits 1961
Act One 1963
The Moonspinners 1964
The Good, The Bad and the Ugly 1967
The Tiger Makes Out 1967
The Angel Levine 1970
Crazy Joe 1973
Cinderella Liberty 1974
Nasty Habits 1977
Movie Movie 1978
Winter Kills 1979

WARNER, H B 1876-1958

H B Warner was born Henry Byron Warner in London. His father, Charles Warner, was a famous British stage actor. Though Warner debuted at his father's theater at age seven he later studied medicine until opting for acting. Success on stage led to a prolific Hollywood film career. He was Christ in *The King of Kings* (1927) and Chang in *Lost Horizon* (1937).

FILMOGRAPHY
King of Kings 1927
Mr Deeds Goes to Town 1936
Lost Horizon 1937
Victoria the Great 1937
Topper Returns 1941
Sunset Boulevard 1950
The Ten Commandments 1956

WAYNE, John 1907-1979

John Wayne was more than a movie star – to millions throughout the world he was the symbol of rugged masculinity. Though even his most fervent admirers would admit that the only part he could ever really play was himself, that didn't make any difference. He became the biggest moneymaker in movie history.

Wayne was born Marion Michael Morrison in Winterset, Iowa. The family moved to Glendale, California, a suburb of Los Angeles, where he picked up his nickname 'Duke.' He had a dog named Duke, and everybody knew the dog's name.

He got a football scholarship to the University of Southern California and spent summers lugging props around a movie studio. Since he was big and looked good in a sombrero, he got bit parts, mainly in westerns. After an injury cost him a football scholarship, he went into acting full time and made a huge number of 'B' or worse westerns. He even became the screen's first singing cowboy, though his singing was dubbed.

Wayne's breakthrough film was *Stagecoach* (1939), directed by John Ford. The film was a huge financial and critical success; it changed the image of the western from a Saturday afternoon entertainment for the kids to a vehicle capable of carrying a real story and first-rate performances.

When World War II broke out Wayne tried to enlist but his age (he was 34) and his old football injury kept him out of the army but not off the screen. From a cowboy hero he became a war hero. After the war it was back in the saddle again for some of his best westerns, including *Red River* (1948).

Wayne's most successful non-western was *The Quiet Man* (1952), about an Irish-American boxer who returns to the old country. Though the film has no shootout, its most

memorable scene is a long brawl between Wayne and Victor McLaglen.

The off-screen Wayne was very much like the characters he played – a tough, hard-drinking, brawling 'man's man' who seemed to prefer the company of his drinking buddies to the sustained company of women. He had three not terribly successful marriages and his divorce from Mexican actress 'Chata' in 1953 was accompanied by charges of drunkenness and violence.

Wayne was outspoken about his hawkish, right-wing politics. He even financed a couple of movies to promote his point of view; however, they were not commercially successful.

John Wayne – the classic Westerner.

Above: Scott, Wayne, Dietrich – *The Spoilers* (1942).

Wayne was stricken with lung cancer in 1964, but after a serious operation he went right back to making movies, including *True Grit* (1969), for which he received his only Oscar. Though he never really recovered his health he continued making movies almost to the end.

FILMOGRAPHY
Mother Machree 1928
The Big Trail 1930
Two Fisted Law 1932
Riders of Destiny 1933
The Man from Utah 1934
Idol of the Crowds 1937
Pals of the Saddle 1938
Stagecoach 1939
The Long Voyage Home 1940
Pittsburgh 1942
The Fighting Seabees 1944
Flame of the Barbary Coast 1945
Back to Bataan 1945
They Were Expendable 1945
Fort Apache 1948
Red River 1948
Wake of the Red Witch 1948
She Wore a Yellow Ribbon 1949
The Quiet Man 1952
Big Jim McLain 1952
The Conqueror 1956
The Alamo 1960
The Man Who Shot Liberty Valance 1962
The Longest Day 1963
How the West Was Won 1963
The Sons of Katie Elder 1965
The Green Berets 1968
True Grit 1969
The Cowboys 1972
Rooster Cogburn 1975
The Shootist 1976

WELCH, Raquel 1940-

Raquel Welch was a beauty contest winner who made it to the top because of her voluptuous body and a clever publicity campaign launched by husband of the time, Patrick Curtis. She was expected to fade with the first wrinkle but she has proved a tough and talented survivor.

FILMOGRAPHY
One Million Years BC 1966
Myra Breckinridge 1970
Fuzz 1972
The Last of Sheila 1973
The Three Musketeers 1974
The Four Musketeers 1975
Mother, Jugs and Speed 1977
The Prince and the Pauper 1977
Restless 1979

WELLES, Orson 1915-1985

Orson Welles was an actor, director, producer and screenwriter. He was also an egotist, a flamboyant character and probably a genius, a man who fought for artistic integrity throughout his career, and who appeared in poor films from time to time simply to earn money to finance his own serious projects.

He had his admirers and detractors. To some he was a self-indulgent charlatan who usurped other people's ideas, and who was moody and difficult to deal with. To others he was simply an artist who failed to live up to his enormous early promise. His admirers point to his originality and flair, his magnificent speaking voice and to his great film triumph, the masterpiece *Citizen Kane* (1941).

Born in Kenosha, Wisconsin, into a wealthy family, Welles was a genuine prodigy with an audacious streak who talked his way into a leading role at Dublin's respected Gate Theatre when he was only 16. He directed the Negro People's Theatre production of *Macbeth* with an all black cast in 1936. By then he'd appeared on Broadway. In 1937 he founded the Mercury Theatre with John Houseman and dramatized H G Wells's *The War of the Worlds* so effectively on radio on Halloween 1938 that listeners panicked and fled their homes.

Welles went to Hollywood, creating a stir with *Citizen Kane*. With its thinly disguised critical depiction of news-paper mogul William Randolph Hearst, the movie brought down the wrath of the Hearst newspapers on Welles's head, seriously affecting the film's commercial success and making it difficult for Welles to continue working in Hollywood. When he directed *The Magnificent Ambersons* (1942), a gem, the studio cut it brutally.

Opposite top: Welles and Joseph Cotton in *Citizen Kane* (1941).

Right: Welles and Joan Fontaine in *Jane Eyre* (1943).

Welles was imposing as Rochester in *Jane Eyre* (1943) and as Claudette Colbert's crippled husband in *Tomorrow is Forever* (1944). *The Lady from Shanghai* (1947) co-starred wife of the time Rita Hayworth, and his conception of *Macbeth* (1948), though boldly unconventional, was hampered by a low budget. Welles went to Europe,

creating a memorable screen role in *The Third Man* (1949). His daring *Othello* (1951), his acting and directing in *Touch of Evil* (1958) and his performance in *The Long Hot Summer* (1958) are all worthy of note. He won a special Academy Award in 1970 for his artistry and the American Film Institute's Life Achievement Award in 1975.

FILMOGRAPHY
Citizen kane 1941
The Magnificent Ambersons
  (narration) 1942
Journey Into Fear 1942
Jane Eyre 1943
Tomorrow is Forever 1944
The Stranger 1945
The Lady from Shanghai 1947
Macbeth 1948
The Third Man 1949
Othello 1951
Moby Dick 1956
Touch of Evil 1958
The Long Hot Summer 1958
Compulsion 1959
A Man for All Seasons 1966
Treasure Island 1972
Voyage of the Damned 1976
The Man Who Saw Tomorrow 1982

WEST, Mae 1892-1980

Mae West owed a lot to sex and sex probably owes a lot to her. She was a gifted blonde comedienne and egomaniac with plenty of brains, a one-of-a-kind original, ahead of her time when it came to notions of sexual freedom for women, able to turn those notions into a vastly lucrative stage and film career.

Born in Brooklyn, New York, Mae never bothered much with school because she was too busy performing, first as an amateur and later in burlesque, billed as 'The Baby Vamp.' At 14 she began appearing in vaudeville and in Broadway revues. It was Mae who introduced the shimmy on stage. She was also a male impersonator. This, plus her tough, 'macho,' guilt-free attitude to sex eventually led to a rumor that she was really a man in disguise. Mae's countless male lovers put the lie to that one.

In 1926 Mae wrote a play called *Sex* which led to her being jailed on charges of obscenity. In 1927 she wrote a play about homosexuality called *Drag*, which was never performed on Broadway. Her 1928 play *Diamond Lil*, however, was an enormous Broadway hit. By now she was a theatrical star, a 1920s celebrity, admired by Cole Porter and other luminaries, but still incorruptibly unrespectable, boldly advertising her habit of picking up virile prize fighters.

Mae went to Hollywood and appeared with George Raft in *Night After Night* (1932), stealing, as he said, 'everything

The incomparable Mae West.

Mae West in the 1970s.

Mae West in the 1930s.

FILMOGRAPHY

Night After Night 1932
She Done Him Wrong 1933
I'm No Angel 1933
Going to Town 1934
Belle of the Nineties 1934
Klondike Annie 1936
Go West Young Man 1937
Every Day's a Holiday 1937
My Little Chickadee 1939
The Heat's On 1943
Myra Breckinridge 1970
Sextet 1977

but the cameras.' She became an enormous film star, breaking box-office records. Lines like, 'Come up and see me sometime,' passed into common usage. She made Cary Grant a star with *She Done Him Wrong* (1933) and vied with W C Fields in *My Little Chickadee* (1939), but by then American Puritanism was on the upswing and censorship ended her movie career.

But she went back on stage and at age 62 started a popular nightclub act, surrounding herself with male body builders. She returned to films near the end of her life. By then she was a legend and a cult figure, a high priestess of sex in a white gown, white furs and a diamond necklace, telling the hypocrites where to get off and showing all of us a good time.

250

WHITE, Pearl 1889-1938

Pearl White played the heroine in the most successful movie serial ever made, *The Perils of Pauline* (1914), and was for a time the most popular female star in films, outdistancing even Mary Pickford. A fascinating personality off-screen, White was a child actress who joined a circus as an equestrienne at the age of 13.

A spinal injury she received falling off a horse forced her to leave the circus. She was working as a secretary at a film company when her good looks won her a role in a western series. She did most of her own stunts, but required a double at times because of her injury. She later attempted dramatic roles but did not succeed and she retired to France.

WHITTY, Dame May 1865-1948

Dame May Whitty, a British actress highly respected on both sides of the Atlantic, was created Dame Commander of the British Empire in 1918 in recognition of her services during World War I. Chiefly a stage actress until she settled in Hollywood during the 1930s, she played strong kindly old ladies on screen better than anyone else in the world.

FILMOGRAPHY
Enoch Arden 1915
Night Must Fall 1937
The Lady Vanishes 1938
Mrs Miniver 1942
My Name is Julia Ross 1945
The Return of October 1948

Above: Richard Widmark in *Warlock* (1959).
Left: Pearl White.

FILMOGRAPHY
The Perils of Pauline 1914
The Exploits of Elaine 1915
The White Moll 1920
Know Your Men 1921
A Virgin Paradise 1921

WIDMARK, Richard 1914-

Richard Widmark was so brilliant playing villains at the start of his film career that he had to battle against typecasting. He evolved into a solid durable star even though his heroes do tend to be tough loners. Weak guys have never been Widmark's forte. Born in Sunrise, Minnesota, he discovered football and acting in college. Acting won.

Radio dramas gave him a start. Broadway came next. When he debuted on screen in *Kiss of Death* (1947) as a psychopathic killer whose chilling laugh terrified audiences, he received an Oscar nomination. Eventually Widmark formed his own movie production company and also began appearing successfully on television.

FILMOGRAPHY
Kiss of Death 1947
Slattery's Hurricane 1949
Panic in the Streets 1950
The Cobweb 1955
Saint Joan 1957
Judgment at Nuremberg 1961
The Bedford Incident 1965
Madigan 1968
Murder on the Orient Express 1974
Rollercoaster 1977
Bear Island 1979

WILDER, Gene 1935-

Gene Wilder, a protégé of Mel Brooks, has specialized in nervous or embarrassed comic characters. Born Jerry Silberman, he took drama classes at the University of Iowa and after graduation studied at the Old Vic Theatre School of Bristol. Wilder joined the Actors Studio and appeared in several Broadway productions.

His film debut was a small but notable part in *Bonnie and Clyde* (1967), but his real success came in Brooks' films, particularly *Young Frankenstein* (1974). Wilder's career slipped as he started writing and directing his own films, but he has been redeemed somewhat with the success of *The Woman In Red* (1984).

FILMOGRAPHY
Bonnie and Clyde 1967
The Producers 1968
Willy Wonka and the Chocolate Factory 1971
Everything You Always Wanted to Know About Sex 1972
The Little Prince 1973
Blazing Saddles 1974
Young Frankenstein 1974
The Adventures of Sherlock Holmes' Smarter Brother 1975
Silver Streak 1976
The Frisco Kid 1979
The Woman in Red 1984
Haunted Honeymoon 1986

WILDING, Michael 1912-1979

Michael Wilding began as a painter and worked in the art department of a British film studio. Wilding then switched to acting and became a polished leading man. In the US he is best remembered as the second husband of Elizabeth Taylor and father of two of her children.

FILMOGRAPHY
The Wedding Group 1935
In Which We Serve 1942
English Without Tears 1944
An Ideal Husband 1947
Under Capricorn 1949
Stage Fright 1950
The Egyptian 1954
The Glass Slipper 1955
The World of Suzie Wong 1960
The Naked Edge 1961
Waterloo 1970
Lady Caroline Lamb 1972

WINGER, Debra 1955-

Debra Winger was born in Cleveland, Ohio, and moved to California when she was six. Debra moved to Israel after graduating high school, but returned home. In 1973 an auto accident left her temporarily blind and partially paralyzed. When she recovered she dropped out of college to pursue her real ambition: acting.

Winger did commercials and television. Then came her first big break. She appeared opposite John Travolta in *Urban Cowboy* (1980). Winger was vulnerable and appealing in the film. Replacing Raquel Welch in *Cannery Row* (1982), her next triumph came in the immensely successful *An Officer and a Gentleman* (1982), with Richard Gere. She was nominated for an Academy Award for her role in *Terms of Endearment* (1983).

FILMOGRAPHY
Urban Cowboy 1980
An Officer and a Gentleman 1982
Terms of Endearment 1983
Legal Eagles 1986
Black Widow 1987

Gene Wilder (*right*) with Marty Feldman in *Young Frankenstein* (1974).

Above: Winger in *An Officer and a Gentleman* (1982).
Right: Shelley Winters with Montgomery Clift in *A Place in the Sun* (1951).

WINTERS, Shelley 1922-

Shelley Winters – today she's fat, dynamic, colorful and exciting. When she started in films she was thin, dynamic, colorful and exciting, one of the sexiest actresses in Hollywood, a star with a capital 'S.'

Born Shirley Schrift in St Louis, Missouri, she was raised in Brooklyn, New York. *A Double Life* (1948) brought her acclaim. She bravely shed her glamor to appear in *A Place in the Sun* (1951) and won Academy Awards as Best Supporting Actress for *The Diary of Anne Frank* (1959) and *A Patch of Blue* (1965). Today the mercurial outspoken Winters plays matronly roles with zest.

FILMOGRAPHY
A Double Life 1948
A Place in the Sun 1951
The Big Knife 1955
The Night of the Hunter 1955
The Diary of Anne Frank 1959
Lolita 1962
A Patch of Blue 1965
Alfie 1966
Harper 1966
What's the Matter with Helen? 1970
The Poseidon Adventure 1972
Pete's Dragon 1977
SOB 1981

Wood and James Dean – *Rebel Without a Cause* (1955).

WOOD, Natalie 1938-1981

Natalie Wood, born Natasha Gurdin, was one of the few child stars to make a smooth transition to teenage and adult roles, becoming a major star in the 1950s. Poor material sometimes hampered her talent but she remained a presence in films. She was married to actor Robert Wagner and her tragic death from drowning was front-page news.

FILMOGRAPHY
Miracle on 34th Street 1947
Rebel Without a Cause 1955
Marjorie Morningstar 1958
Splendor in the Grass 1961
West Side Story 1961
Love with the Proper Stranger 1964
Inside Daisy Clover 1966
Bob and Carol and Ted and Alice 1969
Brainstorm 1983

WOODWARD, Joanne 1930-

Joanne Woodward is far more than simply the wife of superstar Paul Newman. Woodward is an outstanding talent, magnificent in dramas, clever in comedy, with an eye for off-beat roles. She is also politically active in liberal causes.

Born in Thomasville, Georgia, she made her debut in films in 1955, winning a Academy Award for Best Actress for *The Three Faces of Eve* (1957). Husband Newman directed her in the popular *Rachel, Rachel* (1968) and she has won acclaim for her television appearances. Woodward lacks the fire and beauty to be a great star but her achievements have won her enormous respect.

FILMOGRAPHY
A Kiss Before Dying 1956
The Three Faces of Eve 1957
No Down Payment 1957
The Long Hot Summer 1958
From the Terrace 1960
The Stripper 1963
A Big Hand for the Little Lady 1966
Rachel, Rachel 1968
Winning 1969
They Might Be Giants 1971
The End 1978

Joanne Woodward in *Rachel, Rachel* (1968).

before King Kong, and had a long successful career after that film. She appeared in other horror films, but never specialized in the genre. Late in her career she did specialize in mother roles on television.

FILMOGRAPHY
The Wedding March 1928
Legion of the Condemned 1928
Four Feathers 1929
The Texan 1930
Dr X 1932
The Most Dangerous Game 1932
The Mystery of the Wax Museum 1933
Vampire Bat 1933
King Kong 1933
Below the Sea 1933
The Captain Hates the Sea 1934
Murder in Greenwich Village 1937
Wildcat Bus 1940
The Cobweb 1955
Crime of Passion 1957
Dragstrip Riot 1958

WRAY, Fay 1907-

Fay Wray will be forever known as the little blonde whom King Kong loved but Wray was an established star

Fay Wray, terrified by King Kong (1933).

WYMAN, Jane 1914-

A radio singer and chorus girl, Jane Wyman spent ten years playing dumb blondes in film comedies until at last her dramatic talent was recognized. She won an Academy Award for Best Actress for *Johnny Belinda* (1948). Her second husband was actor Ronald Reagan.

FILMOGRAPHY
Brother Rat 1938
Princess O'Rourke 1943
The Lost Weekend 1945
The Yearling 1946
Johnny Belinda 1948
The Blue Veil 1952
Magnificent Obsession 1954
All that Heaven Allows 1955
Miracle in the Rain 1956
Pollyanna 1960
How To Commit a Marriage 1969

YORK, Michael 1942-

Michael York was born in Fulmer, England, and educated at Oxford. The Oxford University Dramatic Society and the Dundee Repertory gave him acting experience and in the late 1960s he began appearing in films. York rose quickly to the status of leading man, at his best opposite Liza Minelli in *Cabaret* (1972).

FILMOGRAPHY
Accident 1967
Romeo and Juliet 1968
Zeppelin 1971
Cabaret 1972
Lost Horizon 1973
The Three Musketeers 1973
The Four Musketeers 1974
Murder on the Orient Express 1974
Great Expectations 1975
The Riddle of the Sands 1979

Above: Gig Young – *The Tunnel of Love* (1958).
Above left: Michael York in *The Last Remake of Beau Geste* (1977).

YORK, Susannah 1942-

Susannah York was a lovely blonde actress born in England and raised in Scotland to whom stardom came when she appeared in *Tom Jones* (1963). Controversy surrounded nude appearances in *The Killing of Sister George* (1968) and *Zee and Co* (1971), but *Images* (1972) brought her a Best Actress Award at Cannes. More recently she has appeared in character roles.

FILMOGRAPHY
Tunes of Glory 1960
The Greengage Summer 1961
Freud 1962
Tom Jones 1963
A Man for All Seasons 1966
The Killing of Sister George 1968
They Shoot Horses Don't They? 1969
Zee and Co 1971
Images 1972
Superman 1978

Right: Susannah York in *Freud* (1962).

YOUNG, Gig 1913-1978

Gig Young was born Byron Elsworth Barr but in his first major film role he played a character named Gig Young and adopted the name. He was a versatile second leading man and was nominated for supporting actor Academy Awards several times before winning an Oscar for *They Shoot Horses, Don't They?* (1969). Young died tragically, apparently shooting his bride of three weeks and then himself.

FILMOGRAPHY
Misbehaving Husbands 1940
The Gay Sisters 1942
The Woman in White 1948
The Three Musketeers 1948
Come Fill the Cup 1951
The City That Never Sleeps 1953
Teacher's Pet 1958
That Touch of Mink 1962
The Shuttered Room 1968
They Shoot Horses Don't They? 1969
The Killer Elite 1975

YOUNG, Loretta 1913-

Loretta Young was ethereally, sweetly beautiful. Graceful elegance and glamorous costumes added to her allure. Born in Salt Lake City, Utah, Young and her two sisters grew up in Hollywood, working as child extras in films.

When Young turned up for a bit role slated for one of her sisters she won the part and a contract; by the mid-1930s she was a major star. Rumors of a love affair with Clark Gable aroused fan interest. Young won an Academy Award for Best Actress for *The Farmer's Daughter* (1947) and became a popular television star before retiring from acting.

FILMOGRAPHY
Loose Ankles 1929
The Devil to Pay 1930
A Man's Castle 1933
The House of Rothschild 1934
Call of the Wild 1935
Ramona 1936
The Story of Alexander Graham Bell 1939
The Farmer's Daughter 1947
Rachel and the Stranger 1948
Mother is a Freshman 1949
Cause for Alarm 1951
It Happens Every Thursday 1953

YOUNG, Robert 1907-

Robert Young was soothing wholesome and kind, a debonair romantic lead at first, later an engaging on-screen husband, and finally television's favorite dad and doctor in 'Father Knows Best' and 'Marcus Welby MD.'

Born in Chicago, Illinois, Young moved to California, becoming one of Hollywood's most durable and prolific performers. He starred in over one hundred movies opposite leading ladies like Joan Crawford, Claudette Colbert, Greer Garson and, most delightfully, Dorothy McGuire. His warmth and charm brought him success even in TV commercials, despite rumors of problems with alcohol and depression.

Robert Young (*center*) headed an all-star cast in *Lady Be Good* (1941).

FILMOGRAPHY
The Sin of Madelon Claudet 1931
Strange Interlude 1931
The House of Rothschild 1934
Spitfire 1934
Secret Agent 1936

HM Pulham, Esquire 1941
Journey for Margaret 1942
Claudia 1943
The Canterville Ghost 1944
The Enchanted Cottage 1944
Claudia and David 1946

Crossfire 1947
Sitting Pretty 1948
The Forsyte Woman 1949
Goodbye My Fancy 1951
The Secret of the Incas 1954